W9-CEI-175

UTTERLY CRAZY

UTTERLY CRAZY

Ripley
PUBLISHING
a Jim Pattison Company

PUBLISHING

Publisher Anne Marshall
Editorial Director Rebecca Miles
Assistant Editor Charlotte Howell
Text Geoff Tibballs
Proofreader Judy Barratt
Researchers James Proud, Charlotte Howell
Indexer Hilary Bird
Art Director Sam South
Project Designer Rocket Design (East Anglia) Ltd
Cover Design Michelle Foster
Reprographics Juice Creative

Executive Vice President Norm Deska
Vice President, Archives and Exhibits Edward Meyer

PUBLISHER'S NOTE
While every effort has been made to verify the accuracy of the entries in this book, the Publishers cannot be held responsible for any errors contained in the work. They would be glad to receive any information from readers.

WARNING
Some of the stunts and activities in this book are undertaken by experts and should not be attempted by anyone without adequate training and supervision.

Cover images: (t) Jalisa Mae Thompson from Atlantic City, New Jersey, is able to roll her tongue and "pop" her eyeballs almost out of their sockets! (c) John Lynch, a 78-year-old retired Bank Manager, has 241 studs and rings on his body, 150 of which are on his face and neck, and hundreds of tattoos, including an image of Marilyn Monroe. (b) Scottish artist David Mach made this portrait of Marilyn Monroe using thousands of colored matchsticks.

Published by Ripley Publishing 2011
Ripley Publishing, Suite 188, 7576 Kingspointe Parkway, Orlando, Florida 32819, USA

2 4 6 8 10 9 7 5 3 1

ISBN 978-1-60991-001-3

Some of this material first appeared in *Ripley's Believe It or Not! Prepare to be Shocked!*

      Library of Congress Cataloging-in-Publication Data
Tibballs, Geoff.
  Ripley's believe it or not! : utterly crazy / [text, Geoff Tibballs ; interviews, Jo Wiltshire].
    p. cm.
  Includes index.
  ISBN 978-1-60991-001-3
  1. Curiosities and wonders. I. Wiltshire, Jo. II. Title.
AG243.T3997 2011
031.02--dc22
              2010047450

Manufactured in China in November/2010 by RR Donnelley
1st printing

First published in Great Britain in 2011 by Random House Books, Random House, 20 Vauxhall Bridge Road, London SW1V 2SA

www.rbooks.co.uk

Addresses for companies within The Random House Group Limited can be found at www.randomhouse.co.uk/offices/htm

The Random House Group Limited Reg. No. 954009

A CIP catalogue record for this book is available from the British Library

ISBN 9781847946683 (UK)

Contents

Ripley's World 6

Epic Endeavors 12

Strange Tales 56

Amazing Animals 100

Weird World 144

Body Bizarre 188

Fantastic Food 232

Beyond Belief 276

The Last Word 320

Index 364

Acknowledgments 384

Ripley's World

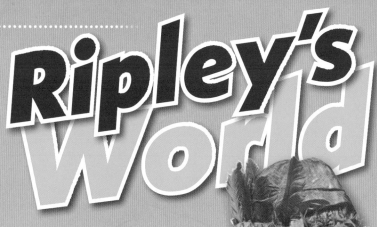

In December 1918, while working as a sports columnist for the New York Globe, Robert Ripley created his first collection of odd facts and feats.

The cartoons, based on unusual athletic achievements, were submitted under the heading "Champs and Chumps," but his editor wanted a title that would describe the incredible nature of the content. So, after much deliberation, the title was changed to "Believe it or Not!" The cartoon was an instant success and the phrase "believe it or not" soon entered everyday speech.

Ripley's passion was travel and by 1940 he had visited no fewer than 201 countries. Wherever he went, he searched out the bizarre for inclusion in his syndicated newspaper cartoons, which had blossomed to reach worldwide distribution, being translated into 17 different languages and boasting a readership of 80 million people. During one trip Ripley crossed two continents and covered over 24,000 mi (39,000 km) "from New York to Cairo and back" to satisfy his appetite for the weird.

Robert Ripley examines a carved coconut head in San Juan, Puerto Rico, in 1940.

Believe It or Not!

by Ripley

Charly ROMANO

MAN WITH RUBBER ARMS

Contortionist Charly Romano was one of many performers who showcased their feats at Ripley odditoriums across the United States.

This souvenir postcard of Romano was on sale in the New York City odditorium in 1940.

Ripley with the "flour girls" of Siam while on a trip to Bangkok in 1932.

Ripley's Legacy Lives On

Although Robert Ripley died in 1949 (after collapsing on the set of his weekly television show) his "Believe it or Not!" cartoons are still produced on a daily basis—just as they have been everyday since 1918—making Ripley's the longest running syndicated cartoon in the world.

Intrepid researchers follow in Robert Ripley's footsteps, continually scouring the world and enabling Ripley's to remain the undisputed king of the strange and unbelievable. With a huge database of incredible facts, people, and events, a massive photographic archive, and a warehouse stuffed with unique exhibits, Ripley's is able to present a celebration of the amazing diversity of our world, without ever passing judgment. From the outset, Robert Ripley encouraged his dedicated readers to submit unusual material and photographs—a tradition that exists to this day. His weekly mailbag sometimes exceeded 170,000 letters! Fittingly, Ripley was once commemorated in a church in his hometown of Santa Rosa, California—a church that was made entirely from a single giant redwood tree!

Ripley's cartoons can still be seen daily across the world.

8

A display in the Ripley's museum in Surfer's Paradise, Australia, features tall man Robert Wadlow, 17-in-tall (43-cm) Alypius—imprisoned in a bird cage by an Egyptian pharaoh for treason—a Paduang woman with brass neck rings, three-legged performer Francisco Lentini, and Avelino Perez Matos who could dislocate his eyeballs from their sockets. Also shown is the tiny Peel P-50 car—big enough for one, and very easy to park!

Ripley's—Believe It or Not!

"ROBO-CUP"

FREEZE

STARTING IN JUNE, PLAYERS AND FANS AT THE 2006 WORLD CUP TOURNAMENT IN GERMANY, WILL BE PROTECTED

BRIAN ANDERSON NEEDED 70 STITCHES FOLLOWING A GREAT WHITE SHARK ATTACK, ESCAPING ONLY AFTER HE REPEATEDLY PUNCHED THE SHARK IN THE NOSE!

www.ripleys.com 3-12

ANDY.

A MUMMY ON DISPLAY AT RIPLEY'S ODDITORIUM IN NEW ORLEANS

MOST ARMY ANTS IN SOUTH AMERICA EAT OTHER INSECTS, BUT TH

The Ripley Museums

Ripley's remarkable collection is now showcased in no fewer than 31 museums across ten countries.

Recent openings include London, England and Bangalore, India. Ripley called his museums "odditoriums," and built the first one in Chicago in 1933. Exhibits here ranged from genuine shrunken heads from the Upper Amazon to *The Last Supper* painted on a dime, and the effect this new museum had on the visiting public was startling. According to Ripley himself: "At Chicago one hundred people fainted every day and we had to have six beds." By the time the New York City Odditorium was opened in 1940, visitors were getting used to the wonderful world of Ripley's—there were only three beds available and "hardly anyone fainted."

This fully-functioning, sparkling Mini Cooper car has been decorated with a mural featuring American icons made from more than one million Swarovski lead crystals. It is currently on display in Ripley's odditorium at Piccadilly Circus in the heart of London, England.

In 1940, the Ripley odditorium was a huge draw at the Golden Gate International Exposition in San Francisco.

Ripley's opened a new odditorium in New York City's Times Square in 2007.

Epic Endeavors

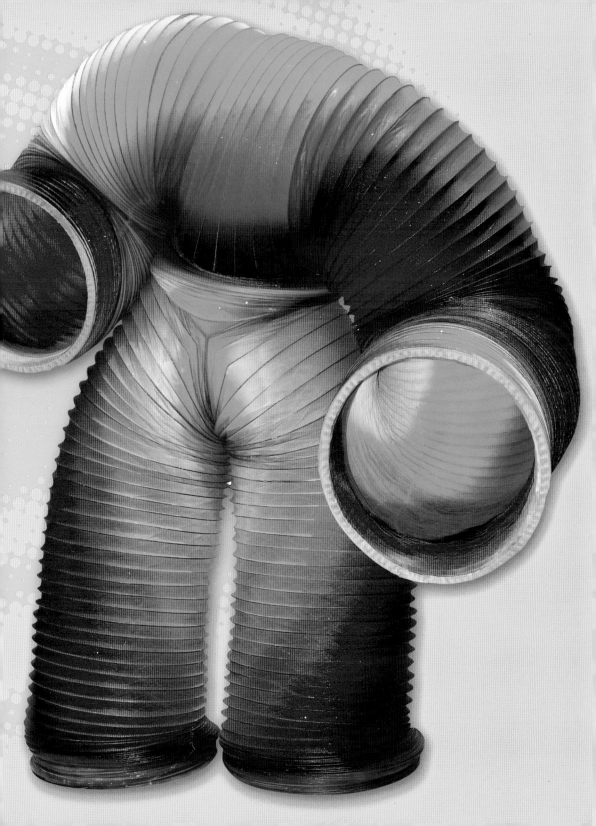

Couch Balloon

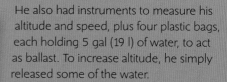

Kent Couch flew nearly 200 mi (322 km) over Oregon in nine hours in July 2007—in a contraption that consisted of nothing more than a lawn chair and 105 brightly colored, helium-filled balloons.

Inspired by Larry "Lawn Chair" Walters, who floated over Los Angeles, California, using weather balloons in 1982, the 47-year-old attached the bundle of 4-ft-round (1.2-m) balloons to his chair and took off from his gas station in Bend, Oregon. He carried a global-positioning device, a two-way radio, a digital camcorder, a cell phone, and a pair of sunglasses.

He also had instruments to measure his altitude and speed, plus four plastic bags, each holding 5 gal (19 l) of water, to act as ballast. To increase altitude, he simply released some of the water.

He traveled as high as 14,000 ft (4,267 m) as he floated eastward and said he could hear cattle and children as he drifted among the clouds. On the ground below, friends and family followed his progress in a convoy of vehicles.

His intended destination was Idaho, but with his water supply running low and mountains approaching, he decided to touch down in a field near Union, Oregon. He completed the descent by popping the balloons.

Afterward, Couch said he would love to do it again. "When you're laying in the grass on a summer day, and you see the clouds, you wish you could jump on them. This is as close as you can come to jumping on them. It was just like being on ice, nice and smooth."

Light Lunch

Wang Gongfu, of Lianyungang, China, eats glass twice a week. He ate his first glass cup when he was 20 and in the intervening 22 years he has eaten more than 440 lb (200 kg) of glass. His favorite is teacup glass, but he is also quite partial to electric lightbulbs.

Wet Ceremony Taiwan's College of Marine Sciences staged its 2007 degree ceremony underwater! At the ceremony, which was held in the aquarium of the National Museum of Marine Biology, the university president wore a diving suit and handed out waterproof certificates to students whose graduation clothes were accessorized with flippers and oxygen masks.

Beer Carrying In 2007, Reinhard Wurz of Australia, carried 32 fl oz (20 liter) glasses full of beer for a distance of 130 ft (40 m).

Balloon Journey
Five-year-old Kelvin Bielunski released a helium balloon from his school in Woodston, England—and three weeks later it was found by a soldier in Iraq, 2,500 mi (4,000 km) away!

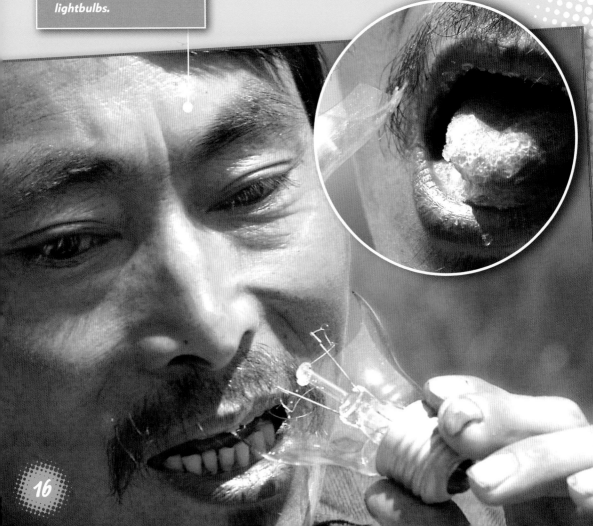

Steel Swallower

This Chinese performer can swallow a stack of steel bars—without suffering any adverse effects.

Smash Hit Dan Wilson from Lodi, California, smashed 64 dinner plates on his forehead in 41 seconds in 2007. The 47-year-old father-of-eight, who also breaks bottles, bricks, and boards on his head, said of his achievement: "I wanted to do something famous before I die and as I don't have the brains, I thought I'd better use my body." He added that he spends about two hours psyching himself up before each challenge, concentrating all his energy on one quarter-sized spot at the top of his forehead.

Stitch in Time While running the 2007 London Marathon, 49-year-old Susie Hewer of Sussex, England, knitted a 4-ft-long (1.2-m) scarf! Susie, who describes herself as an "extreme knitter," still managed to complete the course in under six hours.

Nasal Power A Chinese man pulled a 1$\frac{2}{3}$-ton van and its driver more than 40 ft (12 m) with his nose. Fu Yingjie sucked one end of a thin rope through his right nostril and into his stomach, where he used his abdominal muscles to grip the rope and drag the van.

Loud Clap A man in China can clap his hands almost as loud as the sound of whirring helicopter blades. Seventy-year-old Zhang Quan, of Chongqing City, has had his claps measured at 107 decibels—just three decibels quieter than the sound made by a helicopter. Zhang does not clap very often, however, because the noise is so great that it hurts his ears.

Can Collection Schools across South Africa collected nearly two million tin cans for recycling in just one month in 2007.

Tough Teeth

Joe Ponder of Love Valley, North Carolina, was a well-known strongman who performed lifts using his teeth. Here he is seen lifting a 500-lb (230-kg) mule with his champion choppers.

Let's Rock! On January 27, 2007, Pat Callan of LaCrosse, Wisconsin, headbanged for more than 35 minutes straight at a rock concert.

Hedge Monster John Dobson from Sussex, England, has spent 17 years creating a topiary model of the Loch Ness Monster in his garden hedge. He regularly trims the head, humps, and tail into the 15-ft-high (4.5-m) hedge. He is now growing another monster for his neighbor.

Speed Skipper Olga Berberich, a 23-year-old German fitness coach, completed 251 skips with a rope in one minute in Cologne in September 2007.

Party Girl Evelyn Warburton of Berwick, Pennsylvania, rode to her 100th birthday party in September 2007 in a motorcycle sidecar—wearing a black leather jacket and a cool pair of sunglasses.

Mass Dribble Led by the Indiana Pacers basketball team, around 4,600 people dribbled basketballs through Indianapolis in October 2007.

Keen Typist Les Stewart of Mudjimba, Australia, spent 15 years typing out all the numbers from one to one million in letters, simply because he "wanted something to do." Between 1983 and 1998 he typed for 20 minutes every waking hour—on the hour—eventually filling 19,890 pages. Once he had finished, he threw all the pages out, except for the first and the last sheets. Stewart is no stranger to odd feats—he once put 3,400 stamps on a single envelope.

Color-blind

Florida artist Jay Lonewolf Morales paints beautifully vivid pictures despite suffering from monochromacy—complete color blindness. He can see in only black and white and shades of gray, yet he creates all his paintings with vibrant colors. He says: "I cry every time I paint, because I cannot enjoy the pigments of my labor."

Famous Scenes

Using the alias "Udronotto," Italian artist Marco Pece has re-created Leonardo da Vinci's painting of *The Last Supper* using LEGO® figures. He has also re-created *The Mona Lisa*, and movie scenes from *The Blues Brothers* and *The Graduate*.

Musical Mayhem

F.G. Holt of Nashville, Arkansas, used to demonstrate his ability to control every facial muscle by attaching bells to his eyebrows and playing some well-known tunes. And H.C. Harris, of Jackson, Mississippi, could play the harmonica and whistle at the same time!

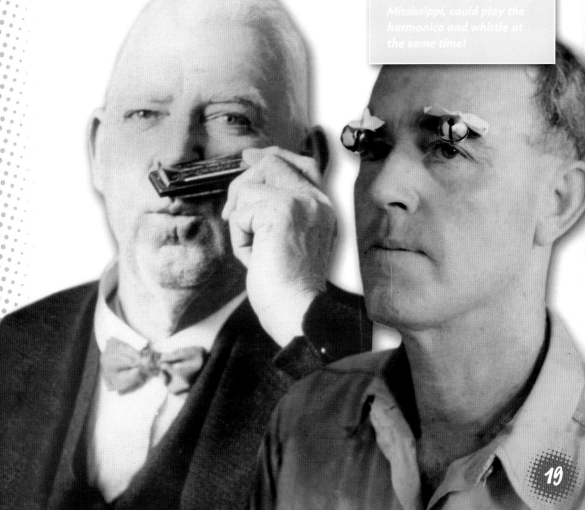

Flat Out

With his legs split, chest bent forward, and chin almost touching the ground, six-year-old Aniket Chindak of Belgaum, India, is so flexible that he can roller-skate under parked cars.

Aniket is a leading exponent of the sport of limbo skating and can also limbo under poles set just 8 in (20 cm) off the ground. Of his car skating he says: "It took three months before I could get my body in the right position. The hardest thing is to go fast enough before I bend down, because that's how you can skate under the car and come out the other side."

Headstrong Appearing on a German TV show in 2007, Kevin Shelley of Carmel, Indiana, broke 46 wooden toilet-seat lids in 60 seconds—with his head! It is not the first time he has used his head for entertainment—he has previously smashed ten pine boards with his head in just over seven seconds.

Globe Runner A man dubbed the British "Forrest Gump" ran around the world over a period of 5 years 8 months. Robert Garside from the town of Stockport in Cheshire, England, ran more than 35,000 mi (56,000 km) and crossed through 30 countries between 1997 and 2003. On the way he was jailed in China, threatened at gunpoint in Panama, and met his future wife in Venezuela.

Worm Dance James Rubec performed a "Worm" break dance move along the turf of the Rogers Centre stadium in Toronto, Ontario, Canada, for more than 98 ft (30 m) in 2007.

Simon Says A total of 1,100 freshmen from the University of Miami gathered at the city's Bank United Center in August 2007 and simultaneously played the mimicking game "Simon Says."

Distinctive Desk Designer Eric Harshbarger has built a full-sized office desk from 35,000 LEGO® bricks for a company in Seattle. The desk weighs around 120 lb (55 kg) and has seven working drawers. After creating the prototype, he had to take it apart and then glue each piece back together to make the desk stronger.

Disney Collection In 2007, Disney unveiled a range of bridal dresses inspired by their fairytale films, including *Sleeping Beauty* and *Beauty and the Beast*. Created by L.A. designer Kirstie Kelly, the dresses cost from $1,500 each.

Wrapped Up New Zealander Alastair Galpin believes in keeping out the cold. In Auckland in 2006, he wore no fewer than 74 socks on one foot. On previous occasions he has worn seven gloves on one hand and 120 T-shirts!

Ontario Superman For five minutes, Rick Ellis of Chatham-Kent, Ontario, Canada, hung suspended in midair from a piece of wood by eight steel hooks that had been inserted into his skin. The hooks—six in his back and one in each calf—had made the 36-year-old scream in agony as they were sunk into his skin, but once suspended he felt fine: "I wasn't in any pain then," he said. "I was at peace with myself. There was a lightness like there was nothing around me. It was like I was flying."

Snakes Alive!

A folk artist in Nanjing, China, can push a snake into his mouth and then pull it out through one of his nostrils!

Body Art

Dubbed the Picasso of LEGO® bricks, Wall Street lawyer-turned-artist Nathan Sawaya creates astonishing masterpieces from the small building blocks beloved by children the world over. Requiring hours of painstaking work, each of his pieces can use more than 250,000 LEGO® bricks in total. Sawaya was bestowed with the honor of becoming a Master Model Builder by LEGOLAND® California in 2004. The pieces shown here were displayed at Nathan's first solo art exhibition, The Art of the Brick, at the Lancaster Museum of Art in Philadelphia, Pennsylvania, in 2007.

Postcard Creations

British artist David Mach creates works of art from postcards. In 2007, he used 8,000 identical postcards of Dubai's Jumeirah Emirates Towers to create a picture of a racehorse that measured 12 x 9 ft (3.6 x 2.7 m).

Still Life
Discovering that his former hometown of Teococuilco, Mexico, had turned into a ghost town over the past 30 years, sculptor Alejandro Santiago decided to repopulate the area with 2,501 clay statues.

Cobra Guard
In September 2007, Harrods Department Store in London, England, used live cobras to guard a $120,000 pair of shoes encrusted with diamonds, rubies, and sapphires.

Hot Stuff
Manuel Quiroz, a 54-year-old taxi driver from Mexico City, Mexico, can eat dozens of spicy chili peppers, as well as rub them on his skin, and even squeeze their juice into his eyes—without feeling any discomfort at all. Quiroz first discovered his awesome talent when he was just seven years old. "Chilies don't sting me," he says. "They have no effect. It's just like eating fruit."

Ball Juggler
Francisco Tebar Honrubia, alias Paco, a Spanish entertainer who has performed with New York's Big Apple Circus, can juggle five ping-pong balls—using only his mouth and sending them up to 50 ft (15 m) in the air. He says the secret of his art is not to let his mouth get too dry.

Giant Crossword
A self-confessed crossword fanatic from the Yemen has created a giant crossword puzzle that is 178 times bigger than any other. Abdul-Karim Qasem spent seven years devising a crossword with 320,500 squares and 800,720 words in its accompanying clue book. He spent hours on end surfing the Internet to find information for his clues and answers, taking great care not to repeat any information in the puzzle.

Eurasian Trek

In September 2007, Australian Tim Cope completed a 3-year, 6,200-mi (10,000-km), solo trek across some of the harshest terrain on the planet, from Mongolia to Hungary, following in the footsteps of the 13th-century Mongolian warlord Genghis Khan.

Tim with Tigon, which means "hawk" in Kazakh, in the Carpathian Mountains.

Tim and his leading horse, Taskonir, taking a dip in the Black Sea in the Ukraine.

In Kazakhstan with his three horses, Tim heads into his first winter of the trip.

En route he endured temperatures ranging from −54°F (−48°C) to 130°F (54°C), had his horses and his dog stolen, and survived a night surrounded by howling wolves hungry for their next meal.

The inspiration for this epic journey was a desire to understand what life is like for the nomadic people who populate the steppes of Asia and Central Europe. When Tim from Gippsland, Victoria, set off in June 2004, he expected his journey to take 18 months, but unforeseen delays, including extreme weather, long border hold-ups, and the death of his father, meant that Tim's epic journey took much longer.

Throughout the trek, Tim traveled with three horses—one to carry him and two to carry food and supplies—even though at the start he could barely ride a horse. He needed 13 horses in total to complete his marathon adventure, and in Kazakhstan he also used a camel to combat the intense heat. At other times he had to ride headlong into fierce blizzards, guided only by a compass.

Young Swimmer Leah Robbins of Norfolk, England, swam 164 ft (50 m) in May 2007—even though she was only two years old! She swam the distance backstroke, which is normally tackled by children three times her age.

Gum Art

Street artists in London, England, use a variety of media to express themselves, including these paintings on discarded pieces of chewing gum. With an estimated 300,000 pieces of gum stuck to Oxford Street alone, the artists will never be short of materials.

Blindfolded Text New Zealand teenager Elliot Nicholls sent a 160-character text message in just 45 seconds… while blindfolded. The 17-year-old sends around 50 text messages a day and has worn out the keypads on four cell phones already.

Polar Trek Explorer Hannah McKeand from Berkshire, England, completed a solo, unsupported 690-mi (1,110-km) trek across Antarctica to the South Pole in less than 40 days in 2006. On skis and dragging a 220-lb (100-kg) sled, she faced temperatures lower than −40°F (−40°C) and winds of more than 70 mph (112 km/h).

Mighty Atom He stood only 54 in (137 cm) tall, but David Moyer of Reading, Pennsylvania, won 23 national titles in weight lifting, held national and world records, and could bench press more than twice his own weight.

Chocolate Chess An English artist has designed a chess set in which you can eat your opponent. Prudence Emma Staite from Gloucestershire, creates chocolate sculptures, and has made a chess set with playing pieces in white and milk chocolate arranged on a solid chocolate board. She also used more than 440 lb (200 kg) of Belgian chocolate to make a life-sized chocolate bed (complete with chocolate duvet and pillow) for England's Alton Towers theme park.

Art in Motion

In October 2006, German artist Carsten Hoeller installed five huge spiralling slides—the tallest being 180 ft (55 m) in height—as part of an exhibit at the art gallery Tate Modern in London, England.

Six Faces

A keen gardener has created replicas of the famous Moai statues on Easter Island in his hedge. Retired banker Michael Geiger used shears to clip six faces into the 12-ft (3.6-m) conifer hedge in his front garden in Billericay, England.

Toy Car

An actual-size replica of a Volvo XC90 unveiled at the 2004 New York Auto Show was built from more than 200,000 LEGO® bricks. The car took a team of five builders two months to construct.

Nail Painter

Instead of using a brush to create his paintings, Indian artist Nangaji Bhati simply grows his fingernails. By applying paint to the tip of his 4-in (10-cm) thumbnail, he is able to produce striking artworks on canvas.

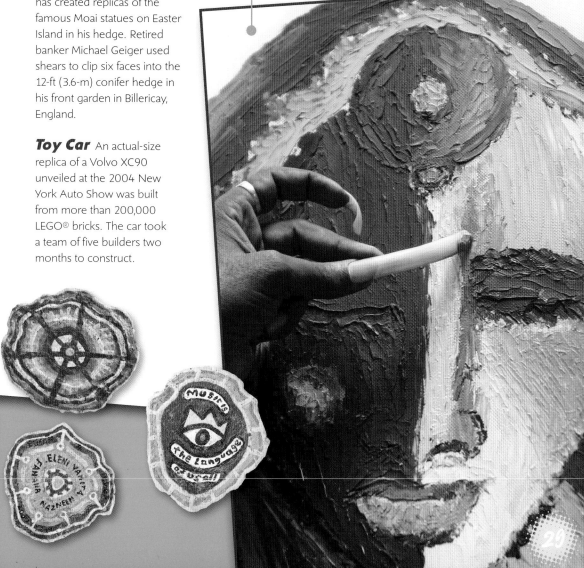

Smashing Time

Yang Yuyin from China's Jiangsu Province can split bricks with one hand. His goal is to split 10,000 bricks in seven hours.

It's the Pits! Breathing air provided by algae watered with urine, an Australian marine biologist lived for 13 days in an underwater steel capsule 10 ft (3 m) long submerged in a flooded gravel pit. Lloyd Godson's survival at a depth of 15 ft (4.5 m) depended on a coil of green algae, which provided air in return for him urinating on the plants each day. Meals came in through a manhole in the capsule and he rode a bicycle to generate electricity, which recharged his waterproof laptop computer.

Dollar Chain On September 24, 2006, residents of St. Michael, Barbados, created a line of dollar coins that measured 1 mi 380 ft (1.73 km) long—adding up to more than $67,000!

Liquid Lunch Five hundred people sampled a lavish dinner party in September 2007—underwater. The feast took place at the bottom of a swimming pool in London, England, but because of the difficulties of eating underwater, each of the three courses consisted of just one mouthful of food.

Veteran Runner Although he never ran a full mile until he was nearly 50, George Etzweiler of State College, Pennsylvania, has been making up for lost time ever since. In June 2007, the active 87-year-old completed the Mount Washington Road Race in New Hampshire— a 7.6-mi (12.2-km) course featuring an uphill climb with a daunting 11.5 percent incline.

Club Juggler Iryna Bilenka of the Ukraine can juggle three clubs for nearly two minutes—while wearing a blindfold!

Strong Eyelids

Most people need both hands to pick up two pails of water— but Li Chuanyong of Guangxi, China, can lift them with just his eyelids! He previously used his mighty eyelids to pull a car 16 ft (5 m) along a road.

31

Miniature Knitting

Imagine a cardigan that is smaller than a dime—or a pair of gloves so tiny that a grain of rice would fit neatly into each finger. These, and other miniature marvels, are the creations of nano-knitter Althea Crome Merback.

"These City-Country socks represent my move from Chicago, Illinois, to Bloomington, Indiana."

"I believe that these tiny cardigans may be among the smallest cardigans in the world!"

Actual Size!

Althea, from Bloomington, Indiana, knits cardigans, sweaters, and jackets on a 1:144 scale and gloves on a 1:12 scale by using fine silk sewing thread, as well as needles made from stainless steel medical wire that is just 0.001 in (0.03 mm) thick. With this method she is able to create garments that have up to 80 stitches per inch.

It is not only the size of her "bug-knit" clothing that amazes people, but also the patterns on them. Her love of art has encouraged her to knit a tiny cardigan bearing a reproduction of a Picasso painting, a sweater with the design of an ancient Grecian urn, and a 2¼ x 1¼-in (5.7 x 3.2-cm) cardigan inspired by the treasures of King Tutankhamun's tomb. She has also knitted a pair of miniature "City-Country" socks—one sock featuring a pattern of the Chicago skyline, the other a country landscape—which sold for $750.

Since 2000, she has created countless items for dollhouse collectors and has had her work featured in the Radical Lace and Subversive Knitting exhibit at the Museum of Arts and Design in New York.

"This sweater has the King of Hearts on one side and the Queen of Hearts on the other. The knitting's so fine that the sweaters are see-through!"

Chinese Acrobats

Su Chuandong, a 63-year-old folk artist, from Wuhan, China, is able to float in a river while spitting fire. A former acrobat and lifeguard, he can also smoke, read a newspaper, and play the bugle while floating on the water.

Woolen House Five-hundred women from across the world—including the U.S.A., Canada, and Europe—knitted for thousands of hours to create a 140-sq-ft (13-sq-m) woolen house. The brainchild of British knitter Alison Murray, the multi-colored "Gingerbread House," displayed in Devon, England, in 2007, was made from millions of stitches. It had 1,000 knitted roof tiles and was surrounded by a knitted garden, with knitted flowers and knitted trees 12 ft (3.6 m) tall.

Stolen Kiss Police charged a woman in Avignon, France, after she was caught kissing a $2-million painting by American abstract artist Cy Twombly. She was apparently so overcome with passion in front of the work that she just could not stop herself.

Rapid Escape Tied with chains and thrown underwater, Akash, a magician from Hyderabad, India, managed to escape from his shackles in a mere 15 seconds!

Tour De Fat More than 3,600 cyclists, some riding homemade contraptions, took to the streets of Fort Collins, Colorado, in September 2007 for the Tour de Fat—an initiative aimed at promoting cycling as an alternative to driving. Many donned fancy-dress costumes, ranging from Miss Piggy to Fred Flintstone.

Vertical Eggs To mark the summer solstice on June 21 in 2005, at 12 noon residents of Chiayi County, Taiwan, made 1,972 eggs stand on end simultaneously.

Sumo Squats At the age of nearly 40, Dr. Thienna, a Vietnamese-born female fitness expert, performed 5,135 sumo squats in one hour in San Francisco, California, in December 2007.

Autograph Frenzy To promote his latest album "West Side," Singaporean pop singer J.J. Lin signed his autograph on 3,052 copies of the album's CD in 2 hours in Tianjin, China, in July 2007.

Teen Texter A 13-year-old girl who sends an average of 8,000 texts a month was crowned U.S. texting champion in 2007. Morgan Pozgar of Claysburg, Pennsylvania, beat off competition from 300 rivals to land the title in New York. She was not short of practice—she sends about 260 texts a day (roughly one every five minutes) to her friends.

Egg-straordinary!

Guo Huochun from Zhejiang, China, can pick up and hold 12 eggs simultaneously in one hand—without any of them cracking.

35

Dizzy Hips

Many people can't run a mile in under eight minutes, but Paul Blair, aka Dizzy Hips, of San Francisco, California, can—and while twirling a hula hoop! He can also hula hoop while skating, skiing, or snow boarding and has performed a routine with a hula hoop measuring 43 ft (13 m) in circumference!

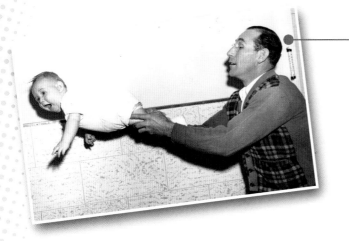

Superbaby

In 1950, strong and supple baby Philip Dellagrotti of Berwick, Pennsylvania, could swing impressively on his father's hands and hold himself out horizontally!

Sculpture Rises A prolonged drought in Utah's Great Salt Lake resulted in a sculpture that had been buried for over 30 years suddenly emerging above the surface. In 1970, artist Robert Smithson used 6,650 tons of black basalt and earth to create "Spiral Jetty," a structure measuring 1,500 ft (460 m) in length that coiled around in the water. For three decades it was visible only from the air until lack of rainfall exposed it to a wider audience.

Long Sari A team of skilled weavers in India worked tirelessly for 14 days in 2007 to create a spectacular green-and-yellow sari that measured an amazing 2,226 ft (685 m) in length.

Simultaneous Skipping More than 3,000 people, ranging in age from ten to 68, assembled in the center of Changsha, China, in July 2007 to take part in three minutes of simultaneous skipping.

Up and Down Mark Anglesey of Yorkshire, England, lifted the back end of a car, weighing 450 lb (204 kg), at least 12 in (30 cm) off the ground 580 times in an hour.

Hay Ride Organized by Bill Buckelew and an army of volunteers, a hay ride on a 500-ft-long (150-m) line of trucks and trailers carried 1,042 people at the 2007 Farm Day celebrations in DeFuniak Springs, Florida.

Car Push In September 2006, Rob Kmet and Teri Starr of Winnipeg, Manitoba, Canada, pushed a Dodge Neon more than 50 mi (80 km) around a racetrack over a period of 21 hours. They trained for the event by lifting weights and jogging in the shallow water of a lake.

Versatile Cook Krishnaveni Mudliar, a housewife from Bhopal, India, can cook nearly 65,000 different recipes. She can prepare recipes from every state in India as well as Italian, Chinese, and Burmese dishes.

Wet Hair Jurijus Levenkovas of Vilnius, Lithuania, performed an underwater haircut in six minutes at an aquarium in July 2006.

Ice World

Every January, part of the northeastern Chinese city of Harbin is transformed into a beautiful ice kingdom. Teams of local and international ice sculptors create a fairytale setting of buildings, people, animals, cartoon characters, and deities using compacted snow and blocks of ice.

Snow and ice sculpting in the region dates back 1,400 years, but the Harbin Snow and Ice Festival originated in 1985. For the 2007 festival, more than 2,000 ice sculptures were crafted from more than 4 million cubic ft (113,000 cubic m) of ice and more than 3 million cubic ft (85,000 cubic m) of snow.

Each year, five million people from across the world converge on the city, drawn by the spectacular ice structures and night illuminations. Most of the sculptures are fitted with colored lights, and at night they glow red, yellow, pink, and blue.

Harbin's famous St. Sophia church was one of the centerpieces of the festival.

Sculptors labored for hundreds of hours to create these superb ice replicas.

Show Stopper

Instead of reaching for the off switch, Germany's Marco Boehm can stop a rotating electric fan with his tongue! He demonstrated his astounding art on a German TV show filmed in Mallorca, Spain, in June 2007.

Echo Skill Daniel Kish of Long Beach, California, is completely blind but can ride a bike using echolocation, just like a bat or a dolphin, to "see" objects with sound.

Float On Keeping his hands behind his head and his toes above the surface at all times, Andrzej Szopinski-Wisla of Poland floated on water for more than two hours in 2006.

Mouth Portrait In Chennai, India, in 2006, S. Rajendran painted a portrait of the then Indian President A.P.J. Abdul Kalam using only his mouth—it took him 151 hours. He produced this amazing piece of art by holding the brush with his tongue.

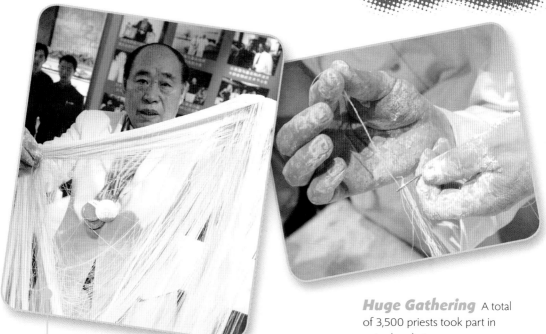

Noodle King

From just 2 lb 3 oz (1 kg) of flour, Li Enhai, of China, can make more than 2,090,000 strings of noodles. The noodles he creates are so fine that 39 can pass through the eye of one needle!

Write On! Subhash Chandra Agrawal and his wife Madhu, from New Delhi, India, are never lost for words. Between them they have had more than 18,000 "letters to the editor" published in newspapers and magazines.

Tough Guy York, Pennsylvania, strongman Chris Rider can perform amazing feats of strength. He can tear two car license plates in half simultaneously, break a baseball bat over his knee, bend an 8-in (20-cm) adjustable wrench, bend a metal horseshoe into the shape of a heart in just seven seconds, and break a 20-oz (567-g) hammer in two.

Huge Gathering A total of 3,500 priests took part in a single religious ceremony at Jaipur, India, in 2007. The ceremony, named Bhoomi Poojan, was held to worship a piece of land before it is put to use, and all of the participating priests dug the earth with pickaxes and hoes.

Big Catch Over the past 25 years, fervent fisherman Dave Romeo of Mount Joy Township, Pennsylvania, has caught more than 25,000 bass! What's more, he keeps a journal detailing every bass he has ever hooked.

Crowded Wave Timing things to perfection, 84 surfers simultaneously rode the same wave at Quebra Mar, Santos, Brazil, in 2007.

Pretty Prank

Walt, a prank-loving employee at a company in Washington, D.C., returned to the parking garage one day to find his beloved Jaguar car covered in 14,000 multi-colored sticky notes! Every inch of the car—including the tires—was covered except for the hood ornament and license plate. It had taken co-worker Scott Ableman and a dozen colleagues less than two hours to pull off the elaborate joke. Luckily, Walt saw the funny side and, once he'd cleaned off the windshield, drove the car home to show his family.

Long Painting In 2007, some 3,500 people in Wakayama, Japan, combined their talents to create a painting that is 15,154 ft (4,620 m) long! It took them more than a month to complete.

Glass Room Ye Fu and Hairong Tiantian lived in a single glass room on a sidewalk in Beijing, China, for a whole month. They were separated by a transparent wall in what they say is a metaphor for the gap in modern family relationships in China.

4,000 Tractors In Cooley, County Louth, Ireland, in 2007, a total of 4,572 vintage tractors plowed a field simultaneously. All of the tractors involved were built before 1977, the oldest dating back 100 years. Farmers traveled from as far away as South Africa, Australia, the U.S.A., and Canada to take part.

Long Line Dance In August 2007, more than 17,000 dancers formed an enormous line dance at the Ebony Black Family Reunion Tour in Atlanta, Georgia.

Cable Car In 2007, Liu Suozhu of Korla City, China, drove his pickup truck for 15 minutes along a 200 yd (180 m) parallel of steel cables that were stretched more than 60 ft (18 m) in the air between two hills.

All Scored Every soccer player in a 12-man squad scored when Bridlington Rangers Blues Under-13s beat Hutton Cranswick United 23–0 in a match in Yorkshire, England, in 2007. As the boys switched positions, even the goalkeeper scored three times.

Multi Tasker Ray Steele of Alva, Oklahoma, could whistle with his tongue sticking out—and chew gum at the same time!

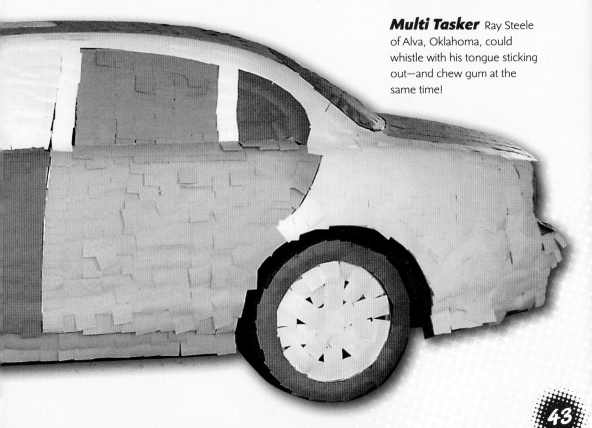

43

High-rise Fred

In 1940, Chicagoan Fred Steinlauf, 18, could be seen riding through the streets of his hometown blindfolded on a 10-ft (3-m) unicycle.

Underwater Hockey

Eight international teams braved the freezing temperatures of an Austrian lake in February 2007 to take part in the first-ever World Underwater Ice-Hockey Championship. Competing under 12 in (30 cm) of ice, the players, wearing wetsuits, masks, and flippers, chased a Styrofoam puck around a "rink" that was 20 ft (6 m) wide and 26 ft (8 m) long. As they had no oxygen tanks, the players resurfaced every 30 seconds for air.

Weight Loss

In just one year, 42-year-old Manuel Uribe of Monterrey, Mexico, shed 440 lb (200 kg)! In early 2006 he weighed a colossal 1,235 lb (560 kg)—over half a ton—but within 12 months his low-carb diet had taken him almost halfway to achieving his ultimate goal of losing 1,000 lb (454 kg).

Tab Belt

Sean Taylor of Stratford, New Jersey, has designed a belt—out of soda can tabs!

Snowmobile Jump

Ross Mercer of Whitehorse, Yukon, Canada, jumped his snowmobile 263 ft (80.3 m) high at Steamboat Springs, Colorado, in March 2007.

Horse Show

As a special attraction at the 2006 Stockholm International Horse Show in Sweden, Oliver Garcia of France rode his horse inside a massive plastic ball.

Strongman Stuart

Stuart Burrell of Essex, England, lifted a 48-lb (22-kg) weight 522 times in one hour!

Gorilla Suit

Ferrari Formula One driver Kimi Raikkonen entered a powerboat race in the Finnish city of Hanko in July 2007 wearing a gorilla suit to disguise his identity.

Helicopter Pull

Lasha Pataraia pulled a 17,050-lb (7,734-kg) military helicopter for a staggering 86 ft 4 in (26.3 m) with only his ear at an airfield near Tbilisi, Georgia. One end of a rope was attached to his ear while the other was tied to the front wheel of the helicopter.

The Regurgitator

In 1939, Dagmar Rothman performed at Ripley's New York City Odditorium astounding crowds by swallowing and regurgitating a live mouse. He smoked a cigarette before and during putting the mouse in his mouth, claiming that the smoke stunned the creature into lying still. Rothman could also place a whole lemon in his mouth.

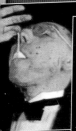

Roller Coaster Ride

PLEASURE BEACH

Richard Rodriguez certainly experienced the ups and downs of life in 2007. The 48-year-old American roller-coaster enthusiast spent 17 consecutive days riding the Pepsi Max Big One at Blackpool Pleasure Beach in northern England.

He got a five-minute break every hour he was on the ride, and could save these up for longer breaks if he preferred. Eating, drinking, and sleeping on the roller coaster, Rodriguez completed nearly 8,000 rides and covered over 6,300 mi (10,140 km)—almost as far as the return journey from Blackpool to his hometown of Brooklyn, New York.

Richard gets ready to bed down for the night on the Big Dipper surrounded by his protective foam padding.

The Big One rises majestically above the beach at Blackpool.

Aqua Golf A marine life aquarium in Fuzhou, China, staged what is thought to be the world's first underwater golf tournament. Five players overcame problems presented by fish, mammals, buoyancy, and water currents to play golf in a tank that was 50 ft (15 m) deep. The result was decided on how long it took to complete the hole rather than the number of strokes taken. The winner sunk the ball in 1 minute 20 seconds.

Hypnotic Power

Canadian hypnotist Ian Stewart is a firm believer in mind over matter. He shows the extreme power of the mind in a demonstration of self-hypnosis in which he endures the shock of more than 100 firecrackers taped to his chest going off with a bang!

Long Beard

Edwin Smith, a miner in the California gold rush of the mid-1800s, liked his beard so much that he let it grow for 16 years. It reached a length of 8 ft (2.4 m) and was so long that Smith had to hire a servant just to wash and comb it.

Hair Dress A model appeared on a catwalk in Zagreb, Croatia, in 2007 wearing a dress made entirely from human hair. Designers at the Artidjana company used 165 ft (50 m) of blonde hair in the dress.

Run Over Patrick Chege of Kenya, allows heavy trucks to run over his chest and gets up afterward without injury!

High Riders In April 2007, two Chilean men drove a car to an altitude of 21,942 ft (6,688 m). After two failed attempts to reach extreme altitudes, driver Gonzalo Bravo and his spotter Eduardo Canales piloted their modified 1986 Suzuki Samurai to the highest slopes of the Ojos del Salado volcano in Chile's Atacama Desert.

Bridge Hop Six hundred people bouncing along on children's Spacehopper toys took part in a simultaneous hop on London's Millennium Bridge in April 2007. The bridge was chosen for the challenge because it wobbled alarmingly when it was first opened to the public in 2000.

Domino Toppling A TV commercial filmed in Salta, Argentina, in 2007 featured 6,000 dominoes toppling in just 14 seconds. The domino trail took two days to construct and also involved 10,000 books, 400 tires, 45 dressers, and six cars.

Turning Tomato

Nicholas Huenefeld calls himself "The Human Ketchup Drinking Machine" —and with good cause. His personal bests are quaffing 13 fl oz (384 ml) of ketchup in just 33 seconds—or 46 fl oz (1.36 l) of the red stuff in six minutes!

Swimwear Shoot In September 2007, 1,010 bikini-clad women assembled at Australia's Bondi Beach for a huge magazine photoshoot.

Tiny Book Teeny *Ted From Turnip Town*, a book produced by the nanotechnology laboratory at Simon Frasier University, British Columbia, Canada, is so small that 20 copies of it can fit on the head a of a pin!

Pulling Pastor The power of prayer helped Reverend Kevin Fast of Cobourg, Ontario, Canada, to pull two firetrucks, weighing a total of 69 tons, more than 98 ft (30 m). He achieved this in 1 minute 15 seconds, but needed two attempts, his first having been halted by a pothole near the finish line.

Underwater Hooper Ashrita Furman of Jamaica, New York, hula hooped underwater for 2 minutes 20 seconds at a dolphin center in Key Largo, Florida, in 2007. While Furman was executing the stunt with a specially made metal hoop and breathing air from a portable scuba tank, the resident dolphins watched intently. "I think the dolphins thought I was totally crazy," said Furman afterward. "Who knows, maybe they'll try it themselves!"

Stone Skipper Russ Byars of Venango County, Pennsylvania, can skip a stone across water 51 times—reaching distances of up to 250 ft (76 m). He started stone-skipping eight years ago for something to do while out walking his dog. He favors smooth, rounded stones about 3–4 in (7–10 cm) across, grips them between his thumb and forefinger and, for maximum distance, adds spin and follow through.

Hug-A-Thon Utah college student Jordan Pearce hugged 765 people in just 30 minutes in 2007. However, the challenge was not all tender-hearted cuddles for the 18-year-old—a boy kicked and screamed to avoid being hugged by her, a man spilled his drink on her, and one girl refused to let go of her.

Penny Line In 2007, 80 penny layers, mostly under the age of ten, set out 2,879 ft (878 m) of pennies in a parking lot at Hancock, Maine, in only 2 hours 26 minutes.

Barrel Ordeal Apart from the occasional toilet break, Dutch philosopher Eric Hoekstra spent an entire week in April 2007 living in a 6-ft (2-m) wine barrel at Leeuwarden University.

Plane Drag Using only his ears, Manjit Singh, 57, from Leicester, England, pulled a 16,315-lb (7,400-kg) passenger jet aircraft 12 ft (3.6 m) along the runway of East Midlands Airport in 2007. Prior to this event, his feats of strength included pulling a double-decker bus using only his hair and lifting 187 lb (85 kg) with only his ears.

Big Foot In November 2007, the Sony Centre for the Performing Arts, in Toronto, Ontario, Canada, unveiled a stocking that measured 90 ft 1 in (27.5 m) long and 37 ft 1 in (11.3 m) wide from heel to toe.

Paper Dresses Thanks to Ed Livingston of Boston Harbor, Washington, women can read what they wear. That's because he makes women's dresses from newsprint!

Undersea Flag On August 2, 2007, Russian divers planted the country's flag 14,000 ft (4,267 m) below the North Pole, on the bed of the Arctic Ocean.

Round of Applause Paramjit Singh of India, can clap his hands more than 11,600 times in just one hour!

The Human Slinky

Romanian circus gymnast Ioan-Veniamin Oprea is able to contort his body into all manner of weird and wonderful shapes inside a colored plastic tube. With the aid of an assistant, he can even create a stunning octopus dance routine.

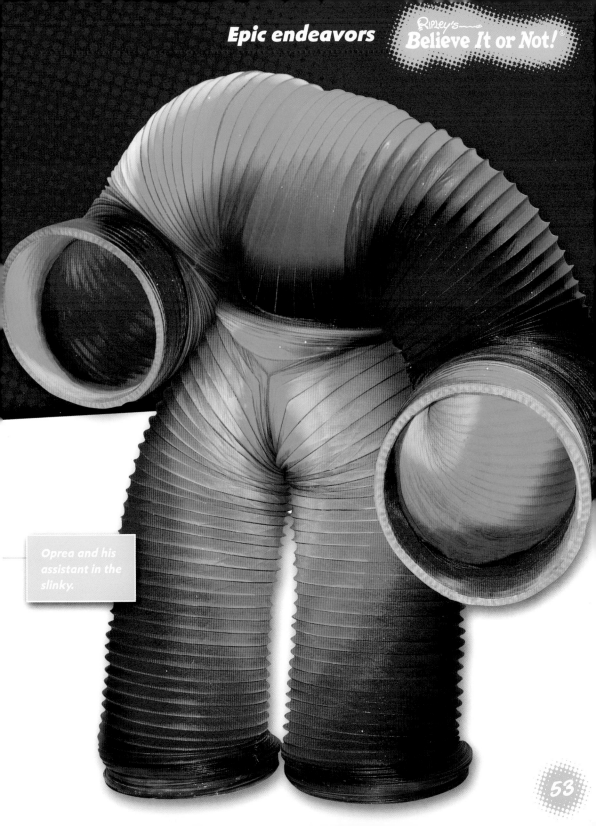

Oprea and his assistant in the slinky.

53

Checkmate K.O.

In November 2007, German policeman Frank Stoldt was crowned world champion of the hybrid sport of chessboxing. Bouts are composed of up to 11 alternating rounds of chess and boxing, representing the ultimate test of brains and brawn. After fending off his American opponent's punches, Stoldt managed to clinch the title with a checkmate in the chess game of the seventh round.

Paddle Power

Margo Pellegrino of Medford Lakes, New Jersey, paddled her kayak some 2,000 mi (3,220 km) along the east coast of the U.S.A. in 2007 from Miami, Florida, to Camden, Maine, covering an average of 40 mi (65 km) a day.

Twister Game

More than 1,400 people played a mass game of Twister at the Rogers Centre Stadium in Toronto, Ontario, Canada, in 2007.

LEGO® Swimmer

A giant plastic figure resembling a smiling LEGO® minifigure was fished out of the sea off the coast of Holland in August 2007. The 8-ft (2.4-m) model with a yellow head and blue body was found by workers in the Dutch resort of Zandvoort. Its origins were shrouded in mystery, but it was believed to have floated from the direction of England.

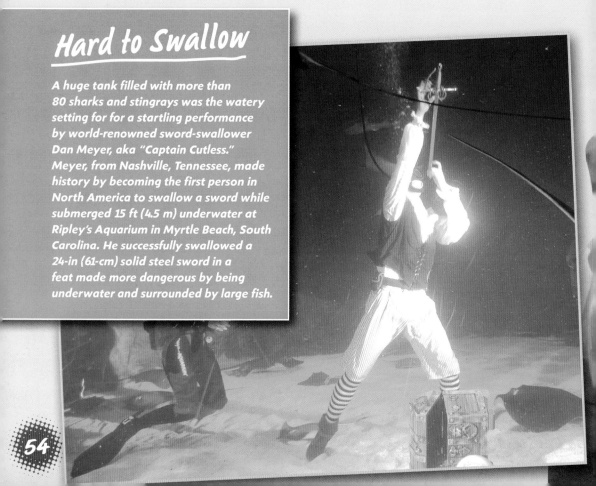

Hard to Swallow

A huge tank filled with more than 80 sharks and stingrays was the watery setting for for a startling performance by world-renowned sword-swallower Dan Meyer, aka "Captain Cutless." Meyer, from Nashville, Tennessee, made history by becoming the first person in North America to swallow a sword while submerged 15 ft (4.5 m) underwater at Ripley's Aquarium in Myrtle Beach, South Carolina. He successfully swallowed a 24-in (61-cm) solid steel sword in a feat made more dangerous by being underwater and surrounded by large fish.

Steely Bite

A performer takes a big bite out of a stainless-steel saucepan lid during festivities to mark Chinese New Year in Beijing in February 2007. His tough teeth managed to bite the lid in two.

Strange Tales

The Blind Adventurer

Miles goes on an underwater scuba walk in the Red Sea, accompanied by his paraplegic friend Mike Mackenzie.

Climbing the icy ridges of the Cairngorms in Scotland presented a formidable challenge.

In April 2007, Miles Hilton-Barber piloted a tiny micro-light aircraft on a 13,360-mi (21,500-km) flight from London, England, to Sydney, Australia. The epic journey took him 55 days and involved 118 stops—but what made it truly amazing is that Miles is blind. The 59-year-old from Derbyshire, England, is no stranger to great adventures. Over the past decade he has circumnavigated the globe, climbed some of the world's highest mountains, trekked 150 mi (240 km) across the Sahara Desert, hauled a sled 250 mi (400 km) across Antarctica, and completed more than 40 parachute jumps.

The amazing micro-light flight from London to Sydney fulfilled another ambition for Miles.

Miles riding an ostrich in South Africa during his circumnavigation of the globe in 2003.

Miles was inspired by his blind brother Geoff, who sailed solo from South Africa to Australia in 1999. "That's what made me realize the problem in my life wasn't my blindness," he says, "it was my attitude to it. The only thing holding me back was five inches—the distance between my ears."

Accompanied by sighted friend Jon Cook, Miles, who has been blind for more than 25 years, has climbed to a height of 17,500 ft (5,335 m) in the Himalayas as well as scaling Mount Kilimanjaro and Mont Blanc, the highest mountains in Africa and Europe respectively.

Miles abseiling down magnificent Table Mountain in Cape Town, South Africa.

Bargain Buy Michael Sparks of Nashville, Tennessee, bought a 184-year-old print of the American Declaration of Independence for $2.48 at a thrift store. Appraisers estimate that it is worth at least 100,000 times that price!

Blindfold Driver At the age of 13, Pat Marquis of Glendale, California, was able to play table tennis and pool, drive a car, read, identify playing cards, or fence—all with his eyes completely covered by a blindfold.

Shovel Race For 30 years The World Snow Shovel Racing Championships were staged at Angelfire, New Mexico, until they were canceled in 2005 on safety grounds. Competitors sat on a snow shovel and sped for 1,000 ft (305 m) down a snow-covered mountain at speeds of over 75 mph (120 km/h).

Unicycle Team A dozen cyclists rode 560 mi (900 km) across New Zealand's South Island in 15 days in 2007— on unicycles.

Firecracker Trail On the last day of Chinese New Year in 2007, festival organizers in Tainan, Taiwan, lit a string of firecrackers over 8 mi (13 km) long!

Simply Breathtaking In August 2007, German diver Tom Sietas managed to hold his breath underwater for 15 minutes 2 seconds— without surfacing once. He breathed in oxygen from a tank for 20 minutes beforehand to help prepare his body for the feat.

Stamp Portraits

Artist Pete Mason, from Hednesford, Staffordshire, England, creates amazing portraits of famous people from thousands of used postage stamps. He sketches each portrait on to a grid before painstakingly cutting the individual stamps to size and sticking them in place. In 2007, he completed a 12,000-stamp tribute to Princess Diana, which measured 7 x 7 ft (2.1 x 2.1 m), to mark the tenth anniversary of her death. His previous works have included prime ministers Winston Churchill and Tony Blair, soccer star David Beckham, and Queen Elizabeth II.

Soldiers Reburied

On November 25, 2007, historical re-enactors dressed up as Napoleonic soldiers and helped to rebury the bodies of 223 French servicemen of the Grande Armée who had died in 1812 near the town of Studenka, Belarus, during Napoleon's invasion.

In a Spin

Eight-year-old Patrick Grieves of Essex, England, accepted a dare from his sister to climb into the family's washing machine—and ended up having to be rescued by ten firefighters after becoming wedged fast in the drum.

Young Bartender
Chris Hardacre of Doncaster, England, is a fully qualified bartender—at 12 years old. His father David is the licensee of the Star pub and now Chris has passed all the exams necessary to serve behind the bar, with adult supervision.

Ballpark Tour
Brothers Brigham and Todd Shearon from Windsor, Ontario, Canada, visited all 30 major-league baseball stadiums in 28 days in 2007—a journey of 14,500 mi (23,000 km).

Long Overdue
In 1650, the Bishop of Winchester, England, borrowed a book from Somerset County Records office but it was not returned to Somerset County Library until 1985—335 years later—by which time it had accrued $6,000 in unpaid fees. The title of the overdue book? *The Book of Fines!*

Headless Corpses
Archeologists on the Pacific island of Vanuatu recently discovered a 3,000-year-old cemetery in which every single body they found had been decapitated.

Groundhog Day
A woman from Ohio has given birth to three children on the same date in different years—odds of more than 130,000 to one. Jenna Cotton of Marysville gave birth to sons Ayden and Logan in 2003 and 2006 respectively, followed by daughter Kayla in 2007—all on October 2.

Hidden Winnings
In 2007, demolition workers at the Sands Casino in Atlantic City, New Jersey, discovered a staggering $17,193.34 in tokens, coins, and bills that had fallen underneath the slot machines.

Cowboy Convention
For more than 20 years, cowboys from all over the U.S.A. and abroad have assembled in Elko, Nevada, each January to read poems and tell stories as part of the National Cowboy Poetry Gathering.

Typewriter Toss
At the annual Typewriter Toss held each April in Springfield, Missouri, contestants stand on an elevated platform and hurl their old typewriters from a height of 50 ft (15 m) at a target on the tarmac below.

Splash Down

Darren Taylor of Denver, Colorado, can achieve a spectacular dive from a 35-ft (10.7-m) platform into a children's inflatable pool containing just 12 in (30 cm) of water. Taylor, who calls himself Professor Splash, has been diving since the age of four and has focused on shallow diving since 2000. "There really is no training for it because it's so dangerous," he says, but adds that his technique is to "skip across the water" when he makes contact with it. Don't try this at home!

Taylor always aims to make a real splash when he lands, because the more water that splashes out of the pool, the more his fall is cushioned.

He knows that with such a small target to aim at, one false move could prove fatal.

Ripley's
Believe It or Not!®

Taylor says that when he stands on the platform he makes sure he never looks down into the tiny pool below.

10m70

10m

9m

8m

7m

6m

5m

4m

3m

2m

1m

KEYAKIZAKA STUDIO

Long Dress

A Chinese man had a 656-ft-long (200-m) wedding dress made for his fiancée. Ken, the groom from Guangzhou, originally intended to make the dress 2,008 m (1 mi) long in tribute to the 2008 Beijing Olympics, but decided to reduce it to 658 ft (200.8 m). It took nearly three months to make and weighed almost 220 lb (100 kg).

Shell Shock An elderly lady in England used a live German World-War-I artillery shell, which could have exploded at any time, as a doorstop for 20 years. The 7-in-long (18-cm) device had been collected by Thelma Bonnett's grandfather in 1918 while he served with the Merchant Navy. Thelma had used it as an ornament for decades in her home in Paignton, Devon. However, a neighbor sounded the alarm in 2007, after which bomb-disposal experts were called in to the home to deal with the shell, which was packed with explosives and had its mechanism primed to fire.

Carcass Contest In the Central Asian sport of *buzkashi*, two teams of horsemen compete to grab a livestock carcass and carry it into their opponent's circle to score points.

Mary Poppins Blown off a six-story building in Zhejiang Province, China, by a sudden gust of wind in May 2007, schoolgirl Zhang Haijing landed softly after her open umbrella slowed her fall.

Skunkfest North Ridgeville, Ohio, is home to an annual Skunk Festival that features pet skunk beauty and costume contests.

Txt Bk *The Last Messages*, a novel by Hannu Luntiala of Finland, consists exclusively of text messages exchanged between the main character and his friends and relatives.

Balloon Wedding

Laura Dakin walked down the aisle at her wedding to Don Caldwell in 2006 wearing a dress made entirely out of twisted balloons. To add to the surreal nature of the Blue Hawaii-themed ceremony at the Viva Las Vegas Wedding Chapel in Las Vegas, Nevada, "Elvis" was on hand and the groom wore Hawaiian shorts. The couple met at a balloon-twisting convention and Caldwell (a.k.a. Buster Balloon) popped the question after stepping from a giant 6-ft (1.8-m) pink balloon.

It took the groom around eight hours to make the wedding dress from more than 200 white balloons.

Festival of Fire

To celebrate the feast of Saint Anthony (the patron saint of animals), horses and riders jump through burning pyres each January in the Spanish village of San Bartolomé de Pinares as part of the Las Luminarias de San Anton Festival.

Cheered on by enthusiastic crowds, more than 100 horses and riders, some carrying small children, brave the flames from 30 bonfires laid out over the 0.6-mi (1-km) course. The controversial ceremony, which dates back hundreds of years, stems from the belief that running through fire will cleanse the village of disease.

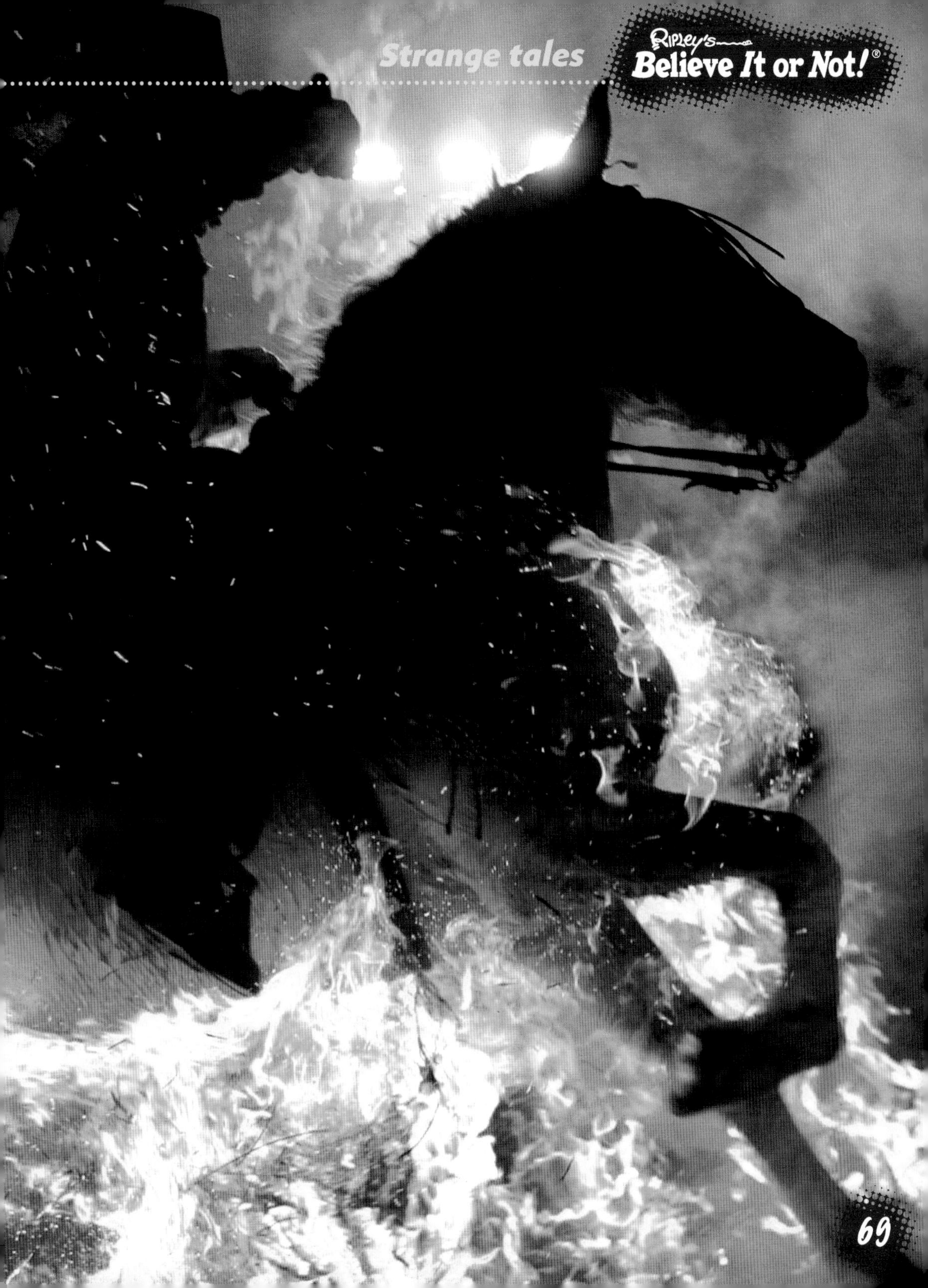

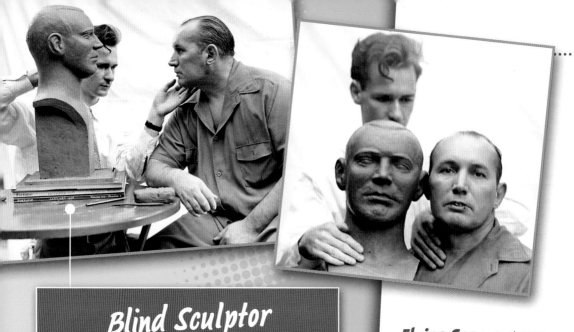

Blind Sculptor

Mark Shoesmith of New York, seen here with his model, sculpted this bust of Robert Ripley in 1938. Remarkably, Shoesmith was blind and achieved Ripley's likeness purely by touching his face.

Flying Car In April 2007, a tornado in Indiana hurled a police cruiser 120 ft (35 m) into the air, but the driver, Detective Shayna Mireles, walked away with only bruises.

Desert Run Charlie Engle (U.S.A.), Ray Zahab (Canada), and Kevin Lin (Taiwan) ran the equivalent of two marathons a day for 111 days to cross the entire 4,000-mi (6,440-km) Sahara Desert on foot in 2007. They ran through six countries—Senegal, Mauritania, Mali, Niger, Libya, and Egypt—and had to cope with temperatures over 100°F (38°C) by day, but sometimes below freezing at night.

Spitting Contest In a Sudanese marriage ritual, newlyweds have a milk spitting competition to decide who will become head of the household.

Skin Binding A 300-year-old book discovered in the center of Leeds, Yorkshire, England, in 2006 is thought to have been bound in human skin. The book was written mainly in French and was published at a time when accounts of murder trials were sometimes bound in the killer's skin.

Bottled Bliss After getting married on a Lake Michigan beach on August 18, 2007, Melody Kloska and Matt Behrs released a bottle containing their wedding vows. A few weeks later, it was picked up by Fred and Lynnette Dubendorf, of Mears, Michigan, who were also married on a beach—28 years to the day before Kloska and Behrs.

Cat Launch At the annual Flying Cat Ceremony in Verviers, Belgium, a toy cat attached to a small balloon is launched from the tower of the Church of St. Remacle. The ceremony is supposedly based on fact—in 1641, an apothecary conducted an experiment in aerodynamics by launching a live cat attached to inflated pigs' bladders from the same tower. The cat is said to have landed on its feet and run off unharmed.

Bun Snatch At the Cheung Chau Bun Festival in Hong Kong, China, contestants climb a 33-ft (10-m) tower stacked with plastic buns and try to grab as many as possible in three minutes. Local belief says that the buns make sure there will be a smooth sailing and a good catch for fishing boats.

Bottle Cap Inn

The Bottle Cap Inn was the appropriate name for this bar in Miami, Florida, that was decorated with more than 300,000 bottle caps in the 1930s.

Patriotic Diner

Customers at a West Virginia diner join waitress Judy Hawkins in singing the U.S. national anthem every day at noon. Hawkins works at the Liberty Street Diner in Charles Town and encourages customers to stop eating and sing along to "The Star-spangled Banner."

Spinster Seat

Icelandic superstition says that an unmarried woman who sits at the corner of a table will not marry for at least another seven years.

Comb Caution

The Japanese believe it is bad luck to pick up a comb with its teeth facing your body.

Balancing Act

Modern-day versions of traditional Japanese raftsmen, known as *kawanami, ride on floating square logs during a festival in Tokyo. The custom dates back to the 17th century when agile Japanese lumberjacks were able to build rafts while standing on floating logs.

Ripley's Believe It or Not!

Sauna Birth
Until the 1920s, babies in Finland were often delivered in saunas, because the heat was thought to be beneficial in warding off infection for the newborn and the mother.

Banned Names
Malaysian parents are issued a list of names that they are not permitted to give their children—including Hitler, smelly dog, hunchback, and 007.

Sleepyhead Day
July 27 is Sleepyhead Day in Finland, where the last person in the house to wake up is dragged out of bed and thrown into a lake or the sea.

Sacred Meteorite
Members of Oregon's Clackamas Indian tribe annually make a cross-country pilgrimage to visit the 15.5-ton Willamette Meteorite, which they consider sacred, at the American Museum of Natural History in New York City.

Frog Ritual
In Rangpur Province, Bangladesh, villagers perform mock weddings with frogs in the belief that the ritual will bring rain.

Tusk Currency
The 14 branches of the Tari Bunia Bank on Vanuatu's Pentecost Island have standard accounts, interest rates, and check books, and an unusual currency—pig's tusks. The tusks are paid into a customer's account, and the more they weigh, the greater their worth.

Cat Curse
In some regions of France people believe that if a bachelor steps on a cat's tail, he will not find a wife for at least a year.

Jumping Devils
At the El Colacho festival in Castrillo de Murcia, near Burgos, Spain, parents who want to protect their newborn babies from evil spirits lay them on the ground and allow grown men dressed as devils to jump over them.

Tongue in Cheek

In Cologne, Germany, in 2007, Britain's Thomas Blackthorne had a powerful jackhammer—a drill normally used for breaking up roads—lowered 10 in (25 cm) down his gullet and turned on for five seconds—and he survived. Blackthorne said his greatest fear was that the pneumatic drill would get stuck in his throat or knock all his teeth out!

Reckless Rockets

The Yenshui Beehive Rockets Festival in Taiwan is so dangerous that spectators wear protective clothing and crash helmets. Even so, each year, dozens of people suffer eye injuries and burns as thousands of small rockets are fired into the air and explode in a cloud of sparks and flames. The spectacular fireworks display is supposed to scare away evil spirits for the start of the Chinese New Year.

Icy Swim In 2004, Lynne Cox of Southern California, completed a 25-minute, 1.2-mi (1.9-km) swim through the polar ice water along the Antarctic shoreline, in water temperatures that would have given most people hypothermia in just five minutes.

Name Dropper At the age of 73, Lowell Davis of Savannah, Missouri, began to write down the names of all the persons he could remember meeting since he was three years old. At 83, in 1983, he had a 69-page binder with 3,487 names.

Flag Expert A three-year-old Indian boy can identify the names of 167 countries from their flag colors. Aazer Hussain of Bangalore learned the flags in just 11 days after his parents bought him a poster of flags of the world.

Bathtub Regatta At the International Regatta of Bathtubs—held in August on the Meuse River at Dinant, Belgium—each craft must have at least one bathtub as part of its design.

Exploding Anvils

Steel anvils are blasted up to 400 ft (120 m) through the air at Laurel, Mississippi, every April during the National Anvil Shooting Contest. Each anvil must weigh at least 100 lb (45 kg) and no more than 2 lb (1 kg) of explosives can be used to blow them up. The contest has its origins in the American Civil War when Yankee troops raided the region, blowing up anvils to destroy weapon-making facilities.

Suicide Race

The Suicide Race at Omak, Washington, is probably the most dangerous horse race in the world. Riders ~~the steep~~

Mighty Finger

Ji Fengshan, 56, of Harbin, China, can lift incredible weights with just one finger. Here he does pull-ups with one finger while carrying a load of bricks weighing 100 lb (45 kg) with another. Ji, who has been perfecting his finger strength for more than 40 years, has also pulled four connected taxis for a distance of 3 ft (1 m)—again with just his middle finger.

Slept On A man in West Virginia carried on sleeping after being shot in the head. Michael Lusher of Altizer didn't realize he'd been shot until he awoke nearly four hours later and noticed blood coming from his head.

Double First In July 2006, 15-year-old Jenna Lambert from Kingston, Ontario, Canada, became the first disabled person to swim across Lake Ontario. Jenna has cerebral palsy, and could use only her upper body—not her legs—to swim, but despite strong winds and waves, she completed the 21-mi (34-km) swim in 32 hours. Then, a year later, her 14-year-old sister Natalie became the youngest person to swim the lake when she made a 32-mi (52-km) crossing from Sackets Harbor, New York, to Kingston in under 24 hours.

Magic Touch In the depths of the Japanese winter, a man wearing nothing but a cotton loincloth wanders through the streets of Inazawa City, while those who try to touch him are doused by "guards" with icy water. Since 767 BC, the Naked Man has been making the journey to a local shrine, supposedly absorbing all the evil and bad luck of the people who touch him. So, every January, at a festival called Hadaka Matsuri, some 10,000 men, equally scantily clad, jostle to touch the naked man as he makes his way through the city.

Sheep March Bringing traffic to a standstill once a year, farmers lead some 700 sheep through the center of the Spanish capital, Madrid. The November sheep march is designed to protect Spain's 78,000 mi (125,500 km) of paths that are used for the seasonal movement of livestock.

Self-amputation After being pinned under a fallen tree for 11 hours, 66-year-old Al Hill of Iowa Hill, California, freed himself by using a pocket knife to amputate his own leg.

Historical Voyage Taking the same route as his ancestor Christopher Columbus had 508 years earlier, Scottish stockbroker Leven Brown rowed single-handed across the Atlantic from Cadiz, Spain, to the port of Scarborough in Trinidad and Tobago. Rowing up to 18 hours each day, Brown completed the 4,278-mi (6,885-km) voyage in five months. Apart from storms, his biggest problem came from whales that wanted to use his 23-ft (7-m) boat as a scratching post!

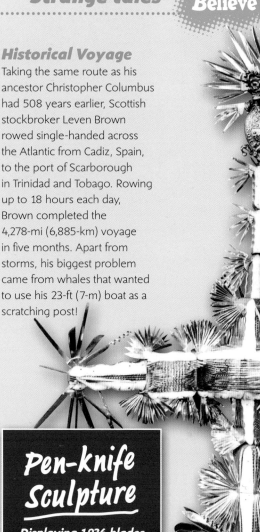

Pen-knife Sculpture

Displaying 1,936 blades in 1936, the "Year Knife" was the creation of cutlery makers Joseph Rodgers & Sons of Sheffield, England. The company started assembling their creation in 1822, with 1,822 blades, and added a new blade every year thereafter.

Optical Illusion

U.S. street artist Kurt Wenner adds the finishing touches to a 3-D work of art at Waterloo Station in London, England.

The classically inspired Wenner has pioneered an art form known as anamorphic, in which a street painting creates an optical illusion by popping up in 3-D when viewed from a certain angle. Here he appears to sit obliviously on a sofa while a taxi crashes through the walls of the house.

American Odyssey

Starting in May 2007, Quinn Baumberger of Stevens Point, Wisconsin, cycled for nine months and traveled more than 19,000 mi (30,600 km) the length of the Americas from Deadhorse, Alaska, to Ushuaia, Argentina. Along the way, he fixed 50 flat tires, was robbed twice, and sprained his ankle in Nicaragua, which put him out of action for two weeks. He replaced his old, worn shirts with those he found on the road.

Parallel Births Identical twins Nicole Cramer and Naomi Sale of Auburn, Indiana, both gave birth to a son at the same hospital on the same day—January 23, 2007.

Clean Sweep Italians moving into a new home use a broom to sweep away evil spirits and sprinkle salt in the corners of the house to purify it.

Pint-size Paparazzi
At age 14, Austin Visschedyk is a paparazzo. Realizing that money could be made from taking photos of famous people near his home in West Hollywood, he and his friend, 15-year-old Blaine Hewison-Jones, most nights head to favorite celebrity hangouts. The pint-size paparazzi, as they have become known, have to be home by 10.30 p.m. and then they work on their photographs before going to bed. Austin has already sold a snap of Adam Sandler exiting a gym for $500.

Mosquito Calling

The Great Texas Mosquito Festival at Clute features a mosquito-calling contest, where people are judged by their interpretations of a mosquito call, and a mosquito legs contest for the men and women with the skinniest legs. The festival is presided over by Willie Man-Chew, a 25-ft (7.6-m) mosquito in cowboy hat and boots.

Poker Run

Thousands of motorbike enthusiasts take part in the annual Key West Poker Run, held in Florida every September. The riders collect their playing cards at five stops between Miami and Key West before playing their hand at the final destination.

Bumpy Ride

Two British students traveled a distance of 9,500-mi (15,300-km) through 14 countries, three mountain ranges, and two deserts—in a car designed 60 years ago. George Vlasto and Max Benitz drove from the University of Calcutta, India, to London, England, in an Ambassador car that was held together by two rolls of duct tape.

Odd Titles

A book titled *The Stray Shopping Carts of Eastern North America: A Guide to Field Identification* was named the oddest book title for 2007 in an annual competition.

Bike Travels

Gregory Frazier of Fort Smith, Montana, has ridden around the world on a motorcycle five times—four solo and the fifth, in 2005, with a 63-year-old grandmother of six on the back of the bike. He has traveled more than one million miles (1.6 million km), riding from Alaska to Tierra del Fuego, and Norway to the tip of South Africa. In the course of his adventures, he has been imprisoned, bitten by snakes, been run over by bulls, had his bike stolen, and has been held up at gunpoint by a Mexican bandit.

Its author, Julian Montague, beat off stiff competition from *Tattooed Mountain Women and Spoon Boxes of Dagestan*, *How Green Were the Nazis?*, and *Better Never to Have Been: The Harm of Coming Into Existence*.

Miss Fatty

A Russian youth-oriented newspaper organizes an annual beauty contest with a difference. At the Miss Fatty contest in Moscow, large ladies try to impress with their skills at such disciplines as skipping.

Cushioned Fall A woman in Nanjing, China, survived a six-story fall in April 2007 after her landing was cushioned by a pile of human excrement. She slipped from a balcony and landed in 8 in (20 cm) of waste, which workers on the street below had just removed from the building's septic tank.

Dummy Run When ventriloquists Eyvonne Carter and Valentine Vox married in Las Vegas, Nevada, their dummies—a baby doll and dog respectively—were present, too. The best man, maid of honor, bridesmaids, and ushers were all ventriloquists, accompanied by their dummies, and the ceremony was conducted by pastor Sheila Loosley—with her dummy, called Digger.

Chicken Wing Hunt

In August 2007, Matt Reynolds led a team of fellow food enthusiasts on a 2,627-mi (4,230-km) trek through New York State in search of the best chicken wings. The Great Chicken Wing Hunt began in Manhattan and ended in Buffalo at the National Wing Festival. Reynolds and his team eventually crowned chef Columbus Grady, of Abigail's Restaurant in Seneca Falls, maker of the best wings in the whole of New York state.

Cardboard Sleds

The annual Colorado Cardboard Classic features sleds made from cardboard and glue. The 2007 event attracted 75 teams and sleds in all different shapes.

Upside Down In 2007,

Antonio Montagno survived three days without food or water—hanging upside down —after a paragliding accident landed him in a tree near Florence, Italy.

Weary Legs In 2007,

Greg Kolodziejzyk of Calgary, Alberta, Canada, traveled 107 mi (172 km) by pedal boat in 24 hours around the city's Glenmore Reservoir.

Furniture Race

Couches, chairs, toilets, baby cribs, trash cans, and even coffins are fixed to skis or snowboards and driven at breakneck speed down a snow-covered mountain in the annual Big Mountain Furniture Race. Held every April since 1970, the event at Whitefish, Montana, marks the end of the skiing season. As well as appearance and speed, points are awarded for accuracy, as there is a target at the end of the run and competitors are scored by how close to it they can stop without actually hitting it.

Feuding Brothers Two

brothers have divided the house that they share with barbed wire because they keep fighting. Taso Hadjiev and his brother Asen from Malka Arda, Bulgaria, have sued each other more than 200 times over the past 40 years but neither can afford to leave the family home—all their money has been spent on lawyers' fees.

Sand Sculpture Indian

sculptor Sudarsan Patnaik created a lifelike replica of the Taj Mahal—in sand. It took him 56 working hours to complete the model, which stood 15 ft (4.5 m) high.

John Davis studied photographs of a real Boeing 747-400 cockpit on aviation websites to make sure that the design for his home version was accurate.

Ripley's
Believe It or Not!®

Behind the exterior of John's modest home lies a replica of a 747 cockpit.

Plane Crazy

John Davis from Coventry, England, has spent eight years and $30,000 constructing an exact replica of a Boeing 747 cockpit in the spare bedroom of his house. The hi-tech simulator, which incorporates an autopilot system, weather radar, and engine sounds, was bought mainly over the Internet. To add to the illusion of real flight, he has erected a 6-ft (1.8-m) screen at the front of the cockpit showing panoramic views of places around the world, from the Alps to the skyline of New York. He even plays mock announcements, instructing passengers to fasten their seat belts to prepare themselves for takeoff.

Same Dress In 2007, Charlotte Middleton of Norfolk, England, became the sixth bride in her family to wear the same wedding dress. The chiffon and satin gown was first worn by her great grandmother in 1910.

Betty Picnic An annual Betty Picnic takes place at Grants Pass, Oregon, in June to celebrate people all over the world who are called Betty or who display Betty-like characteristics!

Hammer Blow Participants in Portugal's So Joo Festival express their attraction to members of the opposite sex by hitting them over the head with a large plastic hammer!

Viking Ship Professor Steven Harding of the University of Nottingham, England, found a 1,000-year-old Viking ship buried under the parking lot of a pub in Merseyside.

Lucky Omen Sitting for a 2007 exam to become a firefighter, Alina Modoran, from Romania, wore her wedding dress. She had come straight from the church and had decided not to change out of her dress because she thought it would bring bad luck.

Hair Sculpture For a 2007 exhibition, Chinese artist Wenda Gu created a sculpture using more than 7 mi (11 km) of braided human hair.

Kayak Crossing

Two Australian adventurers completed a historic crossing of the Tasman Sea by kayak—less than one year after another Australian, Andrew McAuley, died while attempting the same feat. James Castrission and Justin Jones, both from Sydney, finished the arduous 2,050-mi (3,300-km) journey—known locally as "crossing the ditch" —from Forster, New South Wales, to Ngamotu Beach on New Zealand's North Island in 62 days.

Although the kayak was designed to combat 40-ft (12-m) waves, crossing the Tasman Sea proved a daunting prospect and sometimes Jones and Castrission had to paddle in shifts for 18 hours a day.

They arrived in early January 2008 — 20 days later than anticipated after strong winds and stormy seas left them floundering in circles halfway through the trip and nearly forced them to turn back. They also had to fend off the unwelcome attention of sharks.

Their voyage had taken four years' intense preparation, including sleep deprivation and isolation training. Afterward, Castrission acknowledged the value of having a companion to lean on. "Some nights when we were out there," he said, "we had each other to hold through the difficult moments."

When conditions were favorable, the intrepid adventurers were able to paddle at speeds of up to 6 mph (10 km/h).

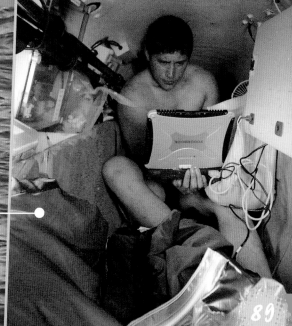

Justin keeping the website account of their epic journey up to date in the kayak's sleeping quarters.

Water Battle

To cleanse the community in readiness for the Buddhist New Year, each April, around 100,000 residents of Chiang Mai, Thailand, soak each other with water pistols in a giant battle as part of the Songkran Festival.

Flying Pumpkins

At the Punkin' Chunkin' Championship staged at Nassau, Delaware, each November, enthusiasts build catapults and mini cannons to launch their pumpkins as far as possible into the sky.

She's Mine!

A couple in Merioneth, Wales, proved just how deep their love was —by getting married 500 ft (152 m) below ground in an abandoned slate mine. Kerry Bevan and Wayne Davies and their 15 guests wore traditional wedding attire with the addition of helmets and gum boots.

Can Do!

In June 2007, three men from Queensland, Australia, sailed nearly 50 mi (80 km) down the Brisbane River in a boat made from beer cans.

Wrapped Up

A Kenyan air passenger flying home from China in 2007 was found to be wearing more than 100 items of men's and women's clothing! He told officials that he had been worried about being charged for carrying excess luggage.

Manilow Sentence

People who break the noise laws in Fort Lupton, Colorado, are given an unusual sentence—they are forced to listen to Barry Manilow music for an hour! The punishment is the idea of Judge Paul Sacco, who claims that offenders who go through the Manilow treatment rarely re-offend. Also on his punishment playlist are The Carpenters, Dolly Parton, and Barney the Dinosaur.

Disk Dragon

Sculptors in China built a huge dragon-shaped lamp from hundreds of used computer disks for a 2007 carnival at Beijing International Sculpture Park.

Fire Ant Festival The October Fire Ant Festival, at Marshall, Texas, is a celebration of all things related to the humble fire ant—including a parade where people dress up as the insects.

Jackpot Joy After winning $10,000 on the Arizona Lottery in 2007, Barbara and Barry Salzman of Henderson, Nevada, immediately bought another ticket with their winnings and won the $15-million jackpot.

Felled Bear In 2007, a man killed a 300-lb (135-kg) black bear that was threatening his family—by throwing a log at it. Chris Everhart felled the bear with a single blow after it raided the family's campsite in the Chattahoochee National Forest in Georgia.

Tornado Terror Caught in a tornado-like storm in New South Wales, Australia, in February 2007, German paraglider Ewa Wisnierska was sucked up in a tornado tunnel to an extraordinary 32,600 ft (9,936 m)—higher than Mount Everest. She ascended at a rate of 65 ft (20 m) per second, causing her to lose consciousness, and in an 80-minute ordeal she survived lightning, a battering from hailstones the size of tennis balls, temperatures as low as −50°F (−45°C), and a lack of oxygen. She reagained consciousness after 45 minutes and eventually managed to come back down to earth 40 mi (64 km) away, covered in ice and gasping for air.

Outsize Album A photo album unveiled in Orlando, Florida, in 2007 was so big that it needed two adults to turn each of its 20 pages. Created for the launch of the 2008 Dodge Grand Caravan, it measured 9 ft (3 m) wide by 12 ft (4 m) tall.

Never a Cross Word! When Aric Egmont of Cambridge, Massachusetts, wanted to propose to Jennie Bass, he decided to do so via a crossword puzzle. At his request, *The Boston Globe* Sunday magazine created a special puzzle where the crossword clues spelled out his proposal.

Round The World

Jamaican-born Barrington Irving of Miami, Florida, flew solo around the world in 2007—at just 23 years of age. His epic flight in a single-engine plane took three months, and on the way he encountered snowstorms, sandstorms, thunderstorms, monsoons, 100-mph (160-km/h) winds, and freezing fog. He named his plane **Inspiration** because, he said, "that's what I wanted my historic venture to be for young people."

Baby Boomerang In 1997, Sadir Kattan of Australia, created a boomerang smaller than the palm of his hand that could be thrown 65 ft (20 m) and returned accurately.

Bad Luck Seventy-five-year-old Phulram Chaudhary of Nepal married a dog in a local custom to ensure good luck. The charm didn't work, as he died three days later!

Rain Prayers For the Tohetohe festival in Nagasaki, Japan, people wearing conical bamboo hats and straw raincoats visit dozens of homes where residents promptly drench them with water! The festival is held each January to pray for rain during the rice-planting season.

Tire Craft Cheng Yanhua traveled more than 1,500 mi (2,400 km) down China's Yangtze River in 2007—on a tire inner tube. Using two small bamboo paddles, and with a basin in the tire for his feet, he took 43 days to get from his home in Jinzhou City to Shanghai.

Making a Splash In the National Cannonball Championships at Toronto, Ontario, Canada, heavyweight divers leap feet-first from a 16-ft (5-m) tower into a swimming pool with the goal of making as big a splash as possible. Burly men plummet into the pool in a variety of costumes— including Michael Jackson, a Viking, and Princess Leia from Star Wars. Competitors are judged on splash, flair, and the ability to tuck.

Math Prodigy In August 2007, Hong Kong Baptist University accepted math prodigy March Tian Boedihardjo as a student—at the age of nine.

Squirrel Find Squirrels in Placer County, California, dug up an ancient artifact in July 2007. The animals were rummaging around in soil at the Maidu Indian Interpretive Center—where it is illegal for human archeologists to dig—when they unearthed a 10,000-year-old carved tool.

Tractor Trek Tractor fan Wolfgang Mueller drove his 44-year-old tractor 700 mi (1,130 km) from Stuttgart, Germany, to Coventry, England, in 2007. He towed a caravan through Luxembourg and France, boarded a ferry at Calais, and drove the tractor sedately through English country lanes. He wanted to visit the place where his beloved Massey Ferguson MF35 had been built—only to find that the factory had been demolished.

Believe It or Not! Blouses

Blouses featuring Ripley's Believe It or Not! cartoons were sold at the Ripley's New York City Odditorium in 1939. During the 1930s, the worldwide-syndicated Ripley cartoons had more than 80 million readers daily.

Perfect Perspective

As a child, Stephen Wiltshire was mute and did not relate to other people. Diagnosed as autistic, he had uncontrolled tantrums, lived entirely in his own world, and did not learn to speak fully until he was nine. Yet he has an incredible talent for drawing and can produce remarkably accurate and detailed pictures entirely from memory.

Stephen Wiltshire

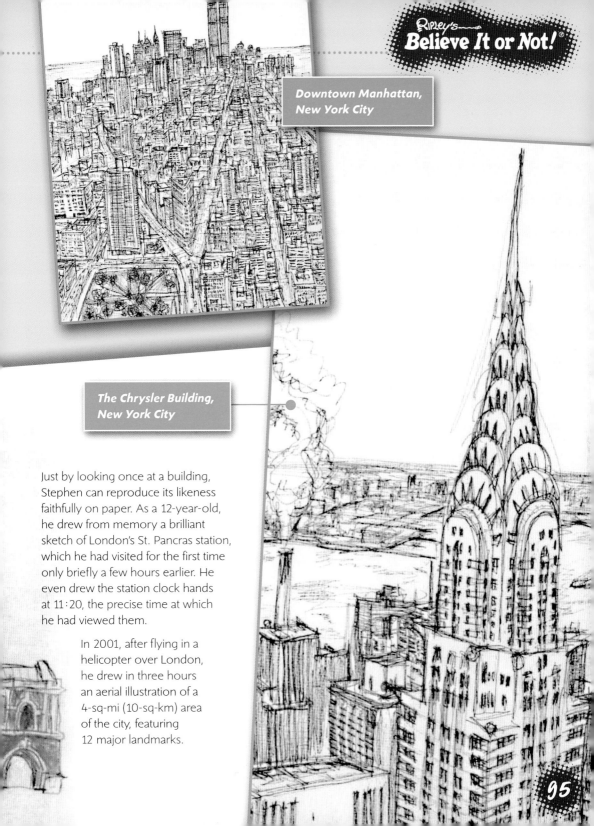

Downtown Manhattan, New York City

The Chrysler Building, New York City

Just by looking once at a building, Stephen can reproduce its likeness faithfully on paper. As a 12-year-old, he drew from memory a brilliant sketch of London's St. Pancras station, which he had visited for the first time only briefly a few hours earlier. He even drew the station clock hands at 11:20, the precise time at which he had viewed them.

In 2001, after flying in a helicopter over London, he drew in three hours an aerial illustration of a 4-sq-mi (10-sq-km) area of the city, featuring 12 major landmarks.

Chainsaw Carving

A sculptor wielding a chainsaw carves a bald eagle at the annual Woodsmen's Field Days festival in New York State. The chainsaw carvers are given 45 minutes to create a sculpture, at the end of which the artworks go to auction. The winner is the sculpture that attracts the highest bid.

Senior Singers A new band made an assault on the U.K. and U.S. charts in 2007—even though they had a combined age of more than 3,000 years! The Zimmers were a group of 40 British seniors who became a surprise Internet hit with their version of The Who's "My Generation," complete with its inappropriate line "I hope I die before I get old."

Memory Boy Eleven-year-old Nischal Narayanam of Hyderabad, India, can memorize and recall 225 random objects in the exact order they are presented to him.

Wad a Find! In 2007, British archeology student Sarah Pickin discovered a 5,000-year-old piece of chewing gum at a dig site in western Finland.

Burning Wheels On Easter Sunday night throughout Germany, giant oak wheels— 7 ft (2.1 m) in diameter and weighing 800 lb (363 kg)— are stuffed with straw, set alight, and rolled down hillsides into the valleys below. It is believed to be a good omen if the wheels are still burning when they reach the valley.

Slow Route Choosing not to fly for environmental reasons, Barbara Haddrill spent six months traveling by bus, train, and cargo ship on a 9,770-mi (15,725-km) journey from Powys, Wales, to attend her best friend's wedding in Brisbane, Australia.

Swan Foreboding To people in Scotland the sight of three swans flying together indicates that a national disaster is imminent.

Parachute Plunge
On his first attempt at skydiving, Benno Jacobs of Bloemfontein, South Africa, fell 3,300 ft (1,000 m) to the ground when his parachute malfunctioned. He walked away with no broken bones!

Scissors Dance

This competitor at a national scissors dance contest in Lima, Peru, has livened up his act by dancing with two crates attached to hooks pierced through his skin. Other dancers perform with nails hammered into their tongue or metal wires driven through their cheeks in a true test of courage and agility. Contestants perform each dance to the accompaniment of a pair of scissors, made from two 10-in (25-cm) pieces of metal.

Hairy Contest Staged at Fairbanks, Alaska, in July, the Hairy Chest, Hairy Legs, and Beard Contest sets out to find the hairiest men in the U.S.A.

Pi Patience In 2006, Akira Haraguchi of Mobara, Japan, recited pi to 100,000 decimal places from memory. It took him more than 16 hours.

Small is Beautiful

A pinhead-sized replica of the Lloyd's of London building sold for $180,000 at an auction in 2007. The model, which was an exact replica of the famous building, took English micro-sculptor Willard Wigan four months to create, using white gold and platinum. The sculpture can be viewed only through a microscope. Wigan, whose previous works include re-creating the Statue of Liberty inside the eye of a needle, said that the Lloyd's of London building was the most difficult piece he has ever made.

Canned Fish

A fish caught off the coast of Iceland in 2007 was wearing a tin can that had grown into its flesh. The fish must have looked into the can and become partly trapped. When fishermen first spotted the halibut, they thought it was wearing tribal jewelry.

Hen-pecked Husband

At the wedding of Terry Morris and Renee Biwer near Bismarck, North Dakota, in August 2006, the bridesmaid was a chicken! Henrietta the hen has been a pet of the groom's for 12 years and even stays in hotel rooms with the couple. The ceremony had a distinct barnyard feel to it, with the bride and groom riding in on horseback and saying their vows from the saddle.

Marathon Swim

In September 2007, Firas al Mualla swam 68 mi (110 km) nonstop across the Mediterranean Sea in 42 hours from Cyprus to his native Syria.

Worm Race

At Banner Elk, North Carolina, each October woolly worms (a variety of furry caterpillar) crawl up a piece of string for a first prize of $1,000. The race derives from the belief that we can forecast the weather depending on the worm's ability to climb the string.

Burry Man Every August, a resident of Queensferry, Scotland, dressed in white flannels and covered from head to toe with the Velcro-like burrs of the burdock plant, parades 7 mi (11 km) through the town. During the journey he drinks whisky through a straw. The Burry Man is believed to date back to a shipwreck victim who, having no clothes, dressed himself in burrs.

Human Flag

Canadian gymnast and acrobat Dominic Lacasse can hold himself horizontally on a bar as a "Human Flag" for 39 seconds—a feat of incredible strength.

Parrot Fashion A four-year-old autistic boy, who has severe learning difficulties and could not speak, learned his first words thanks to his pet parrot. After listening to Barney the macaw, Dylan Hargreaves of Lancashire, England, mimicked the bird's vocabulary.

Amazing Animals

Crocodile Attack

Veterinarian Chang Po-yu lost his arm to the jaws of a saltwater crocodile in Shaoshan Zoo in Kaohsiung, Taiwan, on April 11, 2007.

The vet's forearm was bitten clean through when he reached through iron railings to remove a tranquilizer dart from the 440-lb (200-kg) reptile. Two bullets were immediately shot into the neck of the crocodile, which then dropped the arm. But this story has a doubly remarkable ending. First, the crocodile was unharmed by the gunshots as the bullets didn't penetrate its hide, they merely shocked the croc into opening its mouth; and second, a team of surgeons operated for seven hours to reattach the arm—successfully!

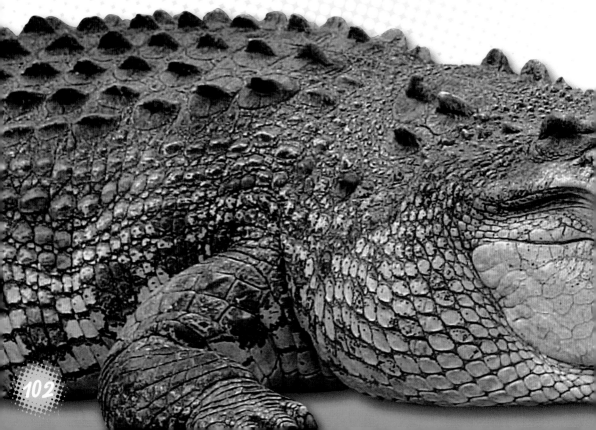

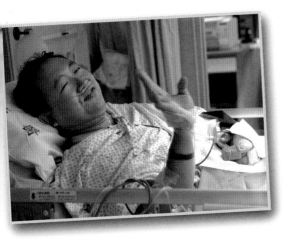

My associate helped me to stop bleeding by pressing on the top of the arm until the ambulance came. When I was on the way to the hospital, the police helped me to take my arm back from the crocodile's mouth.

Right now it's still hard for me to accept this serious damage. I have gone through six large operations and countless small operations. At present, my left arm has no sensation, and the injury is still in the process of recovery. I still need lots of recuperative treatment—for at least two years. Although I can't work right now, I still hope that I could continue to work in the administration or management of the zoo, the treatment of animals… and so on, in the future."

"I am a veterinarian and a director of the zoo. When I anesthetized and treated the crocodile, the animal took my left-hand away suddenly. It was a huge shock in my mind, my limb felt pretty numb.

My left arm caused extreme pain, but I told myself that I must live, I want to take my arm back, and do my best to connect it again.

Ugliest Dog

After finishing second in 2006, Elwood, a Chinese Crested dog, from New Jersey, went one better in 2007 by being crowned the World's Ugliest Dog in the annual contest at Petaluma, California. With the award came a prize of $1,000, no wonder his owner Karen Quigley thinks he's cute.

Croc Plunge Believe it or not, a crocodile suffered nothing worse than a broken tooth after falling from the 12th floor of an apartment block in the Russian city of Nizhny-Novgorod. It was the third time that the pet croc, named Khenar, had tried to escape his captivity by climbing through a window.

Long Lunch Few birds have an appetite to match that of baby robins—they eat 14 ft (4.3 m) of earthworms every day.

Caring Cat A nine-year-old boy with Type 1 diabetes was saved from having a possible seizure by the attention of his cat. Mel-O climbed the ladder to Alex Rose's loft bed in his home in Morinville, Alberta, Canada, walked on his chest, swatted his face and purred in his ear until he got out of bed. When he went to his mother, his glucose levels were found to be dangerously low. Nobody knows how the cat managed to sense low blood sugar.

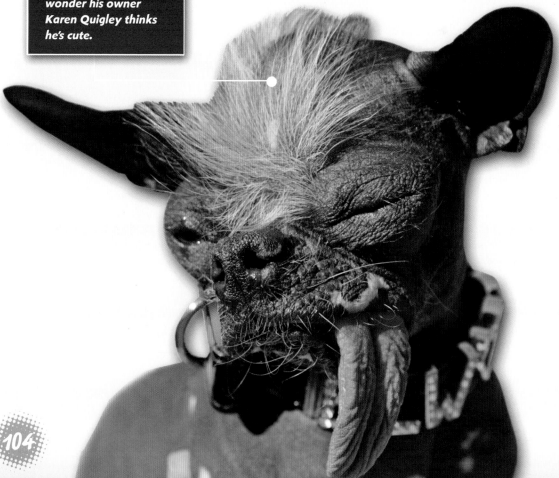

Chewed Cash A pooch named Pepper was in the doghouse in 2007 after eating $750 in cash. The dog was staying with owner Debbie Hulleman's mother in Oakdale, Minnesota, when it found a purse and chewed the contents. It spat out some money and when the family went to clean up the dog's mess outside the house, they noticed a $50 bill hanging out of one pile of poop. They gradually recovered $647 from both poop and vomit, and exchanged the cash for clean currency at a bank.

Too Heavy Young gannets are fed so much fish that they are unable to fly. On leaving the nest, they have to fast for a couple of weeks until they are light enough to get airborne.

Talented Parrot Alex, an African gray parrot, could identify 50 different objects, seven colors, five shapes, and quantities up to six. His owner, Dr. Irene Pepperberg of Waltham, Massachusetts, said he was the intellectual equivalent of a five-year-old child. His last words to her before his death in 2007 were: "You be good. See you tomorrow. I love you."

Tasty Toy A pet bearded dragon, named Mushu, was treated by a veterinarian in Jacksonville, Florida, in 2007 — after swallowing a 7-in (18-cm) rubber lizard.

Brand New Tail

Winter, a two-year-old bottlenose dolphin at the Clearwater Marine Aquarium in Florida, has been fitted with a prosthetic tail. The tail, which helps her to swim naturally, has a silicon sleeve that fits over her stump and a joint made of titanium. She lost her tail fin after becoming tangled in a crab trap at sea.

Great Escape Australian rancher David George spent a week clinging desperately to the branches of a tree to avoid being eaten by crocodiles. Stranded in crocodile country after falling off his horse and hitting his head, George climbed a tree and stayed there for six days and nights, terrified by the red eyes of the hungry crocodiles that were circling expectantly below. Surviving on just a packet of cheese-and-ham sandwiches and a few sips of water, he was eventually spotted by rescuers and winched to safety.

Squirrel Arsonists Squirrels started two fires in eight days at the home of Alan Turcott, of Blue Island, Illinois—by knocking loose and chewing electrical cables.

Untimely Death A kangaroo met an unusual death in Victoria, Australia, after it swam out to sea and was attacked by a marauding shark. Kangaroos usually venture out to sea only if they are ill or in danger.

Red Sheep To cheer up drivers sitting in highway traffic jams in 2007, a Scottish farmer dyed his flock of sheep red! Andrew Jack sprayed his 54-strong flock before releasing them on to the hills next to the busy M8 highway.

Swan Lake A swan on a lake in Germany has fallen in love with a plastic pedal boat. Petra the black swan circles the swan-shaped boat and makes amorous noises at it. She is so in love that when the boat didn't fly south for the winter, neither did she.

Snake Slain When a deadly viper slithered into the intensive care ward of a Croatian hospital, 80-year-old patient Miko Vukovic, who was recovering from heart surgery, jumped from his bed and beat the snake to death with his walking stick.

Fake Burials Animal experts have discovered that gray squirrels fake food burials in order to confuse their rivals if they think they are being watched. To protect their winter food stocks from potential thieves, squirrels put on an elaborate show of burying non-existent nuts and seeds, even covering them over with soil to dupe any thieving onlookers.

Crane Imposter

Staff at a wild bird reserve in Gloucestershire, England, rear Eurasian Crane chicks using crane costumes and crane heads made out of litter-pickers so that the birds do not get too accustomed to humans.

Bath Relief After accidentally setting fire to her home in Northumberland, England, a Rottweiler puppy survived by jumping into the bath and gulping air through the plughole. Peggy had caused the fire by switching on the kitchen stove as she tried to reach her owner's chocolate birthday cake.

Loud Howl The scream of a howler monkey can be heard up to 5 mi (8 km) away. It is so noisy that the sound of a family of howlers traveling through the forest has been mistaken for a thunderstorm.

Pig Country There are more wild pigs than people in Australia, which has a population of 21 million people and 23 million feral pigs.

Back to Life A hamster in Dagenham, England, was miraculously brought back to life after being accidentally cooked. Christmas the hamster was charred when the oven on which his cage was standing was turned on by mistake. When firefighters arrived, he was lying on his back with his legs in the air and his tongue hanging out, but after some oxygen, a rub of his tummy, and a few sips of juice, amazingly he was resuscitated.

Cool Cat

It looks like a wild animal but behaves like a domestic cat. Created by crossing two exotic breeds—a Serval and a Leopard cat—with an ordinary cat, the Ashera is a new breed of domestic cat that resembles a mini-leopard but is playful and affectionate. It grows up to 30 lb (14 kg) in weight and costs a far-from-ordinary $22,000.

Pig-assos

Pigs at a farm in Devon, England, paint works of art on large canvasses with their snouts and trotters. They got into art by accident, when they knocked over some tins of non-toxic paint after running amok at a craft fair.

Grass Addict A dog in Oxfordshire, England, needed life-saving surgery after vets discovered a pound of grass in its stomach. Pie, a Rottweiler–German Shepherd cross, had become so addicted to eating grass that he was unable to digest it and ballooned to three times his normal weight.

French-speaking To strike up a rapport with their new Siberian tiger, staff at the Valley Zoo, in Edmonton, Alberta, had to find a French-speaking keeper. The tiger, named Boris, was born at a zoo in Quebec and only answers commands that are spoken in French.

Maternal Pride A lioness separately adopted three baby antelopes at Kenya's Samburu National Park over the course of a few months. Normally, a young antelope would make a delicious meal for a big cat, but this tenderhearted lioness was fiercely protective of the calves. One day, while the lioness slept, a male lion ate one of the calves. When she awoke from her slumber, the adoptive mother-of-three became grief-stricken and paced around the bush roaring in anger.

Hearty Meal U.S. scientists have discovered that some snakes can survive without food for up to two years by digesting their own hearts. Snake hearts then quickly rebuild themselves after a nutritious meal.

Watch the Birdie!

A pelican resident in St. James's Park, London, England, took a radical departure from its usual diet of fish when it decided to try pigeon instead. The pelican, one of five famous pelicans in this park that lies adjacent to Buckingham Palace, was performing its usual photocall for visiting tourists when it amazed them by scooping a nearby pigeon into its beak. The hapless bird struggled in the beak for a full 20 minutes before the pelican finally swallowed it.

Dances with Buffalo

Some families keep dogs, others keep cats, but the Bridges family of Quinlan, Texas, have a truly unusual pet—a 1300-lb (590-kg) buffalo named Wildthing.

Wildthing has his own room in the house, where he eats and sleeps, and is so tame that he follows his master, R.C. Bridges, everywhere and even used to dance with him. They are best friends and, when Wildthing turned two in 2007, the family staged a birthday party in his room, draping it in ribbons and making a cake of feed and icing shaped like a buffalo patty, topped with a candle.

R.C., a cowboy since childhood, started raising the baby buffalo in 2005. Helped by his son Lloyd, he "halter broke" the young bull even though Wildthing could kick and push with the strength of a fully grown animal. Since then, R.C. has taught Wildthing to pull a plow, and also a chariot on which he takes the family for rides. Wildthing will happily pull R.C.'s daughter Taylor along on a sleigh and another son Will has learned to ski behind him.

Wildthing tucks into a birthday meal in his own special living quarters.

Wildthing spends much of his day in the house, but he also has a pen in the yard.

Wildthing rarely leaves R.C.'s side. Even when R.C. sits down, Wildthing will lie down next to him.

The Bridges family with their big baby, Wildthing. He still has a lot more growing to do.

Color Split

Peavey, a horse belonging to Ann Huth-Fretz of Tiffin, Ohio, has a two-tone eye, with the colors split straight down the middle!

Deadly Head A man in Prosser, Washington State, was hospitalized after being bitten by the decapitated head of a rattlesnake. Danny Anderson beheaded the 5-ft-long (1.5-m) rattler with a shovel, but when he reached down to pick up the severed head, it bit his finger, injecting venom. He took the head to a hospital, and by the time he arrived his tongue was swollen and the venom was spreading. He was released after two days' treatment. The bite was thought to be a reflex action from the snake, as, believe it or not, snake heads can still be dangerous up to an hour after being separated from the body.

Animal Bride To atone for past acts of cruelty to dogs, a 33-year-old Indian farmer married a female dog in a traditional Hindu ceremony in the southern state of Tamil Nadu in 2007. The canine bride, who was bathed before the wedding, wore an orange sari and a traditional floral garland.

Twin Freaks A tiger at Tianjin Zoo, China, gave birth to twin cubs in 2007—one orange, like a normal Bengal tiger, and one white. The mother is a mixed-blood tiger and it appears that, by a genetic freak, each of her cubs has inherited her different colors.

Tiger Attack A stray dog had a lucky escape in January 2008 when it wandered into the tiger pit at Memphis Zoo in Memphis, Tennessee. The 50-lb (23-kg) female retriever-mix jumped over a railing and a wall before swimming across a moat to the center of the enclosure, where it was attacked by a 225-lb (100-kg) Sumatran tiger. Seeing the incident, zoo workers used fireworks and air horns to distract the tiger and, despite being held in the tiger's grasp for several minutes, the dog escaped with nothing worse than puncture wounds to its neck and shoulders.

Painting Pups An art gallery in Salisbury, Maryland, staged an unusual exhibition in 2007—the artists of the exhibits were all dogs! Encouraged by dog-trainer Mary Stadelbacher, the canine Canalettos paint their masterpieces by chewing on a rubber bone with a hole drilled in the middle to hold a paintbrush. In this way they daub paint on the canvas. Each original work is signed with a black paw print in the corner and some of the doggy paintings have already sold for $350.

Fire Rescue

Jango, a Golden Retriever from Trail, British Columbia, Canada, saved his family from a fire by barking as the house filled with smoke. The dog then continued to bark to help the Unger family navigate their way to safety through the flames.

Three Eyes In 2007, a piglet at a Chinese farm was born with two faces. The mutant had one extra-large head, two mouths, and three eyes!

Pooch Hooch Pet-shop owner Gerrie Berendsen of Zelhem, the Netherlands, has devised a new beer—for dogs. The nonalcoholic brew is made from a mix of beef extract and malt.

Two-faced

A two-faced calf, named Star, was born recently at a dairy farm in Rural Retreat, Virginia. The curious creature had three sets of teeth, two lower jaws, and two tongues, but only one mouth. It also had two noses with separate airways, but only a single eye socket with two eyes in it!

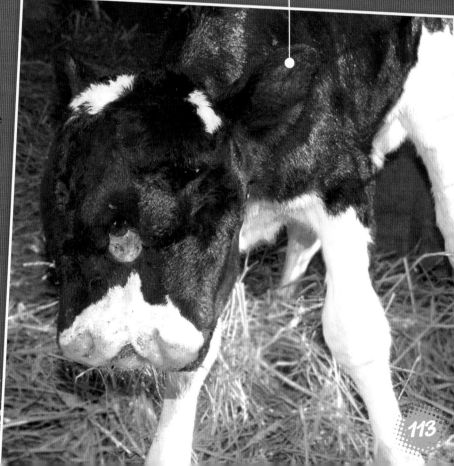

Troubled Triplets

Triplet puppies were born in Virginia in 2007, without any front legs—the first case of its kind in the world. Yet with the aid of daily physiotherapy at a New York animal shelter to strengthen their muscles, the brave little Chihuahuas were soon getting around by standing upright and hopping on their back legs.

Milk Boost Romanian farmers have boosted milk production by playing music to their cows. Cowhands have set up CD players in the stables, and the music relaxes the animals so much that they even come in alone from the fields just to listen to more tunes.

Stuck Duck Eighteen firefighters, three fire trucks, a Land Rover four-wheel drive, and a rescue boat were used in a three-hour rescue to save a trapped duck near Birmingham, England. As crews raced to the scene from 35 mi (56 km) away, residents feared a child had drowned, but it turned out the casualty was Daffy, a white Aylesbury duck who was stranded in a drainage tunnel.

Robot Shark A robot shark was built for the U.K.'s BBC series *Smart Sharks*, containing a hidden camera that filmed sharks live in their natural habitats.

Collie Wobble Kyle, a 14-year-old collie, who is partially blind and is also hard of hearing, survived a 50-ft (15-m) plunge at a Scottish waterfall—called Dog Falls. Despite being the place of Kyle's misfortune, the spot actually gets its name because the water falls in the shape of a dog's leg.

Jumbo Job City officials of Barisal, Bangladesh, hired circus elephants to help them to demolish illegal buildings in March 2007. With a lack of mechanical demolition tools at their disposal, officials called in the elephants, who demolished the buildings in minutes.

Courageous Kittens
An elderly Chinese woman was saved in 2006 when eight family cats fought off a giant cobra that was trying to slither into her bed. As the deadly 6-ft (1.8-m) serpent made its way across the floor, the cats surrounded it, the mother cat stamping on the snake's head and the seven kittens biting its body and dragging it out of the house. As the cats pinned the snake to the ground, the old woman's son beat it to death.

Odd Eyes

A two-year-old cat in Riyadh, Saudi Arabia, has different-colored eyes—one brown and one blue. Appropriately, the cat is a mix of Persian and Siamese.

Purr-fect Passenger
A cat in Wolverhampton, England, amazed passengers by traveling on a bus nearly every day for three months in 2007. The cat jumped on the number 331 bus, always sat at the front, and traveled for two stops before getting off near a fish-and-chip shop.

Cool Cat

Odin, a six-year-old white Bengal tiger who lives at the Six Flags Discovery Zoo in Vallejo, California, has no qualms about diving into water after a piece of meat thrown in by his trainer.

Most cats shy away from water, but Odin loves a cool dip, especially at dinner time. Some scientists believe that because tigers evolved in eastern Asia they dislike excessive heat and may use a refreshing swim as a way to keep cool.

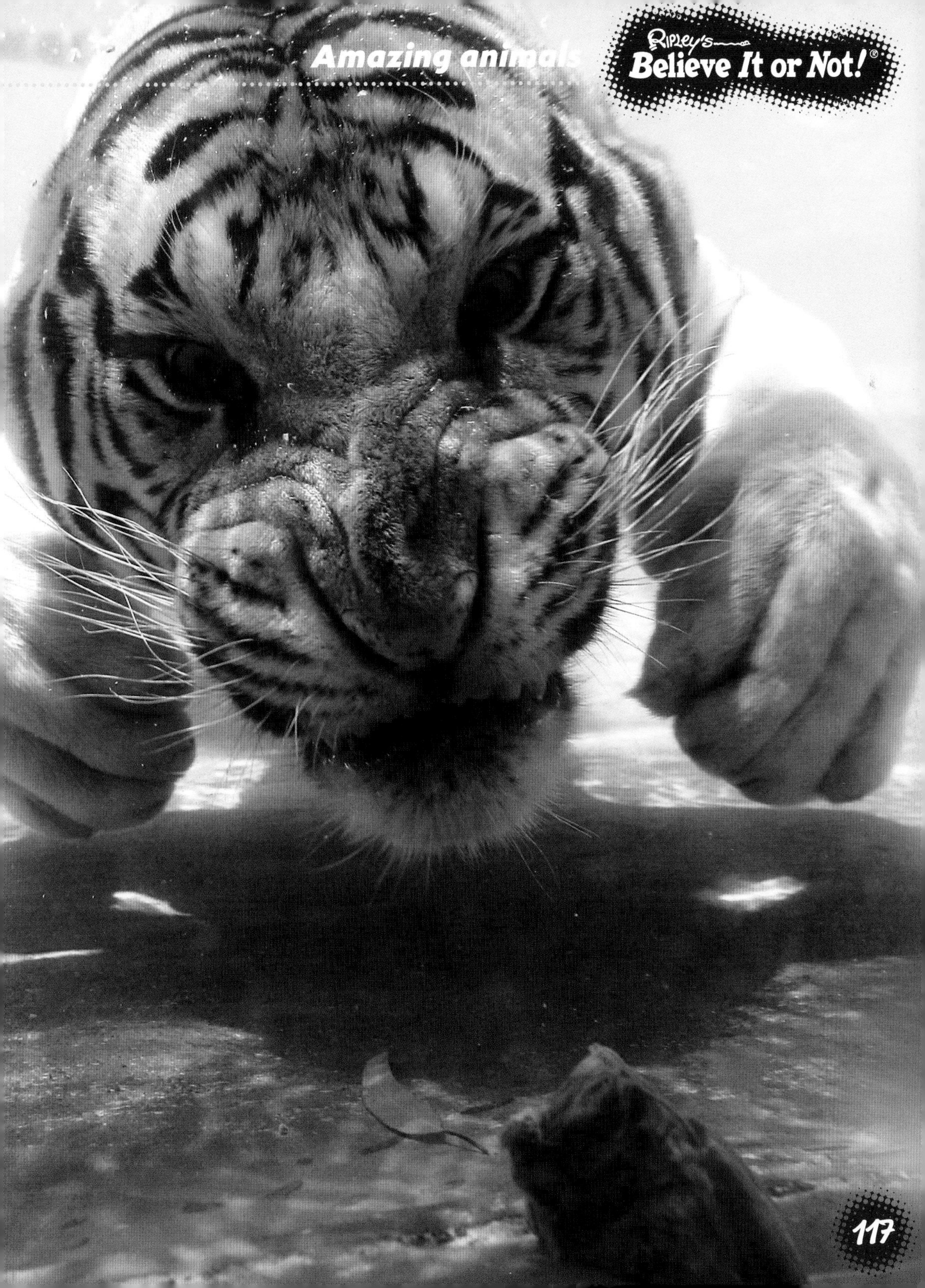

Rescue Dog

An Italian animal-lover has trained Newfoundland dogs to jump out of helicopters and rescue people who are drowning in the sea. Ferrucio Pilenga, from Bergamo, has a team of expert canine swimmers patrolling Italy's beaches, where they have already saved a number of lives.

Penguins Uncovered

In 2004, scientists obtained amazing images of penguins underwater by strapping miniature cameras to the birds' backs. They found that penguins swim together with at least one other bird on about a quarter of their dives for food.

Fishing Bats

Whereas most bats prefer to eat insects, the bulldog bat from Central and South America is an accomplished fisherman. It trails its extra-long legs in the water and grabs fish with its huge hooked claws.

Head Stuck

A cat in Cambridgeshire, England, got its head stuck after trying to pull a mouse out of a jelly jar. The cat was found wandering next to a road with the jar on its head and the mouse just in front of its nose. The cat eventually freed both itself and the mouse by smashing the jar.

Cow-nivore!

A cow in Chandpur, India, eats chickens! When 48 chickens went missing in a month, farmers suspected local dogs—until one night they saw their friendly cow, named Lal, creep in and devour several live chickens.

Blessing in Disguise

Having a leg amputated after getting it caught on a fence would be a disaster for most ducks, but not for Stumpy—because, owing to a rare mutation, he was born with four legs! In fact Stumpy, from Hampshire, England, can actually waddle much faster in pursuit of his lady-friend now that he has only one extra leg to carry.

Dogwatch

A 196-lb (89-kg) Newfoundland dog is the latest recruit to the lifeguards in Cornwall, England. Bilbo's training paid off when he prevented a tourist from entering dangerous currents by swimming in front of her to stop her going out any further to sea. Bilbo has his own lifeguard vest with safety messages written across it.

Kiss-of-Life A man saved the life of his bulldog puppy by giving her the kiss-of-life after she had fallen into an icy lake while chasing ducks and geese. The puppy, named Lucy, had a blue face and paws by the time Randy Gurchin pulled her from the wintry water in Sarpy County, Nebraska, but he revived her by closing her mouth, placing his mouth over her nose, and then breathing into her lungs while pushing on her chest.

Cat-loving Dog Ginny, a Schnauzer–Siberian husky cross, rescued more than 1,000 cats in her lifetime. She had the unique accolade, for a dog, of being named Cat of the Year at the 1998 Westchester Cat Show, in New York. When she died in 2005, at the ripe old age of 17, her memorial service was attended by 300 cats. Her owner, Philip Gonzalez from Long Beach, New York, never trained her—she just knew instinctively when a cat was in trouble. "Ginny loved cats," he said. "And cats loved Ginny."

RESCUE

SURF RESCUE

LIFEGUARD

Penwith District Council
ESAVING NOTICE

BATHE BETWEEN
and YELLOW FLAGS
AVE YOUNG CHILDREN UNATTENDED

Penwith District Council
LIFESAVING NOTICE

BATHE BETWEEN
RED and YELLOW FLAGS
DO NOT LEAVE YOUNG CHILDREN UNATTENDED

LIFEGUARD

119

Sales Dog A dog in Pingdong City, Taiwan, is so clever that she serves customers in her owner's nut shop. The dog—named Hello—can open the refrigerator, pick up the nuts, put them on the counter, and collect money from customers. She also goes shopping by herself, waits patiently in line, and when it is her turn to be served, she puts her front paws on the counter, and gives a bag containing money and a shopping list to the waiting shopkeeper.

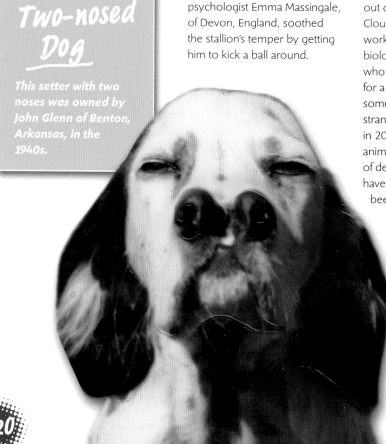

Two-nosed Dog

This setter with two noses was owned by John Glenn of Benton, Arkansas, in the 1940s.

Hidden Passenger Arriving in her hotel room in Niagara, Ontario, Canada, after a two-hour flight from New Brunswick, Mary Martell opened her suitcase—and was amazed to find her cat Ginger inside. The cat had jumped into the case while Mrs. Martell was packing and had even escaped detection by airport security.

Horseplay A dangerous horse has finally calmed down—after learning how to play soccer. Sixteen-year-old Kariba regularly used to throw off riders until horse psychologist Emma Massingale, of Devon, England, soothed the stallion's temper by getting him to kick a ball around.

Toddler Saved When R.C., a German Shepherd–Husky cross, discovered two-year-old Vincent Rhodey outdoors in the freezing cold wearing only a T-shirt, he instinctively sat on the youngster and saved him from hypothermia. The boy had strayed from his home in Canonsburg, Pennsylvania, but R.C. curled up with him for nearly an hour to keep him warm until they were both found.

Dolphin Aid A Florida dog has been trained to sniff out dead or injured dolphins. Cloud, a female Black Labrador, works with her owner, marine biologist Chris Blankenship, who came up with the idea for a dolphin-sniffing dog after some 80 dolphins became stranded off Marathon Key in 2005. Around 30 of the animals died, mainly as a result of dehydration, but they could have been saved had they been located earlier.

Soaring Cindy Cindy, a five-year-old greyhound from Miami, Florida, can jump a bar that is 5 ft 8 in (173 cm) above the ground. Cindy took up high jumping after being rejected for greyhound racing.

Elephant's Buzzword

Despite a huge difference in size and even though their skin is believed to be too thick for them to feel pain from a sting, African elephants are frightened by bees. Researchers have found that entire herds will steer clear of the sound of buzzing bees, and if bees get up elephants' trunks the animals go berserk.

Heroic Chihuahua

A tiny Chihuahua saved the life of a one-year-old boy who was attacked by a rattlesnake. Booker West was playing in his grandparents' backyard in Masonville, Colorado, when the snake lunged, but Zoey the Chihuahua jumped in the way and took the bites. Happily, the brave dog survived.

Parrot Love

A German ornithologist has set up a dating agency—for parrots. Rita Oenhauser runs a bird sanctuary outside Berlin and has brought romance to more than 2,000 pairs of parrots. Courtship between these colorful birds can take up to three months, but once together, loved-up parrots will stay faithful to each other for life.

Doggie Dudes

Four-legged surfing dudes get the chance to shine at the annual Loews Coronado Bay Resort Surf Dog Competition in California. Forty-seven canines took part in 2007, the contest being divided into two sections—the first purely for dogs and the second for dogs and humans surfing together on the same board at the same time. Prizes included a gourmet doggie room service meal at the resort and a basket filled with dog treats.

Hair-raising Yarn

Victoria Pettigrew hated throwing away the hair from her pet Chow's brush after grooming. So one day she decided to spin it into yarn. Her idea has prompted pet lovers across the U.S.A. to wear their pets' hair with pride—in bed, to the shops, and even to the beach.

Victoria's friend Gary used her company to make his hat from his cat Teddie's hair.

From raw fibers through being spun into finished yarn, the pet hair undergoes a thorough cleaning process.

When Victoria's beloved 16-year-old Lhasa Apso dog, Karly, died in 2001, she spun her fur and knitted it into a small scarf. Now customers send hair from their dogs and cats to her

company—VIP Fibers of Denton, Texas—and she spins it into yarn before sending it back to them as maybe a pair of mittens, a scarf, a blanket, a pillow, or, for the more daring, a fun-fur bikini. Such items are proving to be popular keepsakes with which owners can remember their adored pets.

Dog fur is up to 80 percent warmer than sheep's wool, but has to be thoroughly cleaned so that when the yarn gets wet, it does not smell like a wet dog. First the hair is washed in shampoo, then it is put through a process that removes the enzymes that cause odor, and finally it is soaked in softener and conditioner.

Victoria also spins yarn from alpacas, rabbits, horses, and even hamsters, although it may need several years' fur collection to create a hamster blanket!

123

Winged Cat

A cat in China has grown wings! Granny Feng of Xianyang City, was amazed to see what started out as two bumps on her cat's back grow into 4-in-long (10-cm) wing-like sprouts in less than a month in 2007. She said that the wings, which contain bones, make her pet look like a "cat angel."

Confused Cockatoo

Pippa, a 17-year-old cockatoo from Nuneaton, England, spent two weeks trying to hatch a bowl of chocolate Easter eggs! Her owner, Geoff Grewcock, said she saw the delicious-looking eggs on a table and climbed straight on them, because she was going through a "maternal stage." Geoff decided to let her stay on the eggs until she got off them herself—two weeks later.

Wonder Web

A spider's web created in Texas in 2007 measured more than 200 yd (183 m) long! The web at the Lake Tawakoni State Park trapped millions of mosquitoes and was so vast that it totally engulfed seven large trees and dozens of bushes.

Dolphin Rescue

Dolphins rescued surfer Todd Endris from a deadly shark attack off the coast of Monterey, California, by driving the shark away and surrounding the 24-year-old until help could arrive. Endris had been attacked by a 15-ft-long (4.5-m) great white shark, which had rammed him three times and was about to swallow his right leg when he managed to free himself. As the shark moved in for the kill, the bottlenose dolphins swam to his rescue and managed to keep the predator at bay. Talking to journalists, Endris described the rescue as "truly a miracle."

Weighty Worms

If we weighed all the earthworms in the U.S.A., they would be about 55 times heavier than the combined weight of all the American people.

Parrot Joker

An African gray parrot belonging to a New York artist has a vocabulary of 950 words and can even crack jokes! When he saw another parrot hang upside down from its perch, N'kisi squawked: "You gotta put this bird on the camera!" He also uses words in their proper context, with past, present, and future tenses.

Monster Python

Fluffy, a huge python bought in 2008 by Columbus Zoo, Ohio, has a body as long as a small truck and as thick as a telegraph pole. Fed 10 lb (4.5 kg) of rabbits a week, Fluffy is 22 ft (7 m) long and is thought to be one of the biggest snakes currently in captivity.

Ladybug's Ball

A New York City apartment complex released 720,000 ladybugs onto its premises in October 2007 to help clear the grounds of parasitic insects.

Highway Robbery

In 2007, motorists in the Orissa state of India reported that a wild elephant refused to let their vehicles pass unless they gave him food. The elephant stood in the highway, forcing vehicles to stop, and moved aside only when fed with vegetables or bananas.

Snake Shock

While searching for snakes with his granddaughter in 2006, a man in Orion, Illinois, captured a two-headed bull snake.

New Species

Scientists in Indonesia identified 20 new species of sharks and rays during a five-year survey of catches at Indonesian fish markets.

Fowl Play Two chickens in China have become addicted to playing soccer! Owner Mrs. Zhang found an abandoned football and decided to give it to the competitive bantams for fun. Since then they play with the ball every day and can even perform sliding tackles.

Giant Rat In 2007, researchers in a remote jungle in Indonesia discovered a hitherto unknown species of giant rat that is about five times the size of a typical city rat and has no fear of humans. A 2006 expedition to the same stretch of jungle had uncovered dozens of new species of palms and butterflies.

Shed Ordeal A cat locked in a garden shed survived for two months by licking condensation off the windows. Emmy, from Devon, England, was shut in when she followed her owner into the shed, which he then locked up for the winter.

Moose Assault In March 2007, a moose rammed and downed a low-flying helicopter near Gustavus, Alaska! The animal had been shot with a tranquilizer dart, but instead of slowing down it charged the hovering helicopter, damaging the tail rotor and forcing it to the ground.

Donkey Diapers In Limuru, Kenya, the town council is trying to keep the streets clean by ordering local tradesmen to put diapers on their donkeys!

Jar Ordeal A cat survived for 19 days with a peanut-butter jar stuck on her head. Thin and weak through lack of food, the feral cat was saved by the Cain family of Bartlett, Tennessee, who used oil to pry the jar off the animal's head and then nursed her back to health.

Busy Burrows In 1900, a single prairie-dog town in Texas covered 25,000 sq mi (64,750 sq km) and had an estimated population of 400 million animals!

Mynah Offence A mynah bird was placed in solitary confinement at a zoo in Changsha, China, after being rude to visitors. After calling tourists stupid and ugly, eight-year-old Mimi had to stay in a darkened cage for 15 days and listen to recordings of polite conversation in an attempt to improve her behavior and language.

Porky Puppy

After losing its own puppies, Hui Hu, a dog in China's Chongqing municipality, found an ideal replacement—a pig. The arrangement works both ways, as the devoted pig follows its foster mother everywhere.

Caught on Camera

Wondering what his pet tomcat, Mr. Lee, got up to when he went through the cat flap, Jürgen Perthold decided to find out—by fitting a tiny camera to the animal's collar.

A bird table, but no birds…

Please return to:

Thank you!

Mr. Lee wears his owner-made CatCam.

"He goes out the whole day," says Mr. Perthold. "Sometimes he returns hungry, sometimes not, sometimes with traces of fights, and sometimes he also stays out all night. It gave me the idea to equip the cat with a camera."

At first Mr. Lee was not keen on wearing the "CatCam" but he soon got used to it, and his adventures around his home in Anderson, South Carolina, have attracted worldwide attention.

The 2½-oz (70-g) camera, which takes one photo a minute for 48 hours, has shown Mr. Lee looking longingly at bird feeders, exploring garages, hiding under cars with other cats, and even encountering a snake. It has also revealed that the tabby has a girlfriend, although he faces stiff competition from a black tom.

Mr. Lee is not the only cat to be the star of his own feline soap opera. In Los Angeles, California, Julie Peasley has fitted a lightweight camera to the collar of her gray-and-white tuxedo cat, Squeaky. Within days, she had discovered that he likes to hide in the basement of the house next door. With CatCam, no cat's secret will ever be safe again.

I wonder what's in that hole.

Hmm... friend or foe?

It's a jungle out here!

Snakes alive!

Food Cycle Leaf-cutting ants from South America actually grow their own food. They forage for plants and leaves, carry them home and then chew the pieces into a form of compost, which they proceed to spread on the floors of their underground chambers. Eventually, fungus grows on the compost and is eaten by the ants.

Elephants' Picnic In 2007, two elephants escaped from a circus and went strolling around the town of Newmarket, Ontario, Canada, eating grass and trees in neighboring gardens during the early hours of the morning. A woman who saw them couldn't believe her eyes!

Table Manners Gorillas have table manners. A conservation group tracking western lowland gorillas in Africa has discovered that, after eating, they politely wipe their hands and faces with leaves—in exactly the same way that humans use table napkins.

No Sweat! Camels can lose up to 30 percent of their body weight in perspiration and still survive. By contrast, a human would die of heat shock after sweating away just 12 percent of his or her body weight.

Crossbreed A dog in a Chinese village appeared to give birth to a kitten in 2007. The first two puppies in the litter were normal but the third looked just like a cat. Vets in Jiangyan City said that it was really a puppy—it yapped like a puppy—but looked like a cat because of a gene mutation.

Prickly Problem

It looks like mom, it feels like mom, it even smells like mom, but it's actually a brush! However, four tiny, orphaned hedgehogs at a wildlife park in Hampshire, England, knew no better and took a fancy to the center's cleaning brush, because its bristles reminded them of their absent mother.

What a Hoot!

Four tawny owl chicks at a wildlife park in Hampshire, England, were given a stuffed toy owl as their surrogate mother. To keep warm, the orphaned chicks snuggled under the wings of the fluffy toy, which had to be washed regularly because it received so much love and affection.

Freak Calf When Howard Gentry saw eight legs protruding from his pregnant cow, he thought she must be giving birth to two calves. Instead, the fully grown limbs—complete with hooves—all belonged to one eight-legged calf that was stillborn at Gentry's farm in Glasgow, Kentucky, in 2007.

Strong Legs Believe it or not, one leg of a mosquito can support 23 times the insect's weight—while standing on water.

Eagle-eyed Bari Airport in Italy has paid $15,000 to hire Cheyenne, a six-month-old hand-reared golden eagle, to keep its runway free from wildlife. The airport had previously been forced to close the runway because of foxes hunting for mice and rabbits.

Whale Explosion A build-up of gases caused a dead sperm whale to explode onto the streets of Tainan, Taiwan, in January 2004 as it was being delivered to a research center.

Best Friends In 2007, two rare Sumatran tiger cubs and two baby orangutans became inseparable friends in the nursery room of an Indonesian animal hospital. Whereas in the wild, a young orangutan would represent a tasty snack for a tiger, here the abandoned quartet regularly curled up together to sleep.

Fat Cat

This 1935 photograph shows a cat of large proportions that was owned by A.M. Turner of Wimbledon, England. The fat feline weighed a whopping 35 lb (16 kg).

One of a Kind A calf was born in Litchfield, Nebraska, in 2007 with six legs and both male and female sex organs! The extra front and back leg extended from its pelvic area but did not reach the ground. The extra sex organs indicated that twin embryos may have fused during the animal's development.

Spotted House Dog-lovers Goran and Karmen Tomasic of Pribislavec, Croatia, were so upset when their pet Dalmatian, Bingo, was run over by a car that they painted their house white with black spots in his memory.

Talking Cat A cat in China is able to say his own name! The two-year-old cat, from Beijing, says his name, Agui, repeatedly when he becomes nervous or frightened.

In a Flap After shooting a duck for dinner, a hunter told his wife to put it in the refrigerator, which she did. But they didn't eat the duck that night, and when the wife opened the refrigerator door two days later, the duck was still very much alive! Initially, she was shocked at seeing it look up at her, but then she took the injured bird to an animal hospital in Tallahassee, Florida, where it was treated for wing and leg wounds.

Cliff Ordeal A dog survived for two weeks on a ledge 100 ft (30 m) high in Devon, England, in 2007, by eating a dead bird and drinking from a waterfall. Bush the Staffordshire bull terrier had disappeared from his owner's sight when he ran over the edge of the cliff in pursuit of a deer.

Extra Nose A calf in Merrill, Wisconsin, was born in 2007 with two noses. Lucy has a smaller nose on the top of the first, and both noses are functional. Owner Mark Krombholz noticed the extra nose only when he fed her a bottle of milk.

Hiding Place A New Jersey cat survived a house fire in 2007 by hiding in the furniture. The owners of the house in West Orange thought the cat must have perished, but were amazed to find their pet had wedged itself into the couch.

Bug Sniffers Bill Whitstine of Safety Harbor, Florida, teaches dogs to sniff out bedbugs. One of his students, Abbey the Beagle, is such an expert that when she smells bedbugs, she sits down next to them and even points her paw at the affected area.

Pigeon Spies During the 1970s, the CIA strapped cameras—weighing as little as only a few coins—to the chests of pigeons and released the birds over enemy targets. An earlier test, with a heavier camera in the skies over Washington, D.C., failed after two days when the overburdened pigeon was forced to abandon his flight and walk home!

Bushy-tailed Burglar

A squirrel with a sweet tooth raided a Finnish grocery store at least twice a day to steal chocolate candy eggs with a toy inside. The manager of the store in Jyvaskyla said the squirrel always carefully removed the foil wrapping, ate the chocolate, and left carrying the toy.

Heroic Hound A Golden Labrador saved a woman's life in 2007 by giving her the Heimlich maneuver. Debbie Parkhurst of Cecil County, Maryland, was eating an apple when a piece got stuck in her throat. Her choking alerted her two-year-old dog Toby, who stood on his hind feet, put his front paws on her shoulders, pushed her to the ground, and began jumping up and down on her chest, an action that dislodged the apple from her windpipe. As soon as Mrs. Parkhurst started breathing again, the dog stopped jumping and began licking its owner's face to stop her from passing out.

Skinny Pig

The latest designer pet is the skinny pig, a hairless breed of guinea pig first created for laboratory testing 30 years ago. As they are naked, skinny pigs need to be kept warm on cold days, but will also burn if left in the sun for too long without protective suncream.

133

Nail Sculptor

These sculptures of a life-size moose and bison are made entirely from nails. They are the work of artist Bill Secunda from Butler, Pennsylvania, who specializes in creating metal creatures. The moose is made from 95,000 welded nails, weighs 1,800 lb (815 kg), stands 7½ ft (2.3 m) tall, 12 ft (3.6 m) long, and has antlers that are almost 9 ft (2.7 m) wide. The bison, made from 30,000 cut and framing nails, weighs 1,100 lb (500 kg) and is 6 ft (1.8 m) tall, 3 ft (90 cm) wide, and 8 ft (2.4 m) long.

Lobster Lovers In April 2007, a group of animal lovers paid nearly $3,400 to buy 300 lobsters from a Maine fish market—then set them free, putting them back into the ocean.

Jellyfish Invasion In November 2007, billions of jellyfish washed into a salmon farm in Northern Ireland killing every one of the 100,000-plus fish.

Baby Love A Chihuahua dog has been caring for a baby chick at a house in Guiyang City, China. Far from resenting the new pet, Huahua treated the chick as her baby and whenever it strayed too far, she would pick it up gently in her mouth and bring it back to her bed.

Singing Dog A dog has been adding his bark to the hymn-singing at a chapel near Llanelli, Wales. Teddy the Golden Retriever goes to the chapel every Sunday with his owner Nona Rees and joins in with the rousing hymns—although he sometimes falls asleep during the sermons.

Cat Post A cat has been appointed a stationmaster in Japan. Dressed in a railwayman's cap, seven-year-old Tama and his two feline assistants welcome passengers at the unmanned Kishi station on the Wakayama Electric Railway.

Pet Rescue When a man climbed a 60-ft (18-m) pine tree to retrieve his pet cockatoo, he himself had to be rescued by a coastguard helicopter. William Hart, from Montgomery County, Texas, had scaled the tree after the bird, Geronimo, escaped from its cage.

Pet Fox

Instead of behaving like a wild animal, Cropper the fox lives indoors with Mike Towler and his family, eats from a dog bowl, and curls up with the household cats. Towler from the town of Tunbridge Wells in Kent, England, tamed Cropper over a period of several months after the fox contracted a memory-damaging disease that left him unable to make a home or recognize prey.

Eye of the Tiger

Instead of being on the outside of a cage looking in at lions and tigers, Arnd Drossel put himself inside a cage and allowed the big cats to get a close-up. The daring stunt was all part of his 220-mi (355-km) roll through the German state of North-Rhine Westphalia in a ball of steel wire.

Arnd emerging after a night in his ball.

The journey took him across all kinds of terrain.

The 38-year-old performance artist made his unusual journey to raise money for, and awareness of, mental illness. In fact, psychiatric patients from clinics in the region helped him create the rolling globe, which measured just over 6 ft (1.8 m) in diameter, weighed around 265 lb (120 kg), and was constructed out of 250 bent stainless steel rods. When finished, it resembled a massive ball of steel wool.

Drossel set off in April 2007 from his birthplace of Dorsten and finished his roll-athon in his home town of Warburg. He covered around 13 mi (21 km) a day, propelling the ball by simply shifting his weight in a walking motion. As well as "walking," he ate and slept in the ball. Drossel passed through a number of towns on his journey, but, predictably, his most hair-raising moments occurred in the Stukenbrock Safari Park where he came face to face with the eyes of several tigers, not to mention the lions.

That was when—for the first time in his life—he was happy to be inside a strong cage.

The tigers at Germany's Stukenbrock Safari Park are curious about the stranger who has rolled into their paddock.

Feline Stowaway

Taking delivery of a consignment of motorcycle helmets from China, the owner of a shop in North Carolina opened the box to find a cat inside. The animal had managed to chew its way into the cardboard box somewhere in Shanghai and had somehow survived the 35-day sea voyage despite being trapped in a cargo crate without food or water.

Twin Turtle

An aquarium in East Norriton, Pennsylvania, displayed a red-eared slider turtle that had two heads. The reptilian oddity had a pair of front feet on each side, but just one pair of back feet and only one tail.

Flying High

TV producers strapped a miniature camera weighing almost 1 oz (25 g) to a golden eagle and were rewarded with magnificent shots as the bird soared through the air.

Pampered Pet

A wealthy New York hotel magnate left $12 million in her will to her dog. Leona Helmsley doted on her Maltese terrier, Trouble, and also stipulated that when the dog dies, it should be buried next to her.

The Sting

Octopuses have been known to remove the stings from captured jellyfish and attach them to their own tentacles to use as an added weapon.

Snail Trail

The sticky discharge produced by snails as they move along offers the snail such strong protection that they can slide along the edge of a razor blade without cutting themselves.

New Tongue

The tongue louse, a parasite that lives on snapper fish, crawls into the mouth of a fish, eats its tongue, and then itself acts as the fish's tongue for the rest of the fish's life.

Foster Pig

When three tiger cubs at a zoo in Guangzhou City, China, were rejected by their mother, they found an unlikely surrogate mom—a pig. Not only did the cubs gently suckle the pig's milk, they even enjoyed playing with their piglet foster brothers and sisters.

Tattooed Fish Fish in Singapore are being tattooed. A tattoo laser is used to create patterns on the fish's body, including hearts, polka dots, and stripes. The tattooists maintain that the procedure does not harm the fish.

Kitten Savior Zacheri Richardson-Leitman of Cairns, Queensland, Australia, had time to rescue his whole family from a blaze, despite being in bed asleep when his mattress caught fire. How did he do it? His ten-week-old kitten scratched at his face to wake him up and alert him to his burning bed.

Language Barriers When Milo the Jack Russell terrier became trapped in a drain in England in 2007, its rescuers had to talk French to it because the dog used to belong to a family in France and it couldn't understand a word of English.

Auto Sheep Too old to be able to walk alongside his animals, a resourceful Greek shepherd named George Zokos has trained his flock of sheep to follow his car instead.

Nail Hat Yang Decai of Hunan, China, has been attacked so often by an angry owl that he protects himself by wearing a special hat that is fitted with nails protruding from it.

Horned Rooster

This rooster, owned by Jesse Parker of Dequeen, Arkansas, in the early 1930s, had two horns sticking out of the top of its head.

139

Dinner Date A wolf captured in Albania in 2007 became best friends with its dinner! A donkey was put in the wolf's cage as a prospective meal, but instead of hunting it down and eating it, the wolf made the donkey its friend.

Expert Mimics

Australia's lyrebirds mimic a huge range of natural and artificial sounds including other birds, dog barks, car alarms, musical instruments, and even revving chainsaws!

Croc Costume U.S. zoologist Brady Barr studied a group of crocodiles in Tanzania up close while wearing a life-size croc costume to disguise the fact that he's a human!

Seven-legged Lamb

A lamb born in Christchurch, New Zealand, in 2007 was not just one in a million—it was one in several million. The lamb was born with seven legs, making it an extremely rare polydactyl, meaning many-legged animal.

Pie Snatch The 2007 World Pie Eating Championships were thrown into disarray after the organizer's dog woofed the pies. While Dave Williams, who won the title in 1995, was looking after the precious tournament pies at his home in Lancashire, England, his pet dog Charlie managed to sneak in and eat at least ten of them.

Mad Markings

Pete the monocled dog was owned by Harry Lucenay in the 1930s. His startling natural markings helped launch his movie career—Pete was a star in the popular "Our Gang" short movies of the 1930s.

Smart Seagull A seagull turned into a persistent shoplifter by regularly wandering through an open door into a shop in Aberdeen, Scotland, and helping itself to a packet of potato snacks. The bird would wait until there were no customers around and the shopkeeper was standing behind the cash desk.

Chimp Champ A chimpanzee outscored college students in a series of short-term numerical memory tests in Japan. When the numbers were flashed on a computer screen, five-year-old Ayumu proved faster and more accurate than the humans in memorizing the numbers in the correct sequence.

Rapid Growth In just two weeks, the monarch butterfly caterpillar grows to 2,700 times its birth weight. If a 7-lb (3.2-kg) human baby gained weight at the same rate, in a fortnight it would weigh more than 9 tons.

Dog Star

In 1950, the Horden twins of East Falls, Pennsylvania, were the proud owners of a black dog named Rip who had a perfect white-star marking on his chest.

Conjoined Calves

In March 1932, Dr. M.T. Cook of Cumberland, Kentucky, delivered these live conjoined calves that belonged to Gravil Cornett, of Dione, Kentucky.

More Pork A piglet born in Croatia in 2007 had a little extra of just about everything. The piglet, nicknamed Octopig, had six legs, two penises, and two anuses. He was so unusual that farmer Ivica Seic decided to keep him as a pet.

King Hog

A 1,050-lb (475-kg) monster hog, measuring 9 ft 4 in (2.85 m) long, was killed in Alabama in 2007—by an 11-year-old boy. Armed only with a pistol, Jamison Stone pursued the beast for three hours, shooting it eight times before finally firing the fatal bullet. The dead boar was converted into 2,800 sausages.

Odd Couple When Mozambique was flooded in 2002, a dog from the village of Caia became firm friends with a wild monkey. The two played together and the dog even let the monkey ride on its back.

Ele-vision For a TV documentary *Elephants: Spy in the Herd*, a miniature, remote-controlled camera was mounted on a little mobile platform and covered with dry elephant dung. The camouflage was so effective that one elephant picked up the dung cam and walked around with it still filming.

Whale Size A blue whale's aorta—the main artery that supplies blood to the body—is so wide that a fully-grown human could swim through it.

Living Dead When Gan Shugen of Chengdu, China, went to cook a chicken that he had kept in a freezer for two days, he was shocked to find it was still alive. The bird—a gift from a relative—was wrapped in a thick plastic bag with its legs tied, leading Gan to assume it was dead. Instead, despite 48 hours in sub-zero temperatures, it poked its head out of the bag and was soon able to stand.

Artistic Gorillas Gorillas at Franklin Park Zoo in Boston, Massachusetts, are keen finger-painters. Keepers at the zoo claim that the finger-painting helps to keep the apes intellectually stimulated; and it earns them money too—one of their artworks sold for a whopping $10,000!

Garlic Diet Keepers at a zoo in Shanghai, China, have been feeding their penguins garlic to help fight breathing problems and other illnesses associated with the country's rainy season. The keepers hide the cloves of garlic in the penguins' usual meals of fish.

Cash Retriever A British charity, Canine Partners, is training dogs to use cash machines on behalf of their disabled owners. The scheme was inspired by wheelchair-bound Gulf War veteran Allen Parton who was struggling to retrieve his cash from an ATM when his Labrador Endal jumped up to reach for the card, money, and receipt with his mouth.

Lion Kiss

The owner of an animal refuge in Cali, Colombia, is on kissing terms with a fully grown lion! Ana Julia Torres rescued Jupiter the lion from a traveling circus seven years ago and now he repays her kindness by tenderly hugging her with his giant paws through the bars of his cage, and by planting a kiss on her mouth.

Weird World

Birth of an Island

Fredrik Fransson onboard yacht Maiken, *Brisbane, Australia, August 11, 2006.*

We left Neiafu in the Vava'u group of islands in the northern part of Tonga on Friday, August 11, sailing toward Fiji. There was no wind, so we motored along toward an offshore island called Late Island.

Fairly soon we discovered brown grainy streaks in the water. It looked like heavy oil mixed with water. The surrounding water was strangely greenish, like a lagoon, not the deep bluish color that you normally see sailing offshore. As we got further southwest, the streaks turned into heavy bands of floating matter, until the whole horizon was a solid line that looked like a desert.

So far we didn't have a problem, as it was such a thin layer on the surface that it got pushed away by the bow wave, but when we entered the solid field it started to pile up and behaved like wet concrete. The sight was unbelievable; it looked like rolling sand dunes as far as the eye could see. Our speed went from 7 knots down to 1 knot as the pumice stones dragged along the waterline.

Fredrik with the yacht Maiken anchored behind him.

A field of pumice appears to rise out of the deep blue sea.

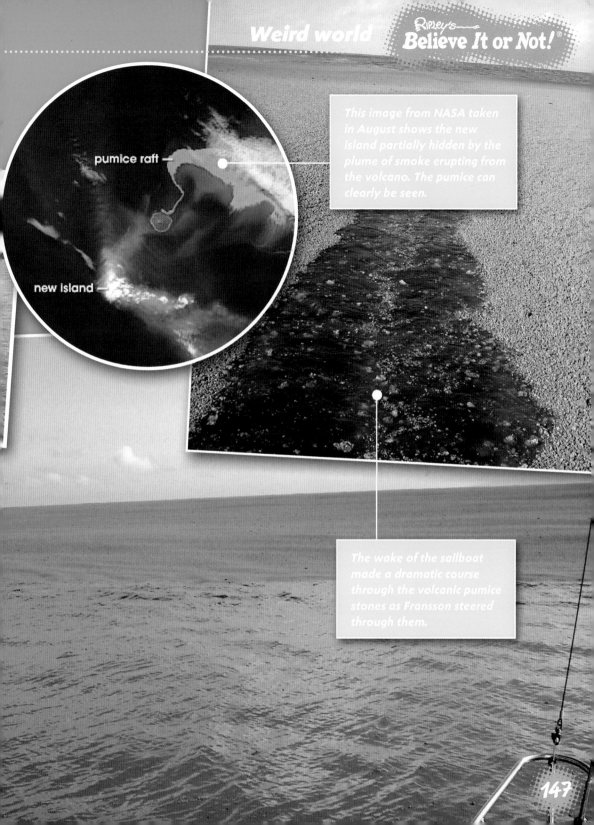

pumice raft —

new island —

This image from NASA taken in August shows the new island partially hidden by the plume of smoke erupting from the volcano. The pumice can clearly be seen.

The wake of the sailboat made a dramatic course through the volcanic pumice stones as Fransson steered through them.

Girl Racer Stephanie Beane of Grafton, Ohio, could roar around the track in a stock car at speeds of 80 mph (130 km/h)—at the age of ten. She made her stock-car debut at the Sandusky Speedway MotorSports Park in June 2007 and finished fifth in a field of 15, most of whom were adult men. She first got behind the wheel of a car when she was just two and started racing at four, learning to ride a go-kart before she could ride a bicycle. She was so successful—often winning trophies that were taller than she was—that she began signing autographs at age six… before she really knew how to write her name.

Armchair Ride

A company from DeMotte, Indiana, has designed a vehicle that enables couch potatoes to drive down the road without leaving the comfort of their armchair. Driven with a joystick and powered by either gasoline or electricity, Armchair Cruisers' range includes a HarleyDavidson chair that reaches speeds of 40 mph (64 km/h), does wheelies, and has an onboard cooler, and a two-seater sofa that can do two 360-degree turns inside an 8-sq-ft (0.74-sq-m) box. The chairs can even be customized with their own built-in stereo system.

Brick Truck Mark Monroe and students at Austin College, Sherman, Texas, created a station wagon that appears to be made of bricks. The Brickmobile is really a 1968 Ford Country Sedan with 839 brick-like ceramic tiles stuck to the bodywork.

Weigh-in The town of High Wycombe in Buckinghamshire, England, is the only place in the world that weighs its mayor publicly. Mayors are weighed at the beginning and end of their year in office to see whether or not they have gained any weight at the taxpayers' expense.

Pure Gold A lump of pure gold that is only as big as a matchbox can be flattened into a sheet the size of a tennis court. An ounce (28 g) of gold can be stretched into a wire 50 mi (80 km) long.

Custom Made

Andy Saunders specializes in taking old cars and turning them into something unrecognizable. The custom-car king, from Dorset, England, is a devotee of 1950s Americana, but gains inspiration from anywhere. He works at an auto center and spends his days studying the shape of windshields, headlamps, and other parts, which he then picks up from scrapyards to use on his latest projects. His crazy creations include a car that looks like a spaceship, a Citroen 2CV redesigned in the style of a Picasso painting (top left), and another vehicle that is just 22 in (56 cm) high (left).

Jet Stool

If Tim Arfons fancies a quick drink, he climbs aboard his jet barstool. Powered by a gas turbine engine, the stool has reached speeds of 40 mph (64 km/h) at a raceway park in Norwalk, Ohio.

Monster Skateboard

In 2007, students at Bay College, Michigan, built a skateboard measuring 31 ft (9.4 m) long and 8 ft (2.4 m) wide, and weighing 2,400 lb (1,090 kg). It can hold 28 people.

Suicide Attack   In

August 2006, a large flock of shearwater birds bombarded a fishing boat off the coast of Alaska for unknown reasons, ramming suicidally against it for 30 minutes.

Underwater Mountains   The longest

mountain range in the world is underwater. The Mid-Ocean Ridge extends about 40,000 mi (65,000 km) from the Arctic Ocean via the Atlantic to the Pacific off the west coast of North America.

Mechanical Man   In

Calgary, Alberta, Canada, there is a 27-ft (8.2-m) mechanical man called Spike, made from locomotive and freight car parts. His body is a boiler, his head and ears are gears, his arms and hands are couplers, and he holds a crankshaft in his right hand.

Roofs Ripped Lead nails ripped from roofs by a tornado were hammered by the wind into beams many yards away at Runanga, New Zealand, on April 20, 1956.

In the Groove Japanese engineers have created "Melody Roads" with specially cut grooves that develop pitched vibrations as a car drives over them.

Magic Menu At the Ninja Japanese restaurant in New York City, waiters perform magic tricks while serving customers their sushi.

Lottery Tree People in Thailand flocked to visit a banana tree in Koh Sireh in 2007 in the belief that it could predict winning lottery numbers. Many claimed to have won prizes after rubbing a mixture of powder and water on the tree's trunk, then waiting to see what number the dried solution resembled.

Pipe Home A man in China has built a home using two cement pipes—and it has become a city attraction. Xin Yucai, 50, of Shenyang City, bought two cement pipes from a construction company and turned them into a real house with windows, a door, and even a chimney. He turned down the offer of living in his daughter's apartment because he loves his new home so much.

Elephant Rock Located in the Valley of Fire in the Nevada Desert is a huge rock that is called Elephant Rock because it is shaped like an elephant. It was formed around 150 million years ago.

Big Stamp An aluminum postage stamp measuring 8 x 6 ft (2.4 x 1.8 m) stands in Humboldt, Saskatchewan, Canada. It was built in 1999 in honor of John G. Diefenbaker, former Canadian Prime Minister, who as a lawyer defended many court cases in the town.

Speed Limo An English inventor has come up with a limousine that can reach 170 mph (275 km/h), and can go from 0 to 60 mph in less than six seconds. Dan Cawley of Manchester, took a Ferrari 360 Modena, chopped it in half, and stretched it by 9½ ft (2.9 m) with a section of hand-built carbon fiber. The resulting eight-seater vehicle is 20 ft (6 m) long.

Luge Racer

Lying horizontally just a couple of inches above the asphalt, Joel King of Sussex, England, reached a speed of 112 mph (180 km/h) on a jet-powered street luge board in August 2007. He says that stopping is the hardest part. "When you've finished you turn the engine off and use your feet to brake, which at over 100 mph is quite interesting!"

Renaissance Man

Decorator Robert Burns has spent more than three years transforming the interior of his modest 1960s house in Brighton, England, into a Renaissance masterpiece. Using art books bought at rummage sales as his inspiration, he has faithfully reproduced the work of 15th-century Italian artists—mostly with emulsion paint from his local hardware store.

The façade of Robert's house conceals the treasures within.

Robert has never been to Italy in his life, nor ever attended art school, but the books have enabled the 60-year-old father-of-four to re-create the beauty of Botticelli on his bedroom walls. A nativity scene with a *trompe l'oeil* (trick of the eye) gold frame dominates the dining room, while cameos of the Virgin Mary and other religious scenes are dotted throughout the house.

The hallway and lounge ceiling are adorned in a mass of fluffy clouds and blue sky, while the landing is decorated in an authentic marble effect.

Whereas Michelangelo, Leonardo da Vinci, and their contemporaries used a mixture of pigments and hundreds of egg yolks, Burns has to rely largely on household paint left over from his decorating jobs.

He adds to the Renaissance feel of the house whenever he is bored or between jobs, because it stops him going crazy waiting for the phone to ring.

Robert applying the finishing touches to a Renaissance masterpiece in his home.

Sitting Tall Michael Mooney of Asheville, North Carolina, rides tall bikes for fun. He regularly rides bikes that are 6 ft (1.8 m) and 12 ft (3.6 m) tall, but in September 2007 he decided to go all the way by riding a bike that was an amazing 44 ft (13.4 m) tall—higher than a two-story house including the roof. He demonstrated it at the Lexington Avenue Arts and Fun Festival, and managed to pedal a few yards before the bicycle toppled over.

Unlucky Strike A diver was killed in the ocean off Deerfield Beach, Florida, in 2007 after lightning struck his oxygen tank as he came to the surface.

Blue Hole

Located on the undersea Lighthouse Reef some 60 mi (100 km) from Belize in Central America is a perfectly circular Blue Hole that measures 1,000 ft (305 m) across and 400 ft (123 m) deep. Filled with dark blue water, the hole was formed 15,000 years ago during the Ice Age when sea levels were lowered by more than 350 ft (107 m), exposing the limestone rock. As fresh water began flowing through the limestone deposits, huge underground caverns formed. Then, as the ocean began to rise again, the caverns flooded and the roof of one cavern collapsed to create this incredible sinkhole. With its breathtaking collection of stalactites, the Blue Hole is now a popular diving venue. At a depth of 130 ft (40 m) the temperature inside the hole is a constant 76° F (24° C).

Green Machine

Students at Warwick University, England, have created an eco-friendly sports car that has a body made from plants, and tires made from potatoes. Eco One uses pulped hemp injected with rapeseed oil for its bodywork, has brake pads constructed from ground cashew nuts, and runs on a fuel of fermented wheat and sugar beet. Even so, it can go from 0 to 60 mph (0 to 97 km/h) in 4 seconds and has a top speed of 150 mph (240 km/h).

Highway Landing

In July 2007, a vintage airplane made an emergency landing on a Wisconsin highway. Pilot William J. Leff from Ohio, brought the 1946 North American T-6G plane down on the northbound lanes of U.S. Highway 41 near Fond du Lac County Airport. The only damage was to the plane's right wing when it hit a number of highway signs.

Horseshoe Tower

The Scarrington Horseshoe Tower in Nottinghamshire, England, is 17 ft (5 m) high and 6 ft (1.8 m) in diameter—and is made up of more than 50,000 metal horseshoes.

Town Resurfaces

Nearly 50 years after being submerged by the creation of an artificial lake, the underwater town of Adaminaby in Australia resurfaced following a prolonged drought in the area. The town was relocated in 1958 when Lake Eucumbene was created as part of the Snowy Mountains Hydro-Electric Scheme. Around 100 buildings were moved to the site of the new town on higher ground, some 300 mi (480 km) southwest of Sydney, but in February 2007 the lake's water level fell so much that the ruins of the old town became visible again.

Big Cheese

A concrete cheese—6 ft (1.8 m) high and 28 ft (8.5 m) in circumference—sits at Perth, Ontario, Canada, to commemorate the mammoth cheese produced in the town for the 1893 Chicago World's Fair. The real cheese weighed 22,000 lb (9,979 kg) and was made using one day's milk from 10,000 cows. It created such a stir that, in 1943, it was decided to build an exact concrete replica.

Beer Mountain

When property manager Ryan Froerer went to check out one of his rented apartments in Ogden, Utah, he found around 70,000 empty beer cans piled high all the way up to the ceiling, completely obscuring the furniture. The cans, which equate to 24 beers a day during the tenant's eight-year stay, were later recycled for $800.

Glass House The Glass House in Boswell, British Columbia, Canada, was built from half a million empty embalming-fluid bottles. It was begun in 1952 by retired undertaker David H. Brown, who traveled western Canada collecting the bottles from friends in the funeral profession and ended up with about 250 tons of them.

Too Weak A 79-year-old woman from Norway was denied a driver's license renewal after losing an arm-wrestling match to her doctor.

Hanging Around Eelko Moorer of London, England, built a set of boots that allows him to hang upside down from safety rails in the subway. The boots have a slot in the heel that hooks over the carriage's handrail.

Shoe House A house near Branddraai, South Africa, is built in the shape of a giant lace-up shoe. Designed by artist Ron van Zyl in 1990, the shoe house has its entrance in the two-story heel and accommodation in the toe.

Fruit Wagon Jackie Harris of Houston, Texas, transformed a 1967 Ford station wagon into the Fruitmobile—a one-of-a-kind car with plastic oranges, apples, pineapples, grapes, and other fruit attached to the bodywork.

Jesus Image A smudge of driveway sealant said to resemble the face of Jesus was sold for more than $1,500 in an online auction. The image was found on the garage floor of the Serio family home in the town of Forest, Virginia.

Iron-eating Tree A sycamore tree in Scotland has literally "swallowed up" pieces of metal over the past 200 years. The Brig o'Turk iron-eating tree has engulfed all kinds of scrap left by the local blacksmith, even a bicycle that a boy left against the tree when he failed to return from World War I.

Tree Bar A pub in South Africa is located in the hollow interior of a 6,000-year-old baobab tree. Inside, the tree is so spacious that the bar can hold 50 people—and because the 72-ft-tall (22-m) tree is still growing, so is the pub.

Name That Town

In 1930, Robert Ripley visited the Welsh town that until recently had the longest town name in the world. Seen here standing at the town's railway station, Ripley was visiting Llanfairpwllgwyngyllgogerychwyrndrobwllllantysiliogogogoch, whose name translates as "The church of St. Mary in the hollow of white hazel trees near the rapid whirlpool by St. Tysilio's of the red cave."

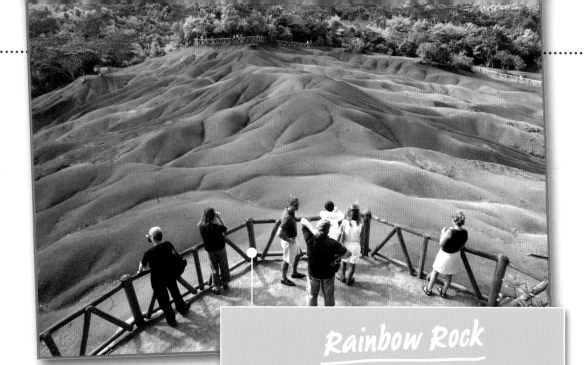

Rainbow Rock

In a stunning natural spectacle, the earth at Chamarel, Mauritius, is divided into seven colors—red, brown, violet, yellow, deep purple, blue, and green. The phenomenon, which is at its most vivid at sunrise, is the result of mineral-rich volcanic rock cooling at uneven temperatures. Bizarrely, the different colors never merge even when it rains, and if mixed together artificially in a test tube, they separate into seven distinct colors again a few days later.

Fish Bike Didi Senft from Storkow, Germany, has built a bicycle in the shape of a fish. The three-wheel monster is 10 ft (3 m) high, 30 ft (9 m) long, and made from 50,000 bicycle bells welded together. It took bicycle fanatic Didi six months to build and, fittingly, his test run in March 2007 was to a local fish restaurant. Senft, who likes to dress up as the devil when riding, also designed a bizarre bike for the 2006 soccer World Cup, which was held in Germany. That 25-ft-long (7.6-m) bicycle had wheels made from 100 soccer balls.

Bear Code Smokey the Bear, the U.S. mascot for forest-fire prevention, has his own postal zip code for fan mail.

Floating Shop Dave's Bait House offers food, drinks, and fishing bait—all from Dave Steiner's 33-ft (10-ft) boat, which he anchors some 6 mi (9.5 km) from shore in the Gulf of Mexico.

Sudden Death The rare *Puya raimondii* plant of Bolivia can take up to 150 years to bloom—and as soon as it does, it dies.

Fake Bill Police arrested a man after he handed over a fake million-dollar bill at a Pittsburgh, Pennsylvania, supermarket and asked for change. When staff refused and confiscated the note, the man became abusive.

Seven-seater Bike

Eric Staller from Amsterdam, Netherlands, has invented a bicycle built for seven. The ConferenceBike, or CoBi, uses three motorcycle wheels and has seven seats in a circle. All seven riders can pedal, enabling the machine to reach speeds of up to 15 mph (24 km/h). One of the riders also takes charge of the steering wheel.

Robot Bank

Asked to come up with a futuristic design for the Bank of Asia building in Bangkok, Thailand, architect Sumet Jumsai took inspiration from his son's toy robot. The 20-story building is shaped like a giant robot and even has two 20-ft (6-m) lidded "eyes" that serve as windows on the top floor. The eyeballs are made of glass and the lids are metal louvers.

Colored Pools

Scattered along the salt flats on the coast of Senegal are a series of small pools filled with different colored water, including red, orange, black, and white. They have been created by women workers digging for salt, which they collect by hand, load into sacks, and sell to neighboring countries. The variety of colors is a result of the high mineral concentration in the soil, the colors being intensified by the shallowness of the water in the pools.

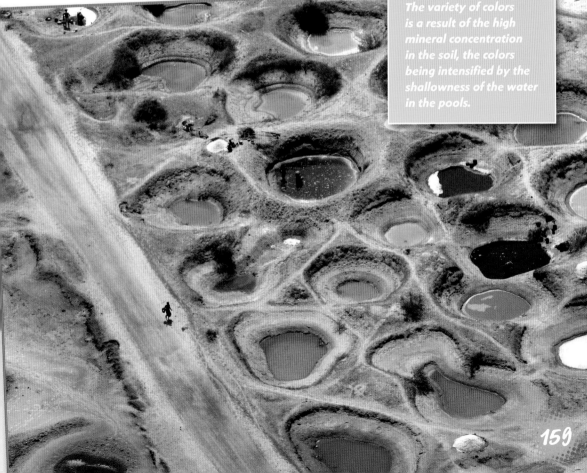

Crystal Car

Ken and Annie Burkitt of Niagara Falls, Ontario, Canada, used more than one million genuine Austrian Swarovski lead crystals to decorate a 2004 Mini Cooper car with images of 11 of the U.S.A.'s most recognizable and enduring iconic emblems.

The mural-style design includes the Statue of Liberty, Mount Rushmore, the U.S. flag, and the famous Hollywood sign. It took four artists six months to place each crystal individually on the "American Icon" by hand. The crystals are all the exact same size and are in 50 different shades of color to represent the 50 states of the U.S.A. Ken Burkitt said: "We wanted to create something that would pay tribute to America in an eye-catching way. The car takes on a completely different look as the lighting changes throughout the day. The crystal design takes on a life of its own."

Inside Out

An art installation in Liverpool, England, allows visitors to see a section of a building turning itself inside out. Called "Turning the Place Over" and designed by Richard Wilson, it consists of an ovoid 26 ft (8 m) in diameter, which has been cut from the façade of a derelict building in the city center and placed on a pivot. Dramatically, the ovoid rotates three-dimensionally like a huge opening and closing window.

The unusual installation seen part way through its rotation.

When the ovoid is closed, you would never guess that part of this building turns itself inside out.

Moving Next Door

A tornado in Lorain, Ohio, in 1928, lifted off the top story of this house and carefully set it down beside it.

Mini Cooper Parade

In June 2007, no less than 273 Minis paraded at Virginia Beach, Virginia, forming a chain more than 5 mi (8 km) long. The cars came from as far away as Connecticut and Indiana.

Spore Release
If a raindrop or a passing animal hits the giant puffball fungus, thousands of spores are puffed out of a hole in the top. In a single day, a giant puffball can release as many as seven billion spores.

Prison Rodeo
The Louisiana State Penitentiary in Angola, which is home to 5,000 inmates, has thousands of acres of farm land, more than 1,500 cattle, a four-year theological seminary, its own radio station, a news magazine, and an annual rodeo.

House Gift
Hollywood photographer Jasin Boland came up with the perfect Valentine's present for fiancée Maria Moral Pena—a gift-wrapped $1-million house. He arranged for the house—in Gloucestershire, England—to be covered in 5,000 sq ft (465 sq m) of white fabric, sprinkled with red hearts, and finished with a giant pink bow.

Colored Snow
Yellow snow and then red snow fell on areas of Russia within a few weeks of each other in 2006. The yellow blizzard was caused by airborne pollution from a gas and oil factory, and the red snow was the result of sandstorms in the neighboring country of Mongolia.

Bumper Crime
A white Ford Ranger pickup truck stolen in Miami, Florida, was recovered five days later. The only things missing were 700 bumper stickers that had been covering the exterior.

Plane Spotters
Nearly 100,000 people arrive daily at the new Suvarnabhumi Airport in Bangkok, Thailand—not to travel, but to sightsee and picnic!

Cuban Park
The José Marti Park in Ybor City, Florida, is actually owned by Cuba. Named after the Cuban writer and independence leader, the park was purchased by Cuba in 1957.

Dolphin Craft

New Zealander Rob Innes and Californian Dan Piazza have designed a watercraft that not only looks like a dolphin, it also behaves like a dolphin. The two-seater Seabreacher uses its 175 horsepower engine to surge through the waves, but because it is made of fiberglass, it is so light that it can fly 10 ft (3 m) in the air even at speeds of 15 mph (24 km/h). The advanced jet-ski is 15 ft (4.5 m) long and has a canopy similar to those seen on U.S. fighter jets.

Heavy Metal

A giant motorbike powered by a tank engine stands 17 ft 4 in (5.3 m) long, 7 ft 6 in (2.3 m) tall—and the engine alone weighs almost 2 tons. Dubbed the *Led Zeppelin* by its creator Tilo Nieber, the bike took a team of welders and mechanics from Zilly, Germany, almost a year to build.

Fog Forest

A lush forest survives in Oman's Dhofar mountains with no rain! The cloud forest is surrounded by deserts and gets most of its water from seasonal fog.

Worm Shower

Clumps of live worms fell from the sky onto the streets of Jennings, Louisiana, in July 2007. They are thought to have been sucked up into the air by a waterspout seen 5 mi (8 km) away, and then dropped on the town.

Forest Flattened

A meteor exploded over Siberia's Tunguska River on June 30, 1908, unleashing the energy of 1,000 Hiroshima bombs and flattening 770 sq mi (2,000 sq km) of forest.

Wealthy Times
Businesses on Times Square in New York City generate about $55 billion a year in revenue—enough to make the city block the world's 76th largest economy.

Shuttle Shuffle
It takes more than six hours for NASA to move the U.S. space shuttle 3.4 mi (5.5 km) from its hangar to the launch pad.

Arabian Cyclone
The first documented cyclone ever to hit the Arabian Sea landed in Oman on June 6, 2007, with maximum sustained winds of 92.5 mph (148 km/h) and affected more than 20,000 people.

Pink City
Officials in Aurangabad in Bihar, India, painted many of the buildings in their city bright pink—thinking that it would help lower the crime rate.

Finders Keepers
Diamonds State Park in Arkansas has a diamond mine where visitors can search for—and keep—any gems they find.

Love Motive
Police in Inglewood, California, arrested a man in April 2007 for stealing 26 cars that he used only to visit his girlfriend.

Virtual Journey
Every Saturday in Delhi, India, around 40 passengers line up for boarding cards—for a plane that never takes off. For $4, Bahadur Chand Gupta offers people who cannot afford to fly the opportunity to experience air travel without ever leaving the ground. His Airbus 300 has only one wing, no lighting, and the toilets are out of order, but passengers happily buckle themselves in for their "virtual journey," watching safety demonstrations and listening to announcements while being waited on by flight attendants.

Floating House

In 1940, R.G. Letourneau of Peoria, Illinois, built a house that he then towed to its destination, across the Illinois River. The watertight steel house, complete with furnace, plumbing, and furniture, did not sit on a barge, but floated happily to its new home.

Mighty Mushroom

A monster white mushroom standing 27 in (70 cm) tall and weighing 41 lb (20 kg) was discovered growing near a coffee farm in Chiapas, southern Mexico, in 2007. The prize specimen of Macrocybe titans had grown to twice its normal size.

Authenticity Scan Zeng, an antique collector in Guangzhou, China, buys plane tickets so that he can go through the airport's X-ray scanners to verify the authenticity of artifacts that he carries with him!

What a Corker! Jan Elftmann of Minneapolis, Minnesota, has decorated her Mazda truck with more than 10,000 wine and champagne corks collected during her 13 years as a waitress in an Italian restaurant. To accompany the truck at art car parades, she wears a ball gown—also decorated with dozens of corks.

Hairy Stone

A stone with thousands of 6-in-long (15-cm) strands of white hair growing on its surface went on display in Dalian, China, in 2005. The stone, which measured 8 in (20 cm) long and 6 in (15 cm) in diameter, was considered to be so rare that it was valued at $1,300,000.

Tropical Alaska It once made 100°F (38°C) in Alaska! Recorded at Fort Yukon on June 27, 1915, it beat its average 27°F (-6°C).

Stress Busters
Customers at the Rising Sun Anger Release Bar in Nanjing, China, are invited to relieve stress by smashing glasses and beating up staff, who wear protective padding.

Chickens Plucked
A tornado in Britain traveled a distance of 100 mi (160 km) on May 21, 1950. The four-hour-long storm actually plucked some chickens completely bare.

Painted Mountain
In 2007, forestry officials in Yunnan, China, hired seven workers to spray-paint parts of Laoshou Mountain green. The barren patch of land had been left an eyesore by years of quarrying, but instead of planting trees, the county government decided to paint the mountainside.

Porky Tribute Rev. Bryan Taylor of Houston, Texas, created the Jeffrey Jerome Memorial Pig car in memory of Victoria Herbert's famous pet pig, Jeffrey Jerome. The pink auto has ears, a snout, and a curly tail.

Exploding Fruit
When the fruit of the South American sandbox tree is ripe, it explodes with such force that the seeds can scatter nearly 200 ft (60 m) from the main trunk. The noise of the explosion fools some people into mistaking it for gunfire.

Mean Mosquito In Upsala, Ontario, Canada, stands a steel and fiberglass monument of a giant mosquito carrying a man and a knife and fork! The hungry mosquito, which is 16 ft (5 m) long and has a wingspan of 15 ft (4.5 m), is holding the 6-ft (1.8-m) man with its legs.

Double Theft York Heiden of Stevens Point, Wisconsin, had his car stolen twice in one day: April 27, 2007.

Pencil-vania

Inside a San Francisco house, artist Jason Mecier has created a wonderful, colorful mosaic from thousands of pencils. He calls it Pencil-vania.

When Jason's friend Jaina Davis bought the 100-year-old property on Potrero Hill, San Francisco, in 1997, she invited her artist friends to design the interior. Jason conceived the idea of connecting the styles of the different rooms by a pencil mosaic winding up the staircase, and

Jason also created a face made of pencils—a futuristic portrait of Jaina aged 88.

was commissioned to create just that. As a result, doors, banisters, and walls have all been decorated with brightly colored pencils that have been glued to the surfaces, inserted in specially drilled holes, or suspended from the ceiling.

Jason's amazing mosaic includes a pencil flower garden, pencil Victorian-style wallpaper, and a futuristic pencil portrait of Jaina, aged 88.

Pencil-vania includes shelves made from pencils, many of which are home to a variety of office supplies.

Work in progress on one of the stairwell walls.

169

No License In June 2007, police in the Netherlands found that an 84-year-old man they had pulled over in a random check had been driving without a license—for 67 years.

Box Wars In a craze that started in Melbourne, Australia, people fight battles wearing suits of armor made of cardboard. The rules of Box Wars—which has spread to Canada, the U.S.A., and Britain—state that only cardboard, tape, and spray paint may be used for armor and weapons. Battles last around 15 minutes each and end when no one is left wearing any cardboard.

Sunny Outlook An Italian Alpine village that never saw any sun in winter fixed the problem by installing a giant mirror. Lying at the bottom of a steep valley and surrounded by mountains, Viganella receives no direct sunlight between November and February, but in December 2006 the mirror —a sheet of steel measuring 26 x 16 ft (8 x 5 m)—was erected on a nearby peak to reflect sunlight onto the village square below.

Crooked House

A crazily shaped building in Sopot, Poland, was inspired by fairytale illustrations and has roof tiles resembling the scales of a dragon. Built in 2003, the 4,780-sq-yd (4,000-sq-m) Centrum Rezydent was created by architect Szotynscy Zaleski, who based his theme on the children's book drawings of Polish illustrator Jan Marcin Szancer. At the heart of the crooked house is a bar named... Wonky Pub.

Ripley's
Believe It or Not!®

Rocket Robert In 1969, Achille J. St. Onge of Worcester, Massachusetts, sent a leather-bound miniature volume of Robert Goddard's autobiography on board *Apollo 11*, the first manned space flight to the Moon. Goddard was a pioneer of rocket building and his space-flown book, with pencil markings by Buzz Aldrin, was later valued at auction as being worth between $25,000 and $35,000.

Big Foot The *Golden Driller* statue, dedicated to the oil industry in Tulsa, Oklahoma, stands 76 ft (23 m) tall and has size 393 DD shoes!

Deep Mine Two of the world's tallest buildings could be stacked on top of each other in the pit of the Kennecott Copper Mine in Utah and still not reach the surface!

Prison Guests A hotel in Liepaja, Latvia, offers guests the opportunity to experience life in a former Soviet prison. The old Karosta jail has been converted into a hotel, but visitors must still sleep on a barren bunk in a damp cell, scrub out the toilets, and are ordered around by the "prison" staff.

Pink Palace

No two columns, doors, or even door handles are alike in the 13,155-sq-yd (11,000-sq-m) Green Citadel in Magdeburg, Germany. The last project of Austrian artist Friedensreich Hundertwasser, who died in 2000, the pink building resembles a child's drawing and, like any Hundertwasser house, there are no straight lines. The $33.8-million development—containing 55 apartments, a hotel, shops, and office space—has roofs covered in grass and the buildings are topped with gold balls.

Cork Source Every nine years since 1820, the Whistler tree of Portugal has had its bark harvested for making corks—yielding enough to cork up to 100,000 wine bottles in a single harvest.

Mirror Image Dennis Clay of Houston, Texas, drives a Volkswagen Beetle—with an identical, upside-down Beetle on top, welded to the roof. He calls his art car creation "Mirror Image."

Piggy Bank The Canadian town of Coleman, Alberta, boasts the biggest piggy bank in the world. The giant cash-collector has been converted from Ten Ton Toots, an old locomotive that used to pull cars in the town's coal mines.

Mountain Toilets Two toilets have been built near the snow-covered summit of France's Mont Blanc. At 13,976 ft (4,260 m), they are the highest washrooms in Europe.

First Rain After two years of abundant rain, grass began to grow for the first time ever on the desert-themed golf course at Cameron's Corner, Australia, in 2007. The unique course straddles three states—South Australia, Queensland, and New South Wales.

Startling Stone

Visitors to a collectors' market in Haozhou, China, in April 2007, could hardly believe their eyes when they saw one of the exhibits—a strange marbled stone that looked like a huge slice of meat.

Taal Tale In the Philippines there is an island in a lake on an island in a lake on an island! The first island is in Crater Lake on Volcano Island in Lake Taal on Luzon Island.

Drifting Apart North America and Europe are moving away from each other at about the same speed as a human fingernail grows—about 6 ft (1.8 m) every 75 years.

Family Ties When an off-duty jail deputy in Nevada was pulled over and charged with driving under the influence, the arresting officer was her husband. Charlotte Moore was driving her 2004 Pontiac when she was stopped by husband Mike, a deputy with the Elko County Sheriff's Department.

Driving Backward In October 2006, a man was stopped by police near the outback town of Kalgoorlie, Australia, after driving backward down a highway for 12 mi (20 km).

Tree-mendous Shock

When a 200-year-old chestnut tree was felled near the town of Bournemouth in Dorset, England, in 2007, villagers were amazed to find a perfect image of a tiny tree imprinted throughout the branch and trunk. Experts said the unusual phenomenon was caused by wood rot.

Snow Donuts

High in Washington Pass, Washington State, in March 2007, avalanche-control expert Mike Stanford found a series of perfectly shaped frozen snow donuts. They had rolled down the mountainside and frozen in place, the biggest being about 24 in (60 cm) high, large enough for Stanford to put his head through the hole in the middle.

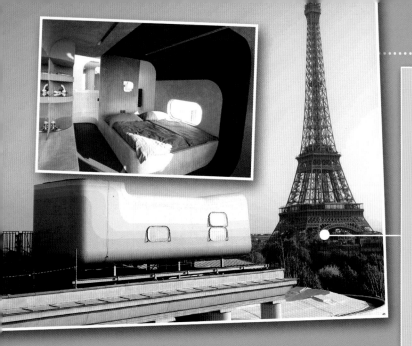

Rooftop Hotel

A one-room hotel opened in Paris, France, in 2007—perched on the roof of a museum. Designed as an art installation by Sabina Lang and Daniel Baumann, the Hotel Everland has stunning views of the Eiffel Tower, a king-size bed, a mini-bar, and breakfast delivered to the door. The creators say guests, who are allowed to stay for one night only, will be part of the exhibit.

Tiny Engine Iqbal Ahmed of Nagpur, India, has built a working steam engine that weighs less than 0.07 oz (2 g). It stands just 0.267 in (6.8 mm) high and is 0.639 in (16.24 mm) long and, with steam generated by ⅓ fl oz (10 ml) water, the brass-constructed engine can run for about two minutes.

Wine Barrels A number of old wine-making barrels have been converted into bedrooms at a hotel in Stavoren, the Netherlands. The 3,830-gal (14,500-l) wooden barrels are large enough to accommodate two single beds, a small living room with TV, and a bathroom with shower and toilet.

Train Push In May 2007, a stalled commuter train in Bihar, India, was able to start again when hundreds of passengers got out and pushed!

Careful Driver A 94-year-old woman from Hereford, England, has driven over a period of 82 years more than 600,000 mi (965,600 km) without even the smallest accident. Muriel Gladwin, who taught herself to drive at age 12, has never even had a scrape—nor has she been booked for speeding.

Oil Field The grounds of the State Capitol in Oklahoma City, Oklahoma, doubled up as a working oil field during most of the 20th century.

Hot Blast In July 1949, a sudden blast of hot air swept across an area of Portugal, causing temperatures to soar remarkably from 100 to 150°F (38 to 65°C) in just two minutes. The heat surge killed countless chickens on local farms.

Thick Ice Ninety percent of the world's total amount of ice is in Antarctica and at the South Pole where it is nearly 2 mi (3.2 km) thick.

Ripley's
Believe It or Not!®

Tree Homes

Canadian designer Tom Chudleigh has created a range of eco-friendly homes that can be suspended from trees or rock faces. Free Spirit Spheres are made from wood and coated in fiberglass to make them waterproof. Accessible only by rope bridge, the 11-ft-wide (3.4-m) houses can sleep four people and are fitted with a kitchen that is complete with microwave, refrigerator, and sink.

177

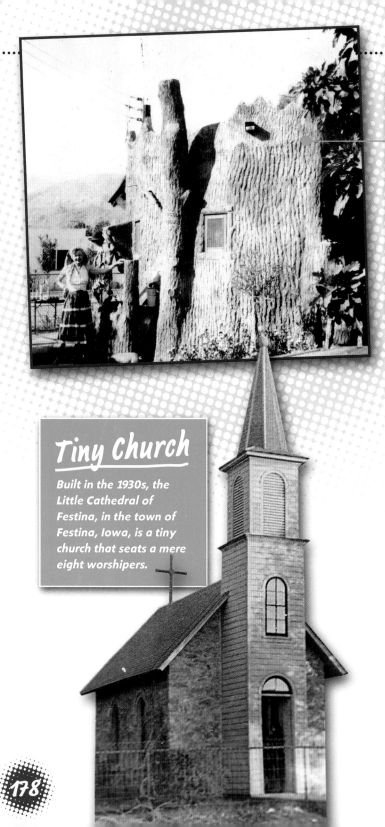

Redwood Residence

This home in Palm Springs, California, was built in the 1950s in the shape of the famous giant redwood tree General Sherman, which stands in Sequoia National Park in California.

Tiny Church

Built in the 1930s, the Little Cathedral of Festina, in the town of Festina, Iowa, is a tiny church that seats a mere eight worshipers.

Ferrari Sale A red Ferrari Enzo with a top speed of 218 mph (350 km/h) was sold for more than $1 million on eBay's U.K. online auction site in 2006. Bidding started at the equivalent of $2.

Cool Bar A new bar in Dubai is the coolest place to hang out—because everything is made of ice. The bar, tables, and chairs at Chillout are made of ice, as are the cups, glasses, and plates. There is also an ice sculpture that depicts Dubai's skyline, and an ice chandelier. A cover charge provides customers with a hooded coat, woolen gloves, and insulated shoes to keep out frostbite.

Lucky Break

A tornado carried away the end of this house in Elgin, Illinois, in 1934, but left every dish in the pantry intact!

Taxi Trip Not wanting to travel by air for her vacation to Greece, 89-year-old Kathleen Searles of Suffolk, England, made the 4,000-mi (6,440-km) journey by taxi instead. Although she could have flown there for $120 and the taxi fare ended up costing her $4,000 and taking three days, she insisted that it was money well spent. Taxi driver Julian Delefortrie said: "When she asked me if I'd like to drive to Europe I replied that I would love to. I never expected her to say Greece!"

Fog Particles Particles of fog are so tiny that it would take seven billion of them to fill a teaspoon.

Name Game Citizens in Wisconsin couldn't agree on a name for their small town, so they decided to pull six letters out of a hat and name it whatever those letters spelled. Thus the town of Ixonia was born!

Tap Tree In April 2006, a tree in San Antonio, Texas, began to spout a constant flow of clean, drinkable water. People visited the tree in the hope that it held miraculous healing powers and was spouting holy water, but it turned out that it had somehow tapped its roots into an underground water pipe.

Mobile Cathedral

Rebecca Caldwell of Oakland, California, has designed a car that looks like a Gothic cathedral, complete with flying buttresses, stained glass windows, and gargoyles. The framework of her "Carthedral" art car is a 1971 Cadillac hearse with a Volkswagen Beetle welded on top.

Silver Beetle

Art car enthusiast William Burge from Houston, Texas, has designed a vehicle with a gargoyle theme. Called "Phantoms," it is based on a 1968 Volkswagen Beetle and proved a scary sight at an automobile fair in Essen, Germany, in December 2007.

Alaskan Tsunami In 1958, an earthquake followed by a rockslide in Lituya Bay, Alaska, triggered a huge tsunami more than 1,720 ft (525 m) high. As the area is relatively isolated and enclosed, the only casualties were two men in a fishing boat.

Chocolate Car A car dealer in Qingdao City, China, coated a Volkswagen Beetle in chocolate for Valentine's Day 2007. The car was covered in plastic wrap, and then 440 lb (200 kg) of melted chocolate was spread over it.

Croc Deterrent

Crocodiles bred in captivity in eastern India have been released into the wild in order to protect endangered animals from poachers. Creatures living in wildlife sanctuaries in Orissa and West Bengal have been threatened by poachers, but the introduction of dozens more crocodiles to the sanctuaries has successfully served as a formidable deterrent.

Spoon Van
Elmer Fleming of Columbia, South Carolina, has covered his Chevrolet pickup in kitchen utensils. He has riveted 1,480 spoons onto the bodywork.

Electric Tricycle
To pull himself along while wearing rollerblades, Swiss figure skater Stephan Soder has designed an electric tricycle with a top speed of 12 mph (19 km/h). The Easyglider X6 has an electric-powered front wheel, a parking brake, a headlight, and three power levels. Optional extras include a music system.

Cave Village
The village of Zhongdong in Guizhou, China, is located within a massive natural cave the size of an aircraft hangar.

Grass Covering

Ephraim Eusebio, of Minneapolis, Minnesota, drives a 1991 Toyota Previa that is covered in artificial grass salvaged from the Guthrie Theater's garbage.

Easy to Spot
Artist Kelly Lyles's converted white Subaru is easy to spot—as it is covered in hundreds of them. Kelly, from Seattle, Washington, has painted the car to look like a leopard, and it has a leopard face on the hood, welded ears, and a tail. Dozens of toy leopards are glued to the bodywork, the interior upholstery is leopard skin, and Lyles herself dresses from head to toe in… leopard skin.

Leaning Steeple
A 15th-century church steeple in Suurhusen, Germany, stands 84 ft (26 m) high and leans at an angle of five degrees—a degree more than Italy's famous Leaning Tower of Pisa.

Boat Revealed
In April 2007, an earthquake near the Solomon Islands, measuring a powerful 8.1 on the Richter scale, pushed coral reefs around 10 ft (3 m) above sea level. It also tossed up a World-War-II torpedo boat that had previously sunk.

Car-toon Truck

New Jersey art teacher Robert Luczun has decorated every inch of a 1928 Model AR Ford Roadster pickup truck with hundreds of comic book, comic strip, and animated cartoon characters.

Combining his twin hobbies of antique cars and comic art, he spent more than 2,800 hours over a period of 15 months airbrush-painting assorted animated icons, from *101 Dalmatians* to *Rat Fink* and *Finding Nemo* to *Dr. Who*. The result is a rolling history of comics from 1896 to the present day.

After months of preparation, Luczun waited another three days so that he could start painting on October 18, 2004—the 108th anniversary of the first published comic, The Yellow Kid, whom he honored with a place on the back of the side mirror.

Each cartoon was hand-drawn twice—once on a paper layout, then again on the vehicle—and every color was masked off to prevent any spray-paint errors. He took much of the truck apart during the project. The desire to cover the entire bodywork—inside and out—forced him to paint in backbreaking positions. While drawing, he put the *Where's Waldo?* figure in at random and finished up with around a dozen Waldos scattered about the vehicle. Luczun's incredible cartoon truck is now a familiar sight at comic book conventions, auto shows, and art car parades.

In the interior of the car, Luczun has used a Nemo toy repainted and converted into a gearshift knob.

Crystal Cave

Mexico's Cueva de los Cristales (Crystal Cave) is home to giant gypsum crystals that are more than 35 ft (11 m) long—over one third as long as the cave itself. By studying fluid samples embedded inside the crystals in the 970-ft-deep (295-m) cave, scientists believe the mammoth structures developed because the temperature there remained just below 136°F (58°C) for hundreds of thousands of years. Volcanic activity created the Naica Mountain some 26 million years ago and filled it with high-temperature anhydrite, which is gypsum without water. Above 136°F anhydrite is stable, but below that it turns to gypsum and, in this case, has formed majestic crystals.

Oxygen Rail
The train service connecting Lhasa, Tibet, to China's rail system operates at such a high altitude that oxygen is provided to passengers, and those over age 60 need medical clearance before they are allowed on board.

Lucky Number
A woman from Devon, England, won the equivalent of $2.6 million in the lottery because she forgot the age of her son. Janet Baddick chooses numbers representing family ages, but used 26 for her son Darren, forgetting that he had turned 27 a few weeks earlier. Luckily, 26 was a winning number!

Cave Dwellers
Centuries-old caves in Andalucia, Spain, have been connected to electricity and water supplies and fitted with modern furnishings in order to provide comfortable homes for people today.

Remote Hotel
Birdsville Hotel and Pub, located in Australia's Simpson Desert, is 900 mi (1,450 km) from the nearest town or city, but still serves 45,000 customers a year.

Thunderstruck
Approximately 1,800 thunderstorms take place across the Earth at any given moment, and the planet is struck by an average of more than 100 lightning bolts every second.

Flying Saucer
A sci-fi fan who admits he knows nothing about computers has spent more than 30 years building his own flying saucer in his garage. Alfie Carrington of Clinton, Michigan, has been putting the machine together using information from aviation books, and so far the project has cost him more than $60,000.

Monster Grasshopper
The town of Wilkie, Saskatchewan, Canada, is home to an unusual monument—a wooden grasshopper measuring 18 x 6 ft (5.5 x 1.8 m) and weighing 4,000 lb (1,815 kg).

Dollhouse Memorial
The grave of Nadine Earles (1929–33) in Lanett, Alabama, is covered by a brick dollhouse with a life-sized doll, a tea set, and toys inside.

Port-a-Potty

Inspired by the sight of a windstorm blowing portable toilets across the tarmac at a drag-car show in Texas, Paul Stender of Brownsburg, Indiana, invented his own jet-powered outhouse. Driven by a 50-year-old, 750-lb (340-kg) Boeing jet turbine, Stender's Port-o-Jet reaches speeds of 46 mph (74 km/h) and shoots out 30-ft (9-m) fireballs in its wake. While in motion, Stender sits on the toilet's original seat and looks out through a hole in the door. He tried to keep the toilet paper, but it kept getting sucked into the engine.

Vanishing Lake In May 2007, a 5-acre (2-ha), 100-ft-deep (30-m) lake in Magallanes, Chile, disappeared in less than two weeks.

Bottle Boat In June 2007, Marcus Eriksen of Long Beach, California, launched a 20-ft (6-m) Viking boat made from 5,000 recycled plastic bottles at Juneau, Alaska. The bottles were held in place by fish net, and the boat's sail consisted of a collection of old shirts. The previous year, Eriksen had sailed a 14-ft-long (4.3-m) boat, the *Fluke*, made from 800 plastic bottles, on a 250-mi (400-km) Californian voyage from Santa Barbara to San Diego.

Secret Apartment Eight artists built and furnished a secret apartment inside a Providence, Rhode Island, shopping mall—and stayed there for four years. They used breeze blocks to build the apartment in a disused space next to a car park and overcame the absence of plumbing by sneaking out to use mall toilets.

High & Mighty

Created by Bob Chandler, of St. Louis, Missouri, the Bigfoot 5 truck is 15 ft 6 in (4.7 m) tall, 13 ft 1 in (4 m) wide, and weighs more than 28,000 lb (12,780 kg). The huge 10-ft (3-m) tall tires, which Chandler bought from a junkyard, had previously been used by the U.S. Army on an Arctic snow train in Alaska during the 1950s.

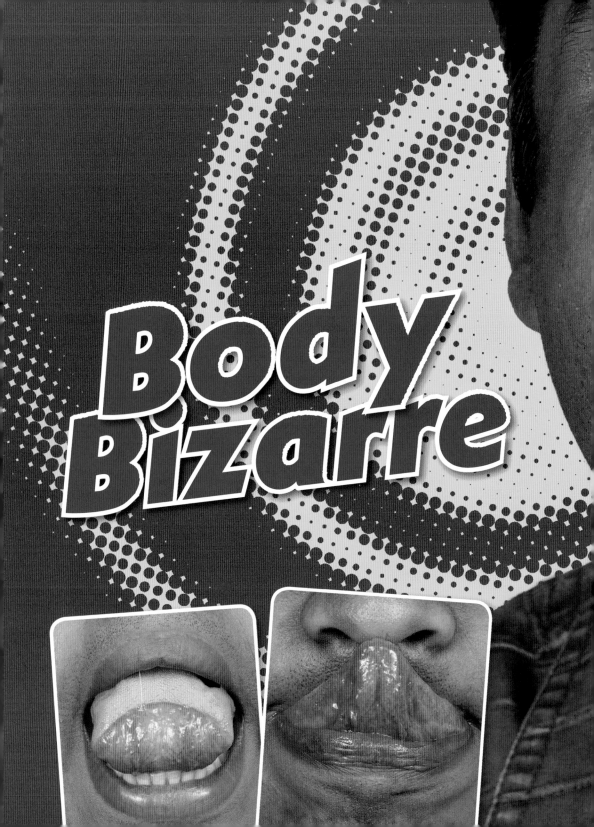

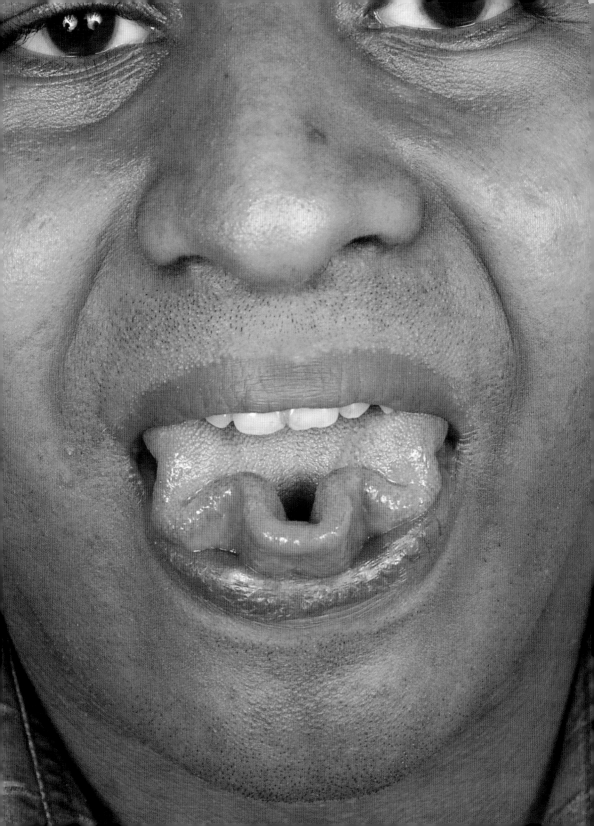

The Human Canvas

Stop! Look very closely and see if you can make out the body parts used as a canvas for these amazing paintings! Chadwick Gray has to remain motionless for up to 15 hours at a time so that artist Laura Spector can paint him. Yet this is no ordinary still life, for the canvas is not a sheet of paper but Chadwick's body.

The completed portrait of Lanna Woman.

Laura paints a Thai portrait onto Chadwick, in Thailand.

> "This painting's original was lost during World War II, so we had to re-create it from a black-and-white photograph."

> "It's rare to find 19th-century portraits in Thailand, so this piece was re-created from the wall of a temple in northern Thailand. The woman represented is the Thai version of Mother Nature—she can water the rice fields with her hair."

It is all part of the New York City collaborative team's Museum Anatomy project, which began in 1996 and sees them re-create old paintings onto a human canvas.

Chadwick admits he suffers for his art and enters almost a meditative trance in order to stay completely still for so long. Sometimes his feats of meditative endurance are made publicly. In 2001, for example, Laura painted a 19th-century portrait of a bride onto his body in the front windows of the Henri Bendel department store in New York.

Chadwick and Laura scour the storerooms of museums across the world for likely subjects, frequently looking for paintings that have been stored and hidden away from public view because of their controversial nature. Chadwick says: "We often had to convince conservative curators, and once, in Prague, even a panel of nuns, to allow us to reproduce rare paintings of the female form onto the often naked male body."

Once the body art is completed, Laura photographs Chadwick and the prints are developed to the same size as the original painting. The resulting photographs reveal a new work of art in which the painting acquires curves and sometimes leaves the canvas unrecognizable as Chadwick's human form.

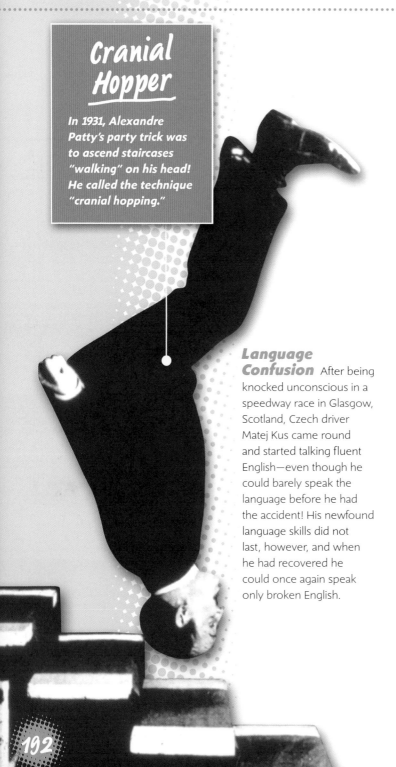

Cranial Hopper

In 1931, Alexandre Patty's party trick was to ascend staircases "walking" on his head! He called the technique "cranial hopping."

Impaled on Spike A five-year-old boy from Sydney, Australia, survived after being speared through the throat by an iron-fence spike in July 2007. The spike plunged 2 in (5 cm) into the throat of Hugo Borbilas, narrowly missing his carotid artery, esophagus, windpipe, all the major nerves in his neck and throat, and stopping just short of his brain. The injury could have killed Hugo instantly, but he managed to pull himself off the spike and yell for help.

Penguin Girl As she had no forearms, only three toes on each foot, and a distinctive walk, diminutive Nany Mae Hill of Keyes, California, was billed in circus shows as the "Penguin Girl." After marrying 6-ft-tall (1.8-m) farmer Benjamin Hill in the 1940s, she wore her wedding ring on the middle toe of her left foot.

Language Confusion After being knocked unconscious in a speedway race in Glasgow, Scotland, Czech driver Matej Kus came round and started talking fluent English—even though he could barely speak the language before he had the accident! His newfound language skills did not last, however, and when he had recovered he could once again speak only broken English.

Hair Mop Thousands of prisoners donated their hair to help soak up spilled fuel following the crash of an oil tanker off the coast of the Philippines in August 2006.

Long Nose Thomas Wedders, who lived in the U.K. during the 18th century, had a nose that measured 7½ in (19 cm) long. He put his pronounced proboscis to good use by joining a traveling freak show.

Horned Man

An 88-year-old man from a village near Zhengzhou, China, has a horn growing from his head. It began to grow in 2006 when he picked at a little bump on his head and it went on to grow steadily over the next few months. Doctors believe it is a form of hyperplasia, an excess of normal body tissue.

Miracle Walker

Born with spina bifida, by the age of 34 Mark Chenoweth was resigned to spending the rest of his life in a wheelchair. Doctors told him he would never walk again. Then, on holiday in Menorca in 1998, against the advice of his doctor, he persuaded a dive center to let him go scuba diving for the first time. He plunged to a depth of 55 ft (17 m) — and when he emerged from the water he found that he could walk again.

"It was just unbelievable," says Mark. "I came out and I could feel my legs like I had never felt them before. They were actually working. The instructor couldn't believe it. He'd seen me arrive in my wheelchair, and now I didn't need it."

Three days later his legs became lifeless again, but back home in Staffordshire, England, he quickly booked his next diving holiday. Since then he has found that the deeper he dives, the longer he can walk for afterward. As a result he now needs his wheelchair only twice a year.

DEPTH DIVED	WALKING PERIOD AFTERWARD
55 ft (17 m)	3–4 days
100 ft (30 m)	2–3 months
130 ft (40 m)	4 months
165 ft (50 m)	8 months

Swollen Fingers

Liu Hua from Jiangsu Province, China, had fingers that were thicker than his arms. His left thumb, index finger, and middle finger were deformed at birth and grew to a huge size before surgeons removed 11 lb (5 kg) of bone and tissue from them in 2007.

Sweet Taste

Humans with a particularly acute sense of taste are able to detect sweetness in a solution that is one part sugar to 200 parts water. In comparison, certain moths and butterflies can detect sweetness when the ratio is one part sugar to 300,000 parts water.

Swallowed Head

A man whose head was swallowed by a great white shark managed to break free from the 10-ft (3-m) monster by lunging at its face with a metal chisel. Eric Nerhus, 41, was diving for sea mollusks off the coast of New South Wales, Australia, in January 2007, when the shark grabbed him head-first. It snatched his head, shoulders, and chest into its mouth, but let go after being struck repeatedly with the chisel. Although the surrounding water was red with his blood, Nerhus escaped with a broken nose and deep bite-marks to his chest.

Rabid Recovery

Teenager Jeanna Giese of Fond Du Lac, Wisconsin, had to relearn how to walk, talk, and function after catching rabies from a bat bite in September 2004. It took more than a year for her to be able to walk unaided, but she still graduated high school with honors in 2007. Jeanna is thought to be the only person ever to have survived the deadly disease, which attacks the nervous system, without having had a vaccination.

Bladder Stone

Doctors in Israel removed a bladder stone from Moneera Khalil that was the size of a grapefruit! The stone measured $5\frac{1}{8}$ in (13 cm) across and weighed nearly 2 lb 4 oz (1 kg).

Half Size

When Frenchman Fabien Pretou married Natalie Lucius at Seysinnet-Pariset, France, in 1990, he towered over her in the wedding photos. For he was 6 ft 2 in (1.85 m) tall and she was half his height at 3 ft 1 in (94 cm).

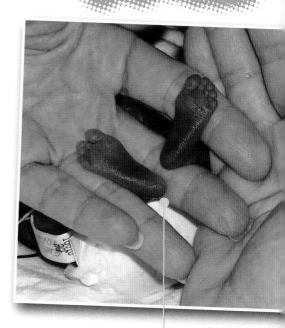

Premature Baby

Born at Miami, Florida, in October 2006, little Amillia Sonja Taylor survived despite a gestation period of fewer than 22 weeks. She spent 21 weeks 6 days in the womb (full-term births are between 37 and 40 weeks) and at birth weighed less than 10 oz (284 g) and measured just 9 in (24 cm) long—that's only slightly longer than a ballpoint pen.

Vodka Drip Doctors in the city of Brisbane in Queensland, Australia, attached a poisoned Italian tourist to a vodka drip in 2007 after running out of supplies of the medicinal alcohol they normally use.

Human Magnet Romanian Aurel Raileanu often finds himself literally glued to the TV. The Bucharest hospital worker has become known as the Human Magnet because spoons, books, lighters, and even a 50-lb (23-kg) TV set, all stick to him.

A Real Mouthful

Despite standing a mere 5 ft (1.52 m) in height, Jackie del Rio of Chicago, Illinois, managed to lift two tables and six chairs— with his teeth!

Muddy Beauty

Visitors to a resort in China's Sichuan Province cover themselves from head to toe in black mud. The mineral-rich mud is said to be beneficial to the skin.

Brief Awakening A woman awoke from a six-year coma—but only for three days. Christa Lilly had been in a coma in Colorado Springs, Colorado, since suffering a heart attack and stroke in late 2000. Then, in 2007, she suddenly woke up and started talking to doctors and family, although she believed it was 1986. However, three days later she mysteriously lapsed back into a vegetative state.

Ear Nest A pair of spiders made their home in the ear of a nine-year-old boy. When Jesse Courtney of Albany, Oregon, felt a faint popping in his left ear, followed by an ache, doctors flushed out two spiders—one dead, the other alive. Jesse was given the spiders as a souvenir and took them to school to show his friends.

Extra Limbs Rudy Santos of Bacolod City, the Philippines, has been promoted as "Octoman" on account of having three legs and four arms. One of the legs is missing below the knee and he also has the small head and ear of his parasitic twin attached to his stomach.

Eight-limbed Girl

A girl born in India with four arms and four legs had the extra limbs removed in a groundbreaking 27-hour operation. Shortly afterward, she was able to stand up and walk for the first time in her life.

Lakshmi Tatma was born a conjoined twin in the impoverished northern state of Bihar. In a rare condition called isciopagus, her twin had stopped developing in the mother's womb and the surviving fetus had absorbed the parasitic twin's limbs, kidneys, and other body parts. Although the twin had a torso and limbs, it had no head and its body was joined to Lakshmi's at the pelvis.

So Lakshmi, who was named after the four-armed Hindu goddess of wealth, was born with two spines, four kidneys, entangled nerves, two stomach cavities, two chest cavities, four arms, and four legs. Many local people revered her as a goddess and lined up for a blessing from the child, but her father, Shambhu, was forced to keep her in hiding after a circus tried to buy her.

In November 2007, the two-year-old underwent an operation at a hospital in Bangalore. As well as removing the surplus limbs, surgeons transplanted a kidney from Lakshmi's twin into her own body, moved her bowels and intestines into a more central position, and amputated the headless twin altogether.

Afterward, when Lakshmi was able to stand up to reach her favorite toy, her mother, Poonam, said: "I had tears in my eyes, it was a dream I thought would never happen."

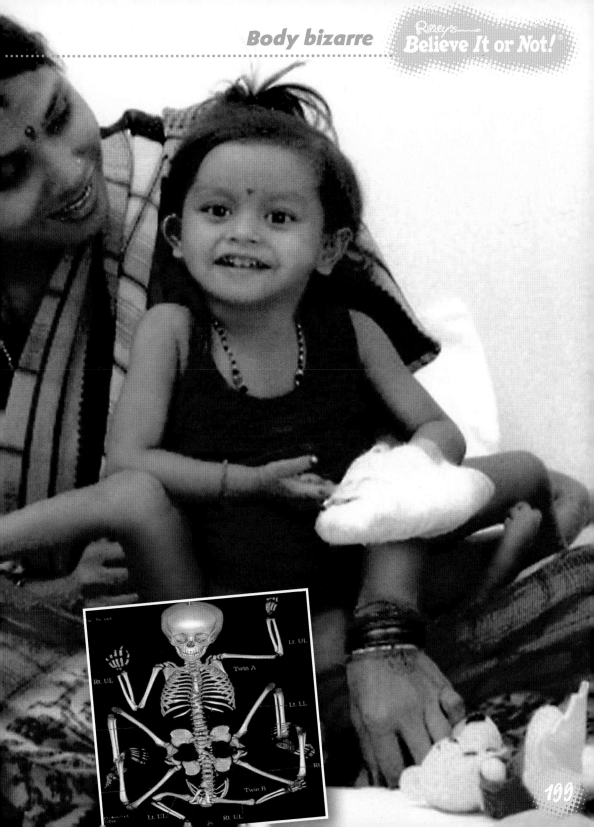

Twin A

Rt. UL

Lt. UL

Lt. LL

Twin B

Lt. UL

Rt. UL

Curved Horn A Chinese grandmother has a 5-in (13-cm) horn growing out of her brow. Ninety-five-year-old Granny Zhao of Zhanjiang City, says the horn, which curves downward and looks like the stalk of a pumpkin, grew from a mole three years ago. It causes her no pain but interferes slightly with her vision.

Half Brain A 39-year-old woman from Wuhan, China, has lived a normal life despite having only half a brain. Although scans showed no gray matter on the left side—the part of the brain that controls language—she has no problem communicating with people.

Eye-popping Claudio Paulo Pinto of Brazil, can pop his eyeballs out of their sockets a distance of at least 0.3 in (7 mm). He once had a job scaring visitors at a haunted house tourist attraction in Belo Horizonte.

Wedged Tooth An Australian rugby player carried on playing for more than three months… unaware that he had an opponent's tooth embedded in his brow. It was only when Ben Czislowski complained of shooting pains that a doctor found the tooth of opposing forward Matt Austin, with whom Czislowski had clashed heads during a match in April 2007.

Knee Images

In December 2006, Amia Fore of Detroit, Michigan, was amazed when she looked in the mirror and saw what appeared to be a face on her right kneecap. A month later another "face" appeared—this time on her left kneecap, the features becoming more pronounced as the weeks passed. A spiritual advisor said the initial image was of Amia's first (unborn) grandchild and that the features would disappear once the baby was born.

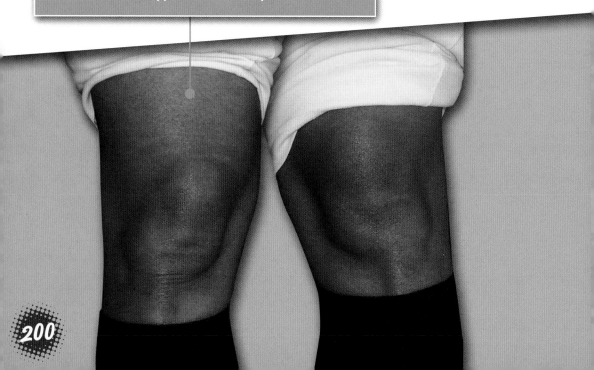

Body Hair

Yu Zhenhuan has thick hair covering 96 percent of his entire body—every inch except for the palms of his hands and the soles of his feet. His eyelashes are so long that they hide his eyes. Also known in his native China as rock singer King Kong, Yu has undergone five operations to remove hair from his nose and recently had another to remove a clump of hair from his ear because it was impairing his hearing.

Unequal Twins Born in Denton, Montana, Donald Koehler (1925–81) experienced an abnormal growth spurt at age ten and stood 8 ft 2 in (2.48 m) tall at his peak. Yet his twin sister was only 5 ft 9 in (1.75 m) tall—a height difference of 29 in (74 cm).

Burial Jars A tribe from Borneo keeps its dead in huge earthenware jars. As the corpse rots, the bodily fluid is drained away and the dried remains are put in another container. The original jars are then re-used for cooking.

201

The Blue Man

A man from California has skin that is permanently blue. Paul Karason of Madera developed the condition 15 years ago after using a homemade silver remedy to treat dermatitis on his face. Despite the unfortunate side effect, he swears by its powers and has even got used to his nickname of Papa Smurf.

Conjoined Twins

This photograph of conjoined twins, Mary and Arrita, was taken in 1924. The girls, from Mexico City, Mexico, were joined at the ribcage.

Pencil Removal A woman in Germany has had part of a pencil removed from her head—after living with it for 55 years. Margaret Wegner was four when she fell over while carrying her pencil. It punctured her cheek and part of it went into her brain, just above her right eye. She has endured nosebleeds and headaches most of her life, but now surgeons in Berlin have managed to remove most of the pencil, although a 1/12-in (2-mm) section was too deeply embedded for them to get out.

Mighty Ming U.S.-based Chinese basketball player Sun Ming Ming stands 7 ft 9 in (2.36 m) tall and wears size 19 shoes. He did not start playing his sport until he was 15, by which time he was already 6 ft 7 in (2 m) tall.

Hiccup Attack Jennifer Mee of St. Petersburg, Florida, started hiccupping on January 23, 2007, and continued for 38 days straight.

Green Blood Surgeons operating on a 42-year-old man in Vancouver, British Columbia, Canada, were alarmed to discover that he had green blood! Tests revealed that he had taken too many doses of a headache pill, which had caused his blood to change color.

German Giant Known as "Le Géant Constantin," Julius Koch (1872–1902) of Reutlingen, Germany, had hands that measured 15 in (38 cm) long—more than twice the size of an average adult hand. He was believed to be more than 8 ft (2.4 m) tall, but his height had to be estimated because his legs were amputated after developing gangrene.

Tattoo Master

At InkLine Studio in New York City, Anil Gupta can reproduce a famous artwork as a tattoo without losing any of the intricate detail from the original painting. He has created postage-stamp-size tattoos of works by Michelangelo, Van Gogh, and Leonardo da Vinci, including a tiny copy of the Mona Lisa and this shoulder-width version of The Last Supper.

Piercing Record

Brent Moffatt from Winnipeg, Canada, pierced himself with 900 surgical needles in 2003 in an effort to break his previous body-piercing record of 702.

Bee Beard Steve Bryans of Alvinston, Ontario, Canada, had his face crawling with 7,700 bees at an annual bee beard contest at Aylmer, Ontario. The bees, which had been smoked into good behavior, were brushed onto competitors' faces and shaped with feathers into beards. They remained in place because they were attracted by their queens, who were caged and tied around the contestants' necks.

Massive Tumor Huang Chuncai, 31, of Hunan, China, is only 4 ft 6 in (1.37 m) tall but he had a facial tumor that was nearly 2 ft (60 cm) long and weighed 33 lb (15 kg). It first appeared when he was four and grew so rapidly that it blocked his left eye, pushed his left ear down to shoulder level, knocked out his teeth, and deformed his backbone. By the time the tumor was removed in 2007, it was hanging down from his face.

Little and Large

Extremes of tall and short people from West (left) and East (right) seen in the 1930s and 1880s respectively.

Second Liver
Jenna Hopkins of Crab Orchard, Kentucky, was born with a second liver growing in her right lung.

Seal and Chimp
Stanislaus Berent of Pittsburgh, Pennsylvania, had hands growing from his shoulders, but no arms—a condition known as phocomelia. Billed in shows as "Sealo the Seal Boy," his act featured a chimpanzee to which he fed cookies.

Denture Drama
A 38-year-old Romanian woman swallowed her lover's false teeth during a passionate kiss. She was rushed to hospital with pains and X rays showed the teeth in her stomach.

Finger Growth
Lee Spievack of Cincinnati, Ohio, lost the tip of a finger in August 2005, but the finger grew back to its original length—and the fingernail on that finger now grows twice as fast as the rest.

Loud Snap Robert Hatch of Pasadena, California, snaps his fingers at a sound level of 108 decibels—almost as loud as a rock concert.

Tough Teeth Cai Dongsheng of Chongqing City, China, can break nails with his teeth. Protecting his teeth with gauze, he has so far snapped more than 22 lb (10 kg) of nails.

Queasy Rider A Japanese motorcyclist carried on riding his bike for more than a mile before realizing that he had lost his leg. The 54-year-old office worker hit a safety barrier but it was only when he stopped a couple of minutes later that he noticed his leg had been severed below the knee.

Pee Power In many parts of Asia, people believe that drinking your own urine cures a variety of ailments—including snakebites, heart disease, chicken pox, infertility, and baldness. Some Japanese women even bathe in their own urine as part of their beauty regime—to improve their skin.

Shark Attack

Attacked by a 2-ft (60-cm) shark while he was snorkeling off the coast of New South Wales, Australia, Luke Tresoglavic had to swim 300 yd (275 m) to shore, walk to his car, and drive to a surf club... all with the shark still hanging on to his leg. The Wobbegong shark, which can grow up to 10 ft (3 m) in length, sank its razor-sharp teeth into Tresoglavic's flesh and refused to let go even though lifeguards flushed its gills with fresh water in a bid to loosen its grip. Tresoglavic was treated for puncture wounds to his leg but, sadly, the shark died as a result of the ordeal and was buried in the Tresoglavic family garden.

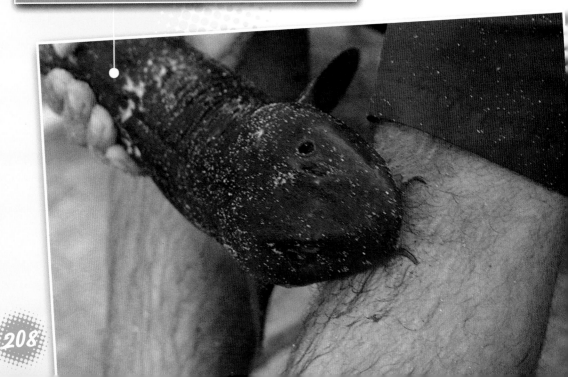

Internal Decapitation

Shannon Malloy survived a car crash in which her skull was separated from her spine—a condition called internal decapitation. At a special surgical unit in Denver, Colorado, doctors drilled five screws into her neck and four into her head to reattach it. Then she was fitted with a metal halo—which consists of rods and a circular bar—to keep her head stabilized, but even during the fitting of the halo her unattached head kept slipping off her neck.

Face Bugs

Doctors thought the painful bumps on Aaron Dallas's head might have been gnat bites or shingles... until the bumps started to move. That was when they discovered five botfly larvae living in an 1/8-in-wide (3-mm) pit near the top of his skull. The tiny parasites were probably placed there by a mosquito. "I could feel and hear them," said Dallas of Carbondale, Colorado. "I actually thought I was going crazy."

Mistaken Identity In October 2007, after overseeing the cremation of a man she thought was her son, a woman was shocked when he turned up alive the next day. Gina Partington had identified a body found in Manchester, England, as her 39-year-old son Thomas Dennison, but 24 hours later he was found alive and well 85 mi (137 km) away in Nottingham.

Snake Bite Matt Wilkinson of Portland, Oregon, spent three days in a coma in 2007 after putting his 20-in (51-cm) pet diamondback rattlesnake into his mouth. He made it to the hospital just in time, as his airway had nearly swollen shut from the venomous bites.

No Pulse Gerard Langevin of Quebec, Canada, was fitted with a new heart but now he has no pulse!

Bao Xishun and Xia Shujuan married in 2007 in traditional Mongolian costume.

A Big Difference

One of the tallest men in the world is Bao Xishun, a former herdsman from Mongolia who is a towering 7 ft 9 in (2.36 m) tall. Bao was of normal size until the age of 16, when he experienced a sudden, unexplained growth spurt, as a result of which he reached his present height just seven years later. In July 2007, after searching the world for a suitable bride, 56-year-old Bao married 5-ft-5-in (1.68-m) Xia Shujuan, a woman from his hometown. She is nearly half his age and more than 2 ft (60 cm) shorter. For the wedding (see left), it took 30 tailors three days to create Bao's outfit.

Mummy Medicine In the 16th century, mummies were thought to possess medicinal properties that could prevent wounds from bleeding. Coated in honey, they were sold in powdered form as pharmaceuticals to be taken orally.

Magic Trick Actor Daniel Radcliffe, best known for his role as Harry Potter in the movies of the same name, can hold his hand on a flat surface and rotate it 360 degrees.

Prolonged Pregnancy An X ray on a 90-year-old woman in Sichuan, China, revealed that she had been pregnant for 58 years. When doctors examined the old lady, they found a dead, distorted fetus in her uterus, dating back to 1949 when she had a still birth.

Two Wombs At a hospital in Bristol, England, in December 2006, Hannah Kersey gave birth to three children from two different wombs. Identical twins Ruby and Tilly were delivered from one womb and a single baby, Grace, was delivered from the other. Kersey was born with an unusual condition called *uterus didelphys*, which leads to the abnormal development of the reproductive organs.

Dinosaur Medicine Villagers in China have spent decades digging up dinosaur bones for use in medicine. The calcium-rich bones are boiled with other ingredients and fed to children to treat dizziness and leg cramps. They are also ground into a paste and then applied directly to wounds to help heal bone fractures.

Hidden Glass Xiao Zhu of China wondered why he always kept crying from one eye—until doctors found that he had had a 1⅓-in-long (3.5-cm) piece of glass buried under his right eye for the past six years. The eye had been injured in a fight, but the operation to repair the injury had missed the shard of glass.

Spoon Surgery In 1942, Wheeler Lipes, a 23-year-old crewman in the U.S. Navy, performed an emergency appendectomy on another crew member using only spoons as retractors and a scalpel blade with no handle. Lipes was not even a doctor—he was a pharmacist's mate—and he carried out the successful operation on a submarine that was cruising 120 ft (36 m) under the South China Sea!

Quarter Boy Johnny Gilmore—alias "Zandu the Quarter Boy"—was born in Marshalltown, Iowa, in 1913 with the entire lower part of his body missing. He used to walk on his hands.

Sand Remedy

Patients in Thailand travel from far and wide to be buried up to their necks in hot sand and then stood on by a doctor. They flock to the northeastern province of Buriram to be treated by witch doctor Pan Rerngprasarn, who believes ancient Cambodian healing can cure anything from cancer to mental illness.

Strange Couple Percilla Lauther from Puerto Rico had a hormonal imbalance that left her with a dark beard and hair all over her body. She was billed in shows as "Priscilla the Monkey Girl" and in 1938 she eloped with performer Emmitt Bejano, "The Alligator-skinned Boy," who suffered from ichthyosis, giving him scaly skin. Together they were promoted as "The World's Strangest Married Couple."

Legless Acrobat Born in Ohio in 1844, Eli Bowen had no legs—just two small feet of different sizes growing from his hips. As a toddler, he used his arms for walking and would hold wooden blocks in his hands, enabling him to swing his hips between his arms. The strength he developed from walking in this manner helped him become a top-class acrobat.

Inuit Family Eight well-preserved, 500-year-old mummies were discovered at an Inuit settlement in Greenland in 1972—a baby, a young boy, and six women. The bodies had been mummified naturally by the sub-zero temperatures and the dry winds in the cave in which they were found.

Pizza Head To mark the opening of his takeout pizza shop, Colin Helsby of Penmaenmawr, Wales, had a slice of ham-and-pineapple pizza tattooed on the back of his head. The tattooist took three hours to complete the artwork, which features three types of ham and chunks of pineapple, as well as strands of cheese dripping down Helsby's neck.

Medical Mishap In 2007, a Brazilian woman discovered that the cause of her persistent stomach ache was a 2-in (5-cm) scalpel that had been left in her body when she gave birth by Cesarean section 23 years earlier.

Phone Light As a result of a power failure, surgeons at a hospital in Villa Mercedes, Argentina, had to finish an operation using the light emitted by cell phones.

Healing Grave Locals say that graves in a churchyard at Launceston, England, can cure a stiff neck if, on May 1, 2, or 3, the ailing person applies dew from a newly dug grave to their neck.

Fiery Treatment

Walnuts and ignited dry moxa leaves are placed on a patient's eyes in Jinan, China, as treatment for eye disease. Taken from the plant Artemisia chinensis, burned moxa leaves are a staple ingredient of Traditional Chinese Medicine.

Tongue in Cheek

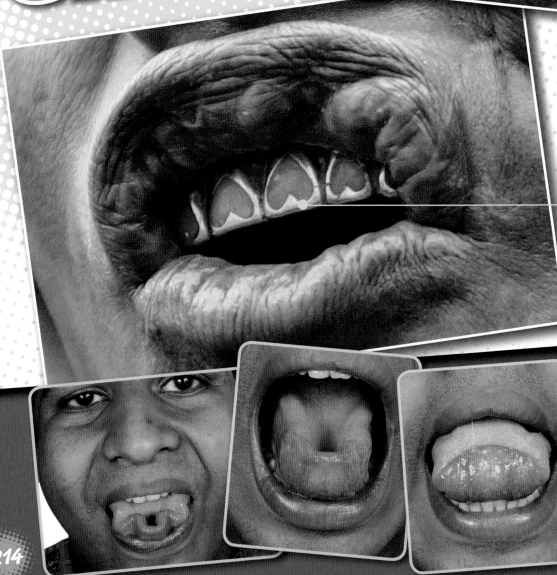

Corpse Export

During the American Civil War, mummies were imported to the U.S.A. so that the extensive linen in which they were wrapped could be manufactured into paper.

Toothbrush Tree

Instead of brushing their teeth, some African tribes in Chad and the Sudan chew on sticks carved from the wood of the *Salvadora persica*, or "toothbrush tree." The wood releases a bacteria-fighting liquid that helps prevent infection and tooth decay.

Stretched Ears

The witch doctor of the Kuria tribe in Tanzania, Africa, used to stretch his ear lobes until they were so large that a child could be passed through them— an act believed to cure the children of their ailments.

Abdominal Growth

Chen Huanxiang of Wuhan, China, was admitted to a hospital in April 2007 for the removal of a whopping 110-lb (50-kg) abdominal tumor.

Frog in the Throat

Ancient Romans would cure toothache by holding a frog boiled in water and vinegar inside the mouth of the patient.

Miracle Cure

Frazer Simpson of Northumberland, England, was accidentally splashed in the face with a corrosive chemical and, rather than hurting his eyes, it miraculously improved his eyesight to the point where he no longer needed glasses to drive.

Edible Gold

A company in Japan has created edible gold shapes that can float in your coffee or decorate your tongue. As well as offering the height of luxury, the gold is said to help refresh the human body.

Gold Crowns

This Bolivian woman has heart-shaped gold crowns on her teeth.

Mohammed Rafi of Kerala, India, can twist his tongue at a 180-degree angle and roll it inside out by flipping his entire tongue backward. He can touch the tip of his nose with his tongue and can also roll it into all sorts of shapes—a flower, a shell, and even a boat.

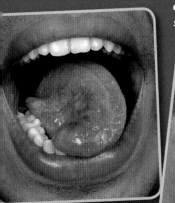

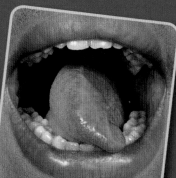

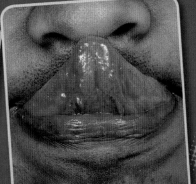

Weird Entertainment

Aristocrats in 19th-century Europe used to buy a mummy, unwrap it, and invite friends over to view the curiosity. The regular exposure to air eventually caused the mummies to disintegrate.

Swallow Please!

A cure for dizziness in 16th-century England was to take a young swallow from its nest during a crescent moon, cut off the bird's head, allowing the blood to run into a vessel containing frankincense, and give the potion to the patient when the moon was waning.

Impalement Horror

Ezra Bias of Spokane, Washington, miraculously survived after being impaled through the head by a 2-ft-long (60-cm) piece of steel bar. He was delivering pizza when a car drove over the bar as it lay in the road, flipping it up into the air, from where if flew through Bias' windshield and into his head.

Bear Necessity

In 16th-century Europe, a cure for fainting was to take fur from the belly of a live bear, boil it in alcohol, and place it on the soles of the ailing person's feet.

Hey, Baby!

Artist Camille Allen from Powell River, British Columbia, applies her knowledge of doll-making and sculpture to create these tiny, highly detailed babies made from polymer clays. Allen, who started this artistic venture when she had some leftover materials from a larger project, uses tiny dentist tools to sculpt the babies' fine features and even applies fine mohair, a strand at a time, to imitate real baby hair.

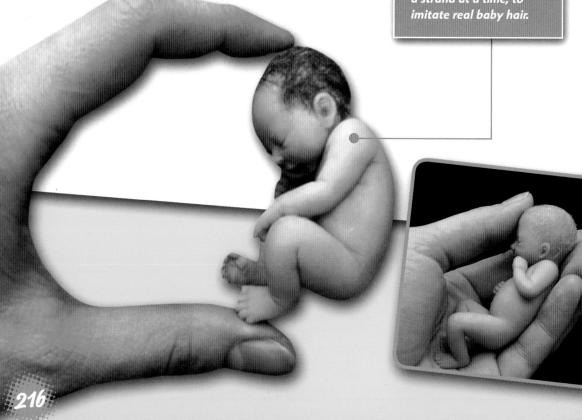

216

Role Model Firefighter John Joseph Conway from Chicago, Illinois, underwent plastic surgery in India to make himself look like Hollywood star Bruce Willis. He spent $1,600 on the operation because he thought Willis' strong jaw was the ideal look for a firefighter.

New Graduate Maurice Yankow of Valhalla, New York, enrolled in medical school at age 63—and became a practicing licensed physician at 70 years of age.

Rare Blood The rarest blood group in the world is a type of Bombay blood known as H-H. It was first discovered in Bombay in 1950, and it is thought that only 57 people in the whole of India have it.

Leg Battle Two men were feuding in 2007 over who had the rightful ownership of a severed leg. John Wood of Greenville, South Carolina, had the leg amputated after a plane crash, but kept it in a barbecue smoker so that he could be buried "whole" when he died. However, the smoker containing the leg was among items that Shannon Whisnant of Maiden, North Carolina, bought at an auction—and he wanted to keep it.

Mermaid Effect A woman from New Zealand with no legs is being fitted with a mermaid's tail so she can pursue her love of swimming. Nadya Vessey had both legs amputated by the age of 16, but has asked the company responsible for the special effects in the *Lord of the Rings* and *King Kong* movies to make her a prosthetic tail molded on to a pair of wetsuit shorts.

Admiral Dot Born in San Francisco in 1858, little Leopold Kahn was discovered by showman P.T. Barnum at age four and dubbed "The Eldorado Elf," later renamed as "Admiral Dot." At 16, Kahn was 2 ft 1 in (63 cm) tall, but he eventually reached 4 ft (1.2 m) and became a deputy sheriff and volunteer firefighter in White Plains, New York, making him the smallest man in the U.S.A. to hold either post.

Hidden Towel When the body of Bonnie Valle from Canton, Ohio, was donated to science after her death in 2002, a green surgical cloth the size of a large hand towel was found behind her left lung. The rolled-up towel had apparently been left there seven years earlier during a surgical procedure on her lungs. Her family said that she had often complained of a funny feeling in her chest.

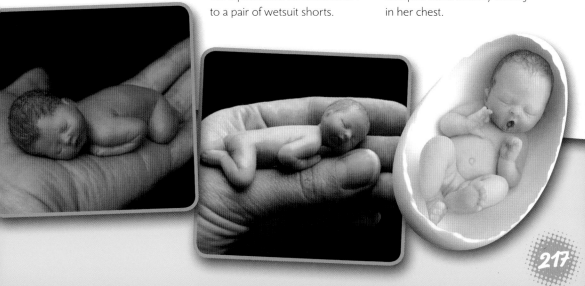

Thick Wrapping

An ancient Egyptian mummy had more than 9,000 sq ft (835 sq m) of wrappings.

Broken Neck

Fourteen-year-old sports fanatic Alfie Tyson-Brown of Dorset, England, led an active life for 10 years—unaware that he had a broken neck that could have killed him at any time. He played rugby, surfed, went mountain biking, and rode roller coasters before doctors finally discovered his life-threatening injury.

Cell Numbers

Our galaxy has more than 100 billion stars, but a human body has about 100 trillion cells.

Wart Remedy

A popular cure for warts was once to put a piece of silver and some rocks in a small sack by the side of the road, in the belief that whoever took the sack would also take the warts. Another wart remedy was to steal a steak and bury it where three roads crossed.

Parasitic Dress

Born in Albany, Georgia, in 1932, performer Betty Lou Williams had a parasitic twin protruding from the front of her torso. The twin consisted of two legs, one arm with three fingers, and a second arm that was little more than a single finger. Sometimes she dressed the twin in tiny clothes and off-stage she kept it hidden under a maternity dress.

Horizontal Strength

Laurence J. Frankel was able to hold himself horizontally on stall bars with a 110-lb (50-kg) weight attached to his back.

Heart Stopping

Three-time New York City Marathon champion Alberto Salazar survived a heart attack at Beaverton, Oregon, in 2007—even though his heart stopped beating for a whopping 16 minutes.

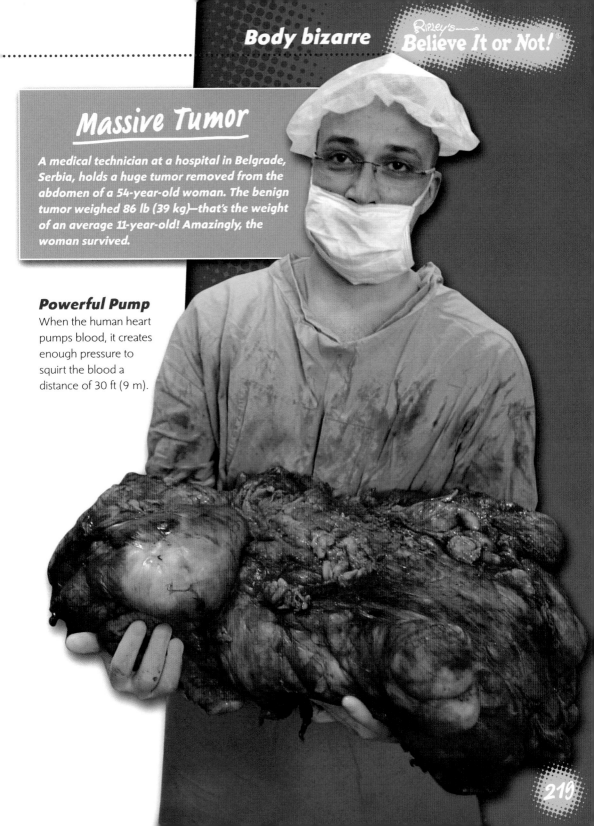

Massive Tumor

A medical technician at a hospital in Belgrade, Serbia, holds a huge tumor removed from the abdomen of a 54-year-old woman. The benign tumor weighed 86 lb (39 kg)—that's the weight of an average 11-year-old! Amazingly, the woman survived.

Powerful Pump

When the human heart pumps blood, it creates enough pressure to squirt the blood a distance of 30 ft (9 m).

Robert Dotzauer of Davenport, Iowa, was able to balance two heavy iron lawn mowers on his chin.

Supersize Cyst When Taquela Hilton of Kellyville, Oklahoma, ballooned to more than 560 lb (254 kg) with a 71-in (180-cm) waist, doctors thought that she was eating too much. Instead, the cause of her weight-gain was a 93-lb (42-kg) ovarian cyst, containing 12 gal (45 l) of fluid. After removing the cyst, one surgeon said: "This was like having a C-section to deliver a 12-year-old. It was a small adult that she was carrying around in her."

Long Wash Dae Yu Quin, a 41-year-old woman from Shanghai, China, has hair that is 14 ft 9 in (4.5 m) long. She has not cut it since she was forced to shave her head as a teenager following a scalp disease. It takes her half a day to wash and dry it!

Timely Recovery

Carlos Camejo of Venezuela was declared dead following a car accident in September 2007, but awoke during his autopsy as the coroner began to cut him!

Beauty Treatment

Drinking the saliva of small birds called swiftlets is said to promote beautiful skin for women in China. The saliva is collected from the binding material of the birds' nests, which are then cleaned and cooked in water.

Brick Bite

The muscles on the sides of a human mouth allow you to bite into things with a force of 160 lb (72.5 kg)—equivalent to the weight of 35 house bricks.

Asthma Cure

The Chinese believe that eating dried seahorses will cure impotence and asthma. Two tons of seahorses are used each year in the Chinese medicine trade.

Shock Discovery

Chinese surgeons operating on a 10-month-old baby girl from Zhoukou found grass growing on her right lung. The 1³/₁₆-in (3-cm) piece of grass was the same type as in the yard at home where she often plays. Doctors say it is possible that grass seed was blown into the baby's nose and through her respiratory system to the lung, where amazingly it found suitable growing conditions.

Supersize Me!

At one point, both Sam Harris of Farmersville, Texas, and Alice Dunbar of Dallas, Texas, were the heaviest man and woman alive, weighing 691 lb (313 kg) and 685 lb (311 kg) respectively.

SAM HARRIS
TEX-KID
FARMERSVILLE, TEXAS
HEAVIEST MAN LIVING. WEIGHT 691 LBS.

Weight 685#

Egg on Face

A British man has a tattoo of a full English breakfast on the top of his head. Dayne Gilbey from Coventry sports a tattoo of bacon, sausages, eggs, beans, and even cutlery. Tattooist Blane Dickinson, who carried out the six-hour artwork, said he now wants to find someone willing to have their face tattooed on the back of their head.

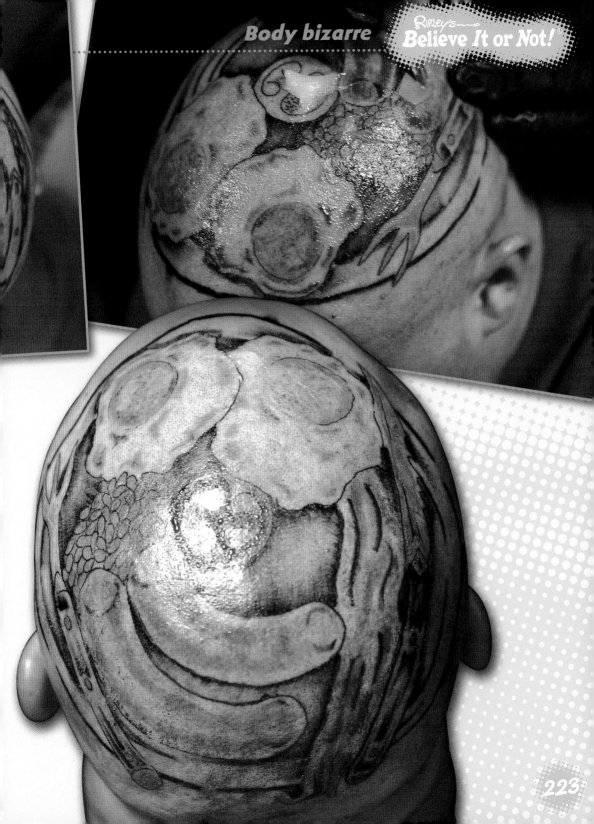

Scorpions!

Dead scorpions and slices of ginger are laid on a patient's face in China in an attempt to cure facial paralysis.

Rare Case Lydia Fairchild of Washington State, is one of only 50 people in the world known to be born with two different sets of DNA, a condition known as "chimerism." Doctors made the discovery in 2002 when she had to prove that she was her chidren's mother.

Long Nails Li Jianping of Shishi City, China, has let the fingernails on his left hand grow for 15 years—and now they are over 3 ft 3 in (1 m) long. He avoids crowded places and always sleeps with his left wrist under his head to stop that hand from moving.

Huge Hairball An 18-year-old from Chicago, Illinois, had a huge hairball weighing 10 lb (4.5 kg) and measuring 15 in (38 cm) long removed from her stomach in 2007. The teenager, who had a habit of eating her hair, complained to doctors of pains in her stomach—where they later found a mass of black, curly hair.

Worm Tea Chong Cha, a Chinese black tea made from the droppings of certain caterpillars, is drunk to prevent heatstroke. Popularly known as worm tea, it is also claimed to help with diarrhea, nosebleeds, and hemorrhoids.

Wrong Leg Surgeons in China trying to correct the limp of a five-year-old boy accidentally lengthened the wrong leg. They said the mistake was due to the boy being anesthetized on his back but then operated on while lying on his stomach. As a result, he had to undergo two more operations—one to extend his right leg, the other to shorten his wrongly extended left leg.

Scissors Found In November 2006, doctors found surgical scissors in the abdomen of a woman from Thenpattinam, India. The scissors had been there for 12 years—ever since a previous operation on the woman in 1994.

Big Tongue Stephen Taylor of the U.K. has a tongue that is 3.74 in (9.5 cm) long, enabling him to insert it into his nostrils!

Long Finger Before surgery, Liu Hua of Jiangsu, China, had an index finger on his left hand that was 12 in (30 cm) long.

Stone Doctor A statue that was covered with magical inscriptions was used for centuries by the ancient Egyptians as a cure for snakebite and scorpion stings. The patient would pour water over the statue and then drink it.

Open Wide!

Live fish dipped in medicinal paste are claimed to be a cure for asthma in parts of India.

Dance Routine The cure for any illness among the Betsileo tribesmen of Madagascar is to put the patient into a trance and then order him to rise from his bed and dance. After a week of this treatment the patient is usually cured—or dead!

Reattached Limb Israel Sarrio of Valencia, Spain, had his arm severed during an accident in January 2004 and doctors sewed it to his leg to keep it alive until they could reattach it properly.

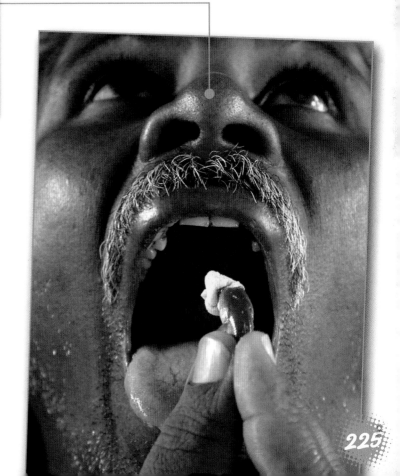

Tongue Splitting

James Keen from Scottsville, Kentucky, shows off his split tongue. He had it split by a piercer using a scalpel heated by a blowtorch and no anesthetic. Although it is said to enhance the pleasure of kissing, the practice is now illegal in some U.S. states, where it is considered tantamount to mutilation.

Lucky Look Women in China undergo cosmetic surgery to look lucky. They ask for less prominent cheekbones, which are said to bring bad luck to their husbands, or to have small blemishes removed from around the eyes or mouth because they, too, are considered unlucky.

Prosthetic Arms Jesse Sullivan of Dayton, Tennessee, has a pair of amazing prosthetic arms that he is able to move merely by thinking about their movement!

Robotic Legs Peng Shulin of China lost his lower body in a 1995 truck accident, but 12 years later doctors in Beijing gave him robotic legs.

Replacement Horn A man in the Yemen has grown two horns. Saleh, aged 102, had often dreamed he was growing a horn on his head and one finally sprouted on the left side 25 years ago. It grew to 1 ft 8 in (50 cm) before falling off but a second one has now grown in its place.

Total Tattoo Lucky Diamond Rich, an Australian performer, has tattoos over every inch of his body—even inside his mouth and ears. Some areas have multiple layers of ink. He has been tattooed by 136 artists in more than 250 studios, in 45 cities and 17 different countries, involving a total tattoo time of 1,150 hours—that's nearly seven weeks.

Mosquito Swarm It would take approximately 1.2 million mosquitoes to drain an average human being of all of their blood.

Cancer Cure In 1588, Jean Nicot, France's ambassador to Portugal, sent tobacco plants to his homeland in the belief that tobacco was a cure for cancer.

Mixed Soup A soup made from herbs and Taiwanese tree lizards is believed to be good for asthma and colds. The cure is apparently most effective when one male and one female lizard are used in the soup.

Baby Teeth A baby in England was born in 2007 with teeth. Megan Andrews from Worthing, Sussex, stunned family by arriving in the world with seven teeth.

Buffalo Drive The cure for any plague that besets the Bhar tribesmen of India is to drive a black water buffalo out of their village—in the belief that it will carry away the disease.

Sweeping Diagnosis Nigerians believe that a man hit with a broom will become impotent unless he retaliates by hitting the hitter seven times with the same broom.

Albino Family All four children of Canada's Mario and Angie Gaulin were born with albinism, giving them pinkish eyes and white hair.

Multiple Digits Jeshuah Fuller of New York City was born in August 2007 with six fingers on each hand and six toes on each foot.

Hair Sandwich To cure a cough in medieval England, a hair from the cougher's head was placed in a bread-and-butter sandwich and fed to a dog.

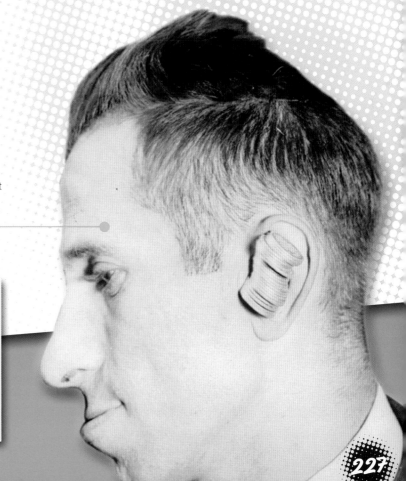

Say What?

Max Calvin, from Brooklyn, New York, never needed to fish for change. He could hold an astonishing 25 quarters in his ear!

Magnificent Mummies

More than 2,000 human mummies line the walls of an underground crypt in Palermo, Sicily—all wearing their finest clothes. To make the spectacle even spookier, their jaws are loosely wired in place so that their mouths appear to be gaping wide at visitors.

Some are stretched out in niches carved into the limestone of the Capuchin Catacombs, but, owing to lack of space, others simply hang from hooks on the walls. The mummies are grouped according to age, sex, and social status, ranging from tiny babies in cribs and rocking chairs to adult lawyers in their best suits and soldiers in uniform. There are also hundreds of coffins, the sides of which have been cut open to reveal the deceased.

The monks of Palermo began mummifying their dead as a status symbol more than 400 years ago. The first Palermo mummification happened by chance. A monk, Brother Silvestro, died suddenly in 1599 and some months later it was found that the limestone and the lack of air in the crypt had combined to mummify his body. Thereafter, his fellow monks decided that

Hundreds of dressed corpses line the walls of the crypt, having been embalmed by the Capuchin monks of the city. Surprisingly, there is no smell.

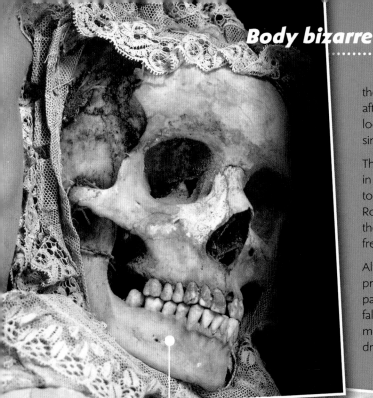

they, too, wished to be mummified after death and soon the wealthier local townspeople began to express similar desires.

The practice was finally discontinued in the 1920s. One of the last people to be mummified was two-year-old Rosalia Lombardo, also known as the "Sleeping Beauty." Her family frequently visited her open coffin.

Although the dry air in the crypt has preserved many of the remains, body parts such as ears and hands have fallen off over the years, and other mummies are now little more than dressed skeletons.

Although the clothes of the Palermo mummies have survived the centuries, many of the bodies themselves have been reduced to skeletons.

On the better-preserved bodies in Palermo, the flesh, the hair, and even the eyes have been mummified.

Bacteria Mass There are 516,000 bacteria per square inch in a human armpit.

Iron Resource If all the iron in the human body were gathered together, there would be enough to make a medium-sized nail.

Holy Snail The Church of St. Leonard in the medieval town of Guingamp, France, was visited for centuries by people from Brittany in the belief they could cure a fever by finding a snail in a cavity in the church walls and carrying it in a pouch.

Lobster Boy Born in 1937, Grady Stiles Jr. from Pittsburgh, Pennsylvania, suffered from ectrodactyly, where the fingers are fused together in groups to form claw-like extremities. Consequently, he was billed in shows as "Lobster Boy."

Tiny Tot When Edith Barlow of Yorkshire, England, was born in 1925, she weighed just over 1 lb (450 g) and was so tiny that for the first six months of her life she was literally wrapped in cotton wool that had been soaked in olive oil. By the time of her death, at age 25, she had grown to a height of only 1 ft 10 in (55 cm).

Swollen Fingers Liu Hua from Jiangsu Province, China, had fingers that were thicker than his arms. His left thumb, index finger, and middle finger were deformed at birth but grew to an amazing size before surgeons removed 11 lb (5 kg) of bone and tissue in 2007.

Neck Tumor Seventeen years after first discovering a strange growth on the back of his neck, 58-year-old Huang Liqian of Chongqing, China, finally had it removed in 2007. In that time it had grown into a huge neck tumor weighing an incredible 33 lb (15 kg).

Egg Remedy An American cure for lowering fever is to soak two cloths in egg whites and put them on the soles of the feet. The egg whites immediately start to draw the temperature down from the brain to the feet.

Well Preserved The mummy of a small girl born in the 2nd century AD was so well preserved when found near Rome, Italy, some 1,800 years later, that her fingerprints could be taken.

Cow Tea An unusual cold remedy in the southern states of the U.S.A. is to drink tea made from dried cow manure.

Human Billboard Edson Alves from Tanabi, Brazil, makes a living by having advertisements tattooed on his body. He walks around with his shirt off, displaying more than 20 tattoos promoting local shops, restaurants, and businesses.

Cockroach Tea In Louisiana in the 1800s, a tea made using cockroaches was a remedy for tetanus, while cockroaches fried in oil with garlic were used as a cure for indigestion.

Spoon Supper A woman accidentally swallowed a spoon 6 in (15 cm) in length while having a laughing fit as she ate a plate of spaghetti in a Sydney, Australia, restaurant in 2007.

Frogs Alive!

Jiang Musheng from China has been eating live frogs to cure his coughs for 40 years.

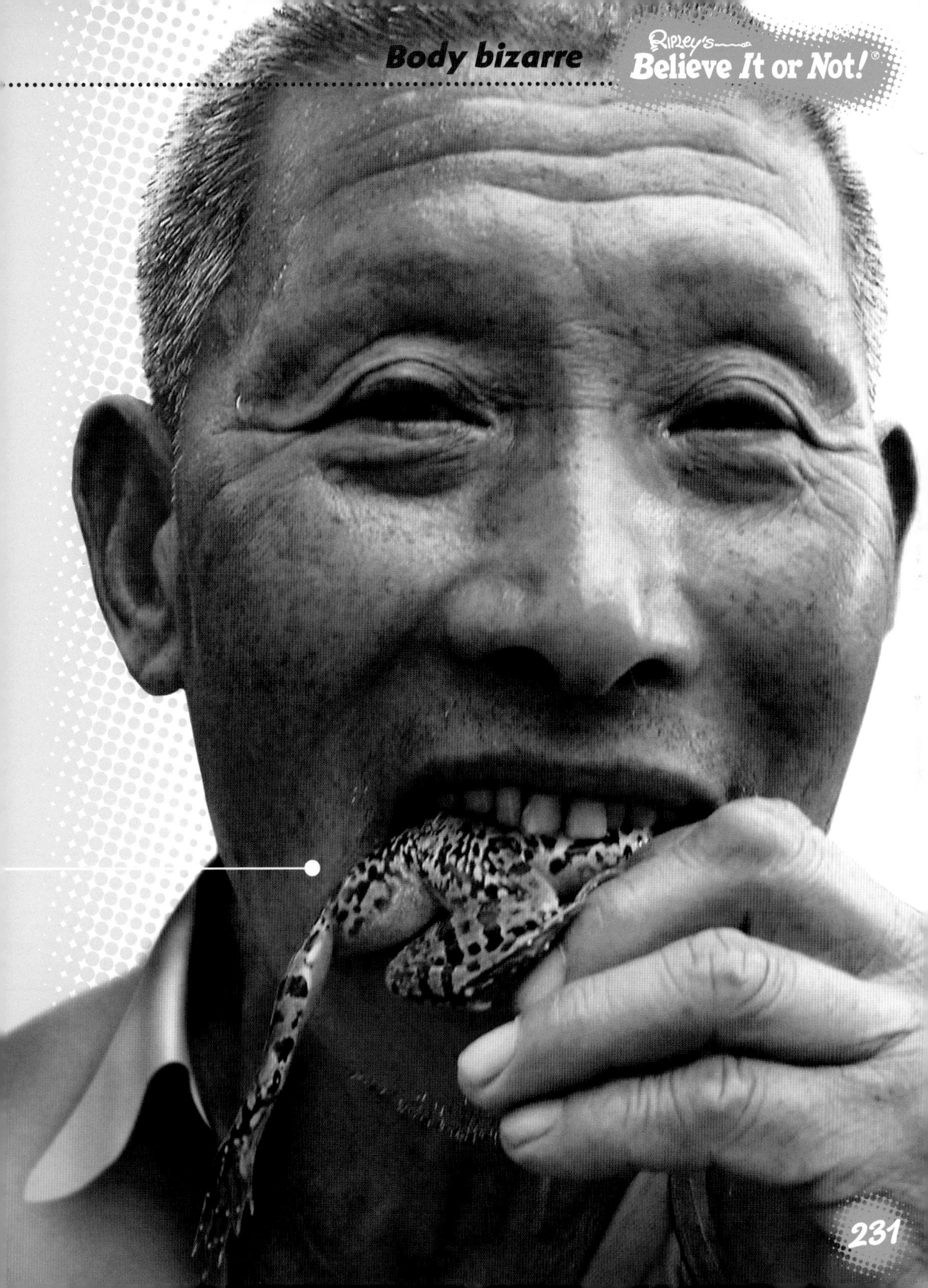

Fantastic Food

Flour Power

Other people see a tortilla as a tasty snack, but Joe Bravo sees it as a canvas on which to create incredible works of art. The Los Angeles artist has earned such a reputation that some of his tortilla paintings sell for more than $3,000. Among those who have bought a Bravo creation is Flea, the bassist with the Red Hot Chili Peppers.

As an art student in the early 1970s, Bravo could not afford canvas, so he chose tortillas instead, reasoning that a staple Hispanic food was the ideal medium for displaying Hispanic imagery. He made a mobile of hanging tortillas—all hand-painted—but it blew apart in the Santa Ana winds. Then, nearly a decade ago, somebody reminded him about it and he started painting on tortillas again.

In his early days he used corn tortillas, but now he uses 26-in (66-cm) flour tortillas, custom-made by a Los Angeles company. He says: "An audience sees a painting on a little regular tortilla, they might go, 'OK.' But to see a really, really big tortilla? That gets their attention."

Brain Food

This unusual-looking sandwich makes a regular appearance on the menu at the Hilltop Inn in Evansville, Indiana, even though it is made from deep-fried cow brains! Its origins are said to date back to a time when German and Dutch immigrants to southern Indiana wasted precious little of anything, especially when it came to animals slaughtered for food. Ketchup anyone?

Frog Remedy Jiang Musheng, 66, of China, has eaten a diet of live tree frogs and rats for the past 40 years. As a young man, he had suffered abdominal pains and coughing until an elderly villager prescribed the unusual remedy. After just one month of eating live frogs, the pains and coughing disappeared.

Ant Cookies Cookies made with *bachaco*, a type of large ant, were served during a demonstration by Venezuelan chef Nelson Mendez at a food fair in Caracas in 2007.

Coffee Sentence King Gustav III, who ruled Sweden in the 18th century, was so convinced that coffee was poisonous that he ordered a convicted criminal to drink himself to death with it. However, the condemned man eventually died of old age instead.

Poppadum Pile Richard Bradbury and Kris Browcott took four hours to stack a pile of approximately 1,000 poppadums to a height of nearly 5 ft (1.5 m) at an Indian restaurant in London, England.

Sheep Supper

Boiled sheep's head served on a bed of rice is the speciality of the Solar de las Cabecitas (House of the Little Heads), a restaurant in the Bolivian capital, La Paz. The dish originates from the Andean mining city of Oruro, where the salty highland pasture gives the lamb its particular flavor.

Serial Swallower Taffy the Springer Spaniel needed an operation in 2007 after swallowing his 40th pair of underpants. The 18-month-old dog, which belongs to vet Eubie Saayman of Staffordshire, England, has also gulped down 300 socks, destroyed 15 pairs of shoes, and once ate the keys to the family's Mercedes car.

Sundae Best In 1988, Mike Rogiani of Edmonton, Alberta, Canada, created an ice cream sundae that weighed a staggering 54,917 lb (24,910 kg). The ingredients—which included 63 different flavors of ice cream—cost about $7,000 and had to be mixed in an empty swimming pool.

Chocolate Sign A giant chocolate billboard in London, England, took a team of ten people 300 hours to build—but it took lucky shoppers in London's busy Covent Garden just three hours to eat. The sign measured 14½ x 9½ ft (4.4 x 2.9 m) and was made of ten chocolate bunnies, 72 large chocolate Easter eggs, and 128 chocolate panels, each of which weighed more than 4 lb (1.8 kg).

Tasty Tarantula

A Cambodian woman munches on a tasty fried spider as she passes through the town of Skuon, which is also known as Spider Town to the locals. The spiders, which are collected from the surrounding countryside, are deep fried in salt and garlic. Customers wash the meal down with a bowl of medicinal tarantula wine, which is served with the rotting spiders' bodies still lying in the bottom of the bowl, with the fangs intact to prevent the medicine from losing its power.

Norwegian Delicacy The local delicacy in the Norwegian town of Voss is smoked sheep's head. Nothing goes to waste except the bare bones of the skull as residents tuck in to the flesh of the entire head, including the sheep's eyeballs, tongue, and ears.

Cockroach Contest With his hands tied behind his back, Shai Pariente ate 13 oven-cooked cockroaches in New York in 2004 to win an iPod in a contest.

Potato Fight In 2007, a woman in Nicholson, Georgia, knocked out her husband with a potato! She picked up the potato and threw it at him during a row and it hit him square on the nose. He decided not to press charges.

Super Soup Cooks in Caracas, Venezuela, prepared a 3,963-gal (15,000-l) pot of soup in September 2007 that was big enough to feed 70,000 people. The soup contained 6,615 lb (3,000 kg) of chicken, 4,410 lb (2,000 kg) of beef, and literally tons of vegetables.

Going Pop More than 500 Canadian boy scouts popped over 1,200 cubic ft (34 cubic m) of popcorn in just eight hours in 2007. Using two giant, homemade machines, the scouts popped at an average rate of two cubic ft per minute into a large bucket at Calgary Zoo, Alberta.

Edible Car A team of British bakers cooked up a cake in the shape of a full-sized Skoda car using 180 eggs, 125 jars of jelly, and 220 lb (100 kg) of sugar. The tires were chocolate frosting, the rear lights were jello, the wipers were licorice, and the engine was filled with syrup.

Eat My Shorts! Los Angeles artist Kasey McMahon has designed a pair of meat shorts, in which pieces of dried meat are glued or sewn on to an ordinary pair of shorts.

Chili Lovers Across the Americas, people were eating chili peppers as long as 6,000 years ago. Recent discoveries from the Bahamas to Peru found starch microfossils of grains from chili peppers alongside remnants of corn, yucca, squash, beans, and palm fruit, suggesting that the ancients used recipes that aimed to make bland tastes more palatable.

Luxury Bagel

Frank Tujague, executive chef of the Westin New York Hotel in Times Square, prepared a $1,000 bagel in 2007. Topped with white truffle cream cheese and goji berry-infused Riesling jelly with golden leaves, the luxury bagel was so pricey because white truffle is the second most expensive food in the world, next to premium caviar.

Monster Donut

To celebrate the release of *The Simpsons Movie* on DVD, Donut King in Sydney, Australia, created a mighty donut that weighed nearly 4 tons—the equivalent of two rhinoceroses. Consisting of more than 90,000 individual donuts, half a ton of pink icing, and 66 lb (30 kg) of sprinklies, it measured 20 ft (6 m) in diameter and took 40 people more than nine hours to build.

Steaming Rats

Piping hot, cooked field rats are one of the dishes on offer at a wild game restaurant in Guangzhou, southern China.

Beer Launch A student from North Carolina has invented a refrigerator that throws cold cans of beer to drinkers. John Cornwell spent $3,000 devising the Beer Launching Fridge, which, when activated by remote control, rotates an arm to line itself up with its target and then catapults the can up to 10 ft (3 m) away.

Pizza Power Patrick Bertoletti just loves pizza—so much so that the Chicago man ate 19 slices in 10 minutes at the 2006 Three Brothers World Pizza Eating Championship in Annapolis, Maryland.

Large Tip A family who were regulars at a Pizza Hut restaurant in Angola, Indiana, were so impressed by their waitress that they gave her a $10,000 tip. After 20-year-old waitress Jessica Osborne had told them she had twice been forced to drop out of college because of lack of money, they returned a few days later with the surprise check.

Butter Potter Harry Potter was magically carved from butter for the 2007 Iowa State Fair in Des Moines. The butter model, the work of sculptor Sarah Pratt, even had Potter's trademark glasses and wand.

Ultimate Takeout An Indian restaurant in Belfast, Northern Ireland, delivered the ultimate takeout meal in 2006—to Manhattan. Steve Francis, a New York dance music producer, ordered the $16,000 transatlantic takeout—complete with fish flown in specially from Bangladesh—after Arif Ahmed's Indie Spice restaurant had served him delicious food at a festival in England.

Chopstick Expert In November 2007, Rob Beaton of Asbury Park, New Jersey, used chopsticks to eat 78 single grains of rice in three minutes.

Fresh Fruit Archeologists in western Japan have unearthed a 2,100-year-old melon—with its flesh still on the rind. They believe it had been preserved for centuries because it had been in a vacuum-packed state in a wet layer below the ground, where it was immune to attack from microorganisms.

Rare Corkscrews Nicholas Hunt of Sydney, New South Wales, Australia, has been collecting corkscrews from around the world for over a decade and now has more than 1,000. One of the oldest dates back to 1838.

Cream Cake In Alanya, Turkey, 285 cooks baked a cream cake 8,840 ft (2,694 m) long, using 159,000 eggs, 12,150 lb (5,512 kg) of sugar, 12,150 lb (5,512 kg) of flour, 1,400 gal (5,300 l) of milk, 5,840 lb (2,650 kg) of bananas, 700 gal (2,650 l) of water, and 1,750 lb (795 kg) of carbonate and baking additives.

Edible Heirloom A hot cross bun has been kept in a family for more than 100 years! Ever since 13-year-old Ada Herbert of Ipswich, England, died holding the bun in 1899, it has been passed down the family's generations. Amazingly, it has never gone moldy and the original cross is still visible.

Cheese Bribe Four police officers in the Campagnia region of Italy were arrested in 2007 for demanding mozzarella bribes from motorists. They were said to have stopped cheese delivery trucks and forced the drivers to hand over the contents or face a large fine.

Luxury Pizza Domenico Crolla, a chef from Glasgow, Scotland, creates a specialty pizza with a $4,000 price tag. It includes Champagne-soaked caviar, Cognac-marinated lobster, smoked salmon, venison, and 24-carat edible gold shavings. It is named the Pizza Royale 007 after the fictional agent James Bond.

Tea Drinker Levi Johnson of Tea, South Dakota, drank 5½ oz (165 ml) of hot Tabasco® sauce—that's nearly three bottles—in just 30 seconds in 2007.

Chestnut Champ In 2007, Joey Chestnut of San Jose, California, ate 182 chicken wings in 30 minutes to win the "Wing Bowl 15" eating contest in Philadelphia. He also consumed 8 lb 10 oz (3.9 kg) of asparagus spears in 10 minutes for a third straight win at the World Deep-fried Asparagus Eating Championship at Stockton, California.

Chocolate Jesus Canadian artist Cosimo Cavallaro created a 6-ft (1.8-m) sculpture of Jesus made entirely from 200 lb (90 kg) of milk chocolate.

Antique Ham The same slab of ham has been on display at the Mecca restaurant in Raleigh, North Carolina, since 1937. The 25-lb (11-kg) ham was first acquired by the grandfather of the restaurant's current owner, Paul Dombalis, more than 70 years ago and has remained an uneaten favorite with customers ever since.

Cake Cathedral George D'Aubney built a 4-ft-tall (1.2-m) replica of the famous landmark St. Paul's Cathedral in London, England. The replica was complete with lights, music, moving parts—and made primarily from fruitcake.

Good Karma Hoping to bring some good karma to his establishment, a restaurant owner in Guangdong, China, paid $75,000 for a single "lucky" fish in April 2007.

Hot Stuff Mark "The Human Vacuum" Lyle ate 8 lb 5 oz (3.75 kg) of chili in five minutes at the 2007 Midwest Chili Eating Championship in Canton, Ohio.

Private Pub In response to a 2007 ban on smoking in public places, including bars and pubs, Kerry Morgan of Briton Ferry, Wales, built a private 90-seat pub in his own home.

Prized Lychee

Known as the "king of fruit," the lychee has always been popular in China. Few, however, have been sold for anything like the price of this one, which went for a huge 555,000 yuan ($67,000) at auction in Zengcheng City, China, in 2002. It came from a 400-year-old tree, named Xiyuangualu, which yields only a few dozen lychees each year.

Prize Pumpkins

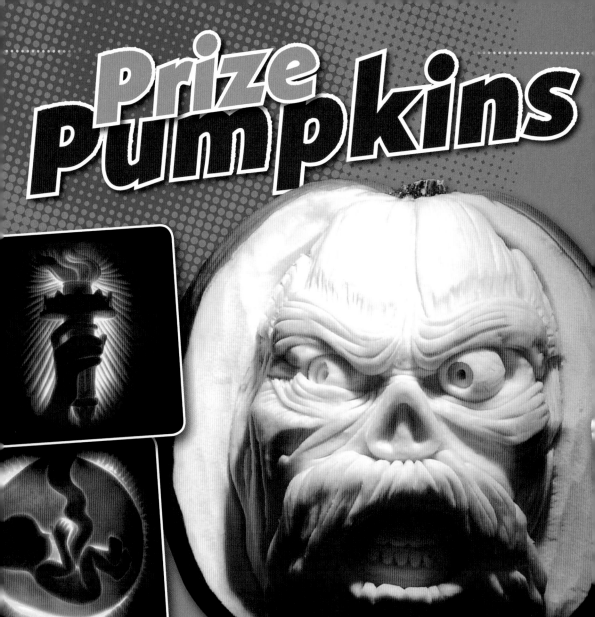

Like thousands of American youngsters, Scott Cummins used to carve out a pumpkin to make a jack-o-lantern for Halloween. But whereas others mastered just the basic eyes, nose, and mouth, Cummins has gone on to create amazingly intricate works of art from the fruit.

The junior high school teacher from Perryton, Texas, has been carving pumpkins since he was 16. His extensive portfolio includes portraits of Leonard Nimoy, Albert Einstein, and George W. Bush; characters such as Gollum from the *Lord of the Rings* and Winnie-the-Pooh; lifelike animal heads; expressive faces born of his own imagination; the Statue of Liberty; and a beautiful baby in the womb. Each carving takes him just a couple of hours.

Sometimes the shape of the pumpkin dictates the face; at other times he has an idea of what he wants to create and looks for a pumpkin of appropriate form and size. He begins by scraping away the inside of the pumpkin and the tough orange skin. For the actual carving, he uses a variety of implements—sharpened spoons, ice-cream scoops, knives, drill bits, and even saw blades—and is always on the lookout for new tools.

Finally, he lights many of the carved pumpkins with a 30-watt bulb, and, as the light shines through the thinner areas of the rind, his fantastic creations acquire an eerie, almost mystical appearance.

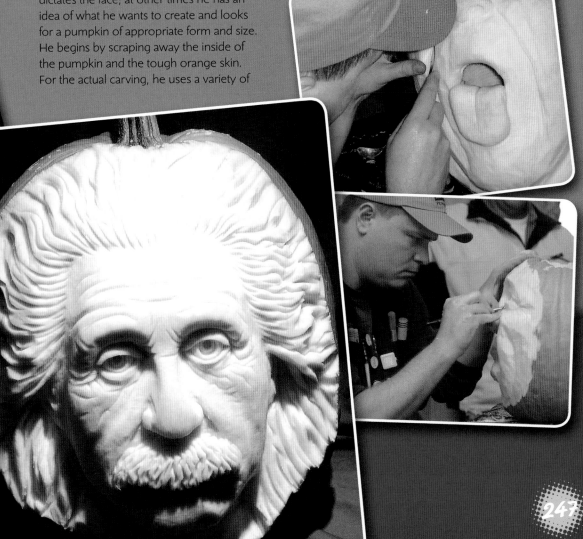

Latte Art

Visitors to a café in Melbourne, Australia, often find a face, a flower, or a butterfly staring back at them from the cup. The artistic frothy designs are all the rage among the city's baristas who use the coffee cup as a canvas and even take part in special latte art competitions. The patterns are created either by manipulating the flow of milk from a jug into an espresso or by etching, using stencils, powders, and milk foam.

Costly Cocktail Visitors to a nightclub in London, England, can buy a cocktail costing $70,000. The Flawless cocktail, which has to be ordered in advance, consists of a large measure of Louis XII cognac, half a bottle of Cristal Rose Champagne, brown sugar, Angostura bitters, and a few flakes of 24-carat edible gold leaf. But what really makes the drink so expensive is at the bottom of the glass where, once you have supped the whole drink, there is a beautiful 11-carat white diamond ring.

Rich Dessert A restaurant in the Sri Lankan resort of Galle is charging $14,500 for a dessert, which comes with a chocolate sculpture and a large gemstone. The Fortress Stilt Fisherman Indulgence consists of cassata, mango, pomegranate, Champagne, and an 80-carat aquamarine stone.

The Big Bite Staff at Wild Woody's Chill In Grill in Roseville, Michigan, made a corned beef sandwich in 2005 that weighed a staggering 5,672 lb (2,573 kg). Measuring 12 x 16 ft (3.6 x 4.8 m) and being 17 in (43 cm) thick, the sandwich had a filling made up of 1,131 lb (513 kg) of corned beef, 150 lb (68 kg) of mustard, 260 lb (118 kg) of white American cheese, 531 lb (240 kg) of lettuce, and an amazing 3,600 lb (1,635 kg) of white bread.

Naked Lunch In 2007, a restaurant in Greenville, Maine, offered a free prime rib sandwich to anyone willing to plunge naked into Moosehead Lake. The Black Frog Restaurant called its sandwich the Skinny Dip.

Orange Cure Sara Jane Trout of Aspinwall, Pennsylvania, ate 3,248 oranges in 1938 as a cure for diabetes.

Drip Feed

At a hospital-themed restaurant in Taipei, Taiwan, customers drink from intravenous tubes suspended from the ceiling. The waitresses are dressed as nurses, crutches hang from the walls, a wheelchair is parked in the lobby, and the sign for the bathrooms is marked "emergency room."

Sensational Sausage

Butchers put the finishing touches to a mammoth sausage that is the star of the show at the annual Sausage Festival in the Serbian village of Turija. The sausage was created by 12 butchers and measured a whopping 6,627 ft (2,020 m) in length. It was made from the following impressive list of ingredients: pork from 28 pigs, 110 lb (50 kg) of salt, 4 lb 6 oz (2 kg) of pepper, 88 lb (40 kg) of paprika, and 11 lb (5 kg) of garlic.

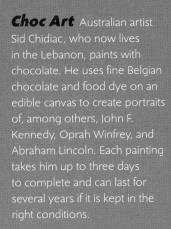

Choc Art Australian artist Sid Chidiac, who now lives in the Lebanon, paints with chocolate. He uses fine Belgian chocolate and food dye on an edible canvas to create portraits of, among others, John F. Kennedy, Oprah Winfrey, and Abraham Lincoln. Each painting takes him up to three days to complete and can last for several years if it is kept in the right conditions.

Insect Treat For centuries, farmers in Santander, Colombia, have harvested queen ants as a tasty treat for local consumption. They now export the ants abroad as gourmet delights.

Tiny Sushi Sushi on single tiny grains of rice is served at the Omoroi Sushiya Kajiki Sushi Restaurant in Fukuoka, Japan.

Colossal Cake To celebrate the centennial of Las Vegas in May 2005, a giant birthday cake was baked that measured 102 ft (31 m) long, 52 ft (16 m) wide, and 20 in (50 cm) high. It weighed 130,000 lb (59,000 kg), had 34,000 lb (15,420 kg) of icing, —that is 23 million calories!

Birthday Cake To celebrate the 230th birthday of the U.S.A., caterers in Fayetteville, Arkansas, baked a 230-layer cake for the Fourth of July, 2006. The cake, which stood 2 ft (60 cm) high and weighed more than 100 lb (45 kg), took 21 hours to bake.

Fish Hook A man eating fish at a restaurant in Shanghai, China, got a fish hook stuck in his tongue. At first he thought it was a bone, but when he discovered blood all over his mouth, he was taken to hospital where the hook was removed.

Ketchup Capital Already home to a 170-ft (52-m) ketchup bottle (in the form of a disguised water tower), Collinsville, Illinois, temporarily acquired a sister attraction in July 2007—a ketchup packet 8 x 4 ft (2.4 x 1.2 m), capable of holding around 127 gal (480 l) of tomato sauce.

251

Dog Food Two students from the town of Swindon in Wiltshire, England, sat in a paddling pool in 2005 and ate dog food while fellow students pledged money to charity in return for covering them in baked beans, baking flour, and cornflakes.

Hot Stuff A two-year-old boy in Assam, India, has become addicted to Bhut Jolakia, the world's hottest chili. Young Jayanta Lahan has eagerly devoured the chilies ever since he first tried them while his mother was cooking when he was eight months old. He can eat about 50 of these chilies in three hours without suffering any ill effects—they are so hot that they would make most of us cry involuntarily and suffer a burning sensation in the stomach. The Bhut Jolokia is one hundred times hotter than a Jalapeno pepper and has half the potency of weapon-grade pepper spray!

Large Slab In May 2007, the Northwest Fudge Factory of Levack, Ontario, Canada, produced a slab of fudge that measured 45½ ft (13.9 m) long, 6½ ft (2 m) wide, and 4 in (10 cm) thick, and weighed 5,038 lb (2,285 kg).

Price of Love

A Japanese chocolate made for Valentine's Day 2006 was encrusted with 2,006 diamonds and priced at 500 million yen ($4.4 million). The chocolate was designed in the shape of the continent of Africa.

Chocolate Igloo

Marco Fanti and his co-workers created a 9,200-lb (4,173-kg) igloo totally out of edible chocolate for the Eurochocolate Fair in Perugia, Italy, in 2006.

The Vermonster

Ian Hickman from Sterling, Virginia, has tamed The Vermonster—a 6-lb-15-oz (3.1-kg) Ben & Jerry's ice cream sundae. Although the dessert—which contains 20 scoops of ice cream, four bananas, three cookies, a brownie, hot fudge, whipped cream, and 18 teaspoons of topping—is designed to be eaten by a group of people, Hickman devoured it single-handedly in just 9 minutes 22 seconds.

Giant Calzone

In 2007, a restaurant in Madison, Wisconsin, created a huge calzone pizza measuring 19 ft 4 in x 2 ft 5 in (5.9 x 0.74 m) and weighing more than 100 lb (45 kg).

Apple Picker

Fifty-year-old Claude Breton picked 30,240 apples, a total weight of 805 lb (365 kg), in eight hours in September 2007 at the orchard in Dunham, Quebec, Canada, where he works. Apple picking has been his passion for more than 30 years, and even when he works in a different job, he still spends his vacation picking apples.

Paws for Thought

Chinese chef Wang Wei Min presents a plate of barbecued dogs' paws at a Chinese restaurant in Tokyo, Japan, in 2006. Apparently, Japanese diners are generally unaware that dog is served in Chinese restaurants in their country, but this dish would leave them in little doubt!

Gingerbread Houses

Some of the most beautiful buildings in the world are displayed each year at the Grove Park Inn, Asheville, North Carolina—and they're all made out of gingerbread. First staged in 1993, the National Gingerbread House Competition draws sugar-and-spice creations from all over the U.S.A.

An enchanting gingerbread church won Virginia Pilarz third place in 2006.

Trish MacCallister took third prize with a festive gingerbread house in 2005.

BAKERY

A bejewelled gingerbread model of St. Basil's Cathedral in Moscow earned Nancy Kyzer first place at the 2005 contest.

Patricia Howard of Winter Springs, Florida, won the coveted Grand Prize with this snowy scene at the 2006 National Gingerbread Competition. She retained her title in 2007.

Organic Restaurant

Guolizhuang is China's first speciality penis restaurant. Every item on the menu at the Beijing diner is an animal's organ—yak, donkey, horse, dog, goat, deer, and ox. The luxury dish is Canadian seal's penis at $440. It has to be ordered in advance.

Scotch George

George Washington, the first president of the U.S.A., also ran one of the largest whiskey distilleries in North America.

Banana Bunch

A bunch of bananas harvested in Holguin, Cuba, in 2007, contained more than 300 bananas. The bunch was 3 ft 10 in (1.2 m) high and weighed 125 lb (57 kg). Amazingly, the plant was growing in a clay soil to which no fertilizers had been added—apparently, water was the only catalyst needed for such enormous growth.

Vanilla Ice

Using an extra-large spoon of his own invention, Ed "Cookie" Jarvis of New York City, ate a whopping 1 gal 9 fl oz (4 l) of vanilla ice cream in only 12 minutes. He says he avoided the dreaded brain freeze by eating his ice cream with the spoon facing downward toward his tongue, rather than upward toward the roof of his mouth.

Burger Mission

Jay Barr of Cape Coral, Florida, makes an hour-long 150-mi (240-km) flight to Kissimmee, Florida, ten times a year—just to buy hamburgers. He buys them in packs of 24 from the nearest Krystal fast-food restaurant. The Krystal company was so impressed by Mr. Barr's devotion to their burgers that it unveiled a hamburger box and drink cup with Barr's face and an airplane printed on them.

Beer Bonanza

The strong, steady hands of Bavarian waiter Clemens Pichl could carry 35 beer steins, full of beer, at the same time in Old Heidelberg, Pittsford, New York in 1935.

Squirrel Pancakes

A hotel in Cumbria, England, served up free gray squirrel pancakes. The squirrels were all caught in the grounds of the Famous Wild Boar Hotel at Crook and served in Peking duck-style wraps. Customers said the squirrel meat tasted like rabbit.

Bread Model

A British artist baked a life-size model of herself out of bread and then invited visitors to the exhibition to eat it.

Ancient Mushroom

U.S. scientists say that a mushroom found embedded in a piece of amber in Myanmar is 100 million years old—an age that makes it 20 million years older than any other known mushroom fossils.

Fat Feast

Croatian conceptual artist Zoran Todorovic fed human fat and skin from liposuction clinics to visitors to his exhibition in Zagreb.

Skinny Diner

This slender eatery in 1940s Miami, Florida, was a mere 50 in (130 cm) wide. It stretched back 52 ft (16 m), however, so it could fit in a long line of hungry diners.

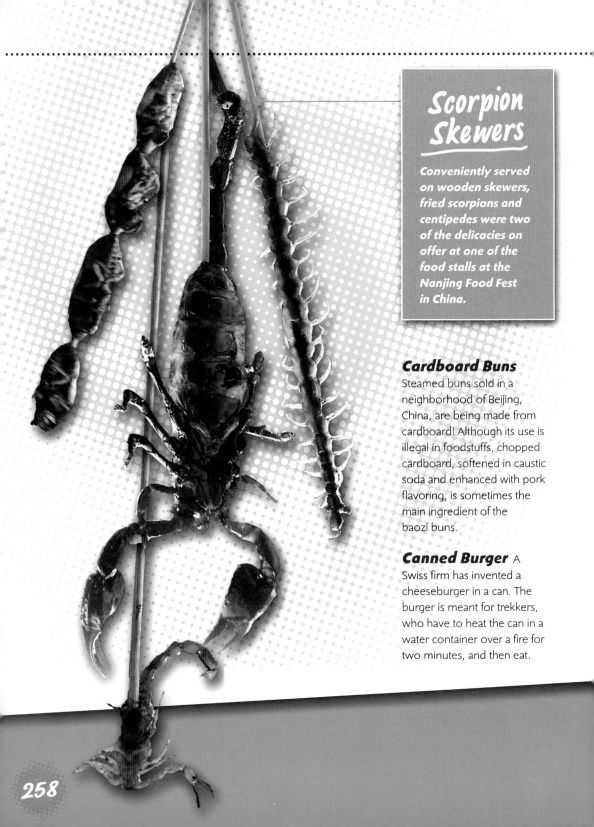

Scorpion Skewers

Conveniently served on wooden skewers, fried scorpions and centipedes were two of the delicacies on offer at one of the food stalls at the Nanjing Food Fest in China.

Cardboard Buns

Steamed buns sold in a neighborhood of Beijing, China, are being made from cardboard! Although its use is illegal in foodstuffs, chopped cardboard, softened in caustic soda and enhanced with pork flavoring, is sometimes the main ingredient of the baozi buns.

Canned Burger A

Swiss firm has invented a cheeseburger in a can. The burger is meant for trekkers, who have to heat the can in a water container over a fire for two minutes, and then eat.

Worm Man Wayne Fauser, alias The Worm Man, from Sydney, Australia, eats live earthworms, either in sandwiches or just plain.

Banana Splits There are more than 300 banana-related accidents a year in Britain, most involving people slipping on skins.

Chocolate Sin Two hundred years ago chocolate was considered to be a temptation of the devil. In some Central American mountain villages, no one under the age of 60 was allowed to taste it and churchgoers who defied the ruling were threatened with excommunication.

Super Bowl Pupils at a school in Warwickshire, England, cooked a bowl of porridge that was big enough to feed 300 people. The porridge was made from 44 lb (20 kg) of oats and 13 gal (50 l) of milk and, when it was made, weighed 145 lb (66 kg).

Snake Snack Shyam Atulkar from Nagpur, India, catches snakes and sometimes eats them alive! "I like the taste of snakes," he says, "especially the tail end, which tastes like raw mutton. The head and neck taste somewhat bitter because of the poison."

Cheesy Hit More than 1.5 million people have logged on to an Internet site to watch a round of Cheddar cheese as it slowly matures in a storeroom in western England.

Gravy Wrestling The first-ever World Gravy Wrestling Championships were held in Lancashire, England, in 2007. Eight teams took part, wrestling each other in a swimming pool filled with lukewarm gravy!

That's Crackers!

A factory in the Japanese town of Omachi is the proud producer of rice crackers that contain the added protein of digger wasps. The jibachi senbei or "digger wasp rice cracker" is a delicacy that has been specially commissioned by a Japanese fan club for wasps. Fan-club members say that the extra ingredient adds a waspish note to the traditional flavor of the crackers.

Food-scapes

Photographer Carl Warner creates beautiful, realistic landscapes with a secret ingredient—they're all made of food.

He makes forests from broccoli, clouds from cauliflower or mozzarella cheese, mountains from bread, and buildings from Parmesan cheese. What appears to be a natural view of a sunlit fishing boat at sea turns out to be a pea pod "boat" resting on a "sea" of smoked salmon, bordered by pebbles made from soda bread and potatoes, and a beach of brown sugar.

Carl from Kent, England, has been perfecting his amazing artworks—called "Foodscapes"—for the past few years. He says: "I begin by drawing a conventional landscape using classic compositional techniques, as I need to fool the viewer into thinking it is a real scene." He plans each image carefully, scouring supermarkets for ingredients. Finding the right shaped broccoli to use for a tree is crucial to his art.

With the help of model-makers, he then creates the set on a table top that measures 8 ft (2.4 m) wide. Each set takes up to three days to build and photograph. The various foodstuffs are either glued or pinned in place. Next, the scenes are photographed in separate layers, from foreground to background and sky, to stop the food wilting under the lights. Then the individual layers are put together on a computer to achieve the final image.

A smoked salmon and soda bread sunset scene looks good enough to eat.

Ripley's— Believe It or Not!

This idyllic scene of a small village set in rolling countryside is made of dozens of different foodstuffs.

The spectacular broccoli forest scene is so realistic that Carl says it is the one he is most proud of.

Krystal King

Joey Chestnut, 23, of San Jose, California, ate 103 Krystal burgers in just eight minutes at the Krystal Square Off IV World Hamburger Eating Championship at Chattanooga, Tennessee, in October 2007—that works out to 13 burgers per minute or one burger every 4.6 seconds! After his incredible eating feat, Joey Chestnut said all he wanted to do was take a nap and digest his food. Chestnut's achievement in becoming the first person to eat 100 Krystal burgers in 8 minutes confirmed his position as the world's leading competitive eater.

Big Bird As part of an annual contest with his sister Andra to see who can cook the biggest Thanksgiving turkey, Rich Portnoy, of Minneapolis, Minnesota, basted a bird weighing 72 lb (33 kg). The giant turkey needed 15 hours of roasting in a 36-in-wide (90-cm) oven.

First Auction A bottle of 81-year-old scotch was sold for $54,000 in 2007—in New York State's first liquor auction since Prohibition. Although Prohibition ended in 1933, the state continued to ban the auctioning of spirits until August 2007.

Massive Mug In April 2007, a Panama coffee producer brewed a 750-gal (2,840-l) cup of coffee. Café Duran took four hours and used 300 lb (135 kg) of coffee to fill a 9-ft (2.7-m) tall mug.

Stir-fry Crazy Helped by 20 assistants, chef Nancy Lam made a stir-fry weighing 1,543 lb (700 kg) in London, England, in 2004. It was made from 153 lb (69 kg) of green cabbage, 489 lb (222 kg) of Chinese cabbage, 449 lb (204 kg) of white cabbage, 413 lb (187 kg) of carrots, and 21 lb (9.5 kg) of baby corn.

Robot Waiter Japanese engineers have invented a robot 3 ft 8 in (1.2 m) tall that can serve breakfast. Called Twendy-One, the robot has long arms and 241 pressure sensors in each hand, enabling it to perform such chores as picking up a loaf of bread without crushing it, putting toast on a plate, and fetching ketchup from a refrigerator.

Light-boiled Egg English inventor Simon Rhymes from Chippenham, Wiltshire, has devised a machine that boils the perfect egg, using lightbulbs instead of water. The eggs are lowered into the machine and heated by four halogen bulbs. After cooking the egg, the gadget even slices off the top so that bread can be dipped into the yolk.

Choc Star In 2005, Madame Tussauds created a life-size model of musical supremo Sir Elton John—in chocolate. Made to the singer's measurements, it was built from 227 lb (103 kg) of chocolate and took more than 1,000 hours to create. The finished product was displayed at the London, England, tourist attraction in a special air-conditioned tent to stop it from melting.

Grass Eater Gangaram, a man in Kanpur, India, has been eating more than 2 lb (900 g) of grass a day for many years. He says it gives him energy and that, although he can do without food, he cannot live without grass.

Preserved Gift A circle of friends has been handing around an old fruitcake as a Christmas present for more than 20 years. Christopher Linton-Smith, Steve Glum, and Tim Arnheim were friends at Stetson University, Florida, and started sending each other the $2.99 world-famous Claxton, Georgia, fruitcake as a joke in 1986. Each Christmas it is passed on to one of the group—even though none of them actually likes fruitcake.

Sweet-toothed Bear A man returned to his van in Vernon Township, New Jersey, in 2007 to find that it had been raided by a bear that had moved it 40 ft (12 m) down the street. Police believe the bear broke in to the van through the window because he could smell the Halloween candy. As he reached for the candy, the bear is thought to have dislodged the parking brake, causing the vehicle to roll down the hill.

Top Ten Unusual Ice-cream Flavors

Tomato & basil
Black olive
Licorice
Beer
Rosemary

Thyme
Lavender
Chewing gum
Violet
Rose

Nice Ice!

An ice-cream parlor in Nice, France, sells tomato-flavored sorbet. Fenocchio offers 70 beautifully presented flavors of ice cream and sorbet, including such wacky tastes as tomato and basil, black olive, rhubarb, lavender, and gingerbread.

Royal Meal In 1999, chef Rick Royal and students from the Art Institute of Los Angeles School of Culinary Arts created a crème brulée with a diameter of 23½ ft (7 m). It was made from no fewer than 3,600 egg yolks.

Scorpion Addict Hasip Kaya of Turkey has become addicted to eating live scorpions. The father-of-two has been eating them since childhood and enjoys them so much that villagers search under rocks to find him fresh supplies.

Dairy Delight Stew Leonard's, a family-owned foodstore with outlets in Connecticut and New York, has the world's largest in-store dairy plant, packaging more than 10 million half-gallon (2 l) cartons per year. That's enough milk to fill a straw reaching from Earth to the Moon and halfway back!

Solo Feast A Thanksgiving meal for ten people was devoured by just one person in 15 minutes in 2007. Competitive eater Tim Janus from New York City consumed a 10-lb (4.5-kg) turkey, 4 lb (1.8 kg) of mashed potatoes, 3 lb (1.4 kg) of cranberry sauce, and 2 lb (1.1 kg) of beans… and still had room for dessert—an entire pumpkin pie.

Ancient Fruit In 2007, a museum in Staffordshire, England, displayed a 116-year-old orange. The blackened, dried-up fruit came from the lunchbox of coal miner Joseph Roberts, who was fatally injured in an underground explosion in 1891—sadly, before he got to eat his orange.

Chocolate Finger A man in Mainz, Germany, found part of a human finger in his chocolate bar. The fingertip, complete with nail, was right in the middle of the bar. A police officer said: "I suppose it went unnoticed because there were nuts in the chocolate and it was hard to tell the difference."

Popcorn Ball A popcorn ball measuring 8 ft (2.4 m) in diameter, 24 ft (7.5 m) in circumference, and weighing 3,415 lb (1,549 kg) was manufactured at Lake Forest, Illinois, in October 2006.

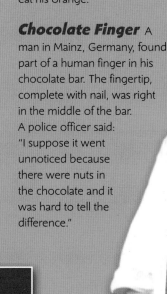

Pie-maker Extraordinaire

Mrs. W. E. Updegraff of Vinita, Oklahoma, made 60 pies in just 45 minutes, every weekday for a period of no less than 23 years. During this time she baked more than an astonishing 380,000 pies!

Starbucks Adventurer

For more than ten years, a contract computer programmer named Winter has been on a mission to drink a cup of coffee in every Starbucks store in the world.

Poughkeepsie, NY

Incline Village, NV

Carmel, NY

Freeport, NY

The idea originated in 1997 at his local Starbucks in Plano, Texas, and by October 2007 he had visited 7,103 stores in the U.S.A. (92.7 percent of the total) and 457 international stores, from Montreal to Madrid and Paris to Hong Kong.

Winter, whose travels are documented in the movie *Starbucking*, started out averaging around ten stores a day, although in 1999 he managed 28 in one day at Portland, Oregon. The only problem is that Starbucks continues to open new stores every week around the world and has no plans to slow down!

Chicago, IL

East Wenatchee, WA

Seekonk, MA

Grand Rapids, MI

Edmonston, AB

Candy Man

A snowman Pez dispenser on display at the Burlingame Museum of Pez Memorabilia in California weighs 85 lb (38.5 kg) and stands 7 ft 10 in (2.4 m) tall—that's 20 times the size of a normal Pez dispenser. It can dispense 6,480 pellets of Pez candy.

Ate Lenses Stopped by police for a breath test in 2007, a 19-year-old man from Ontario, Canada, took out his contact lenses and ate them—and then tried to eat his shirt and socks, too.

Frog Feast Visitors to the annual four-day Fellsmere Frog Leg Festival in Florida routinely eat around 6,000 lb (2,720 kg) of crispy fried frogs' legs.

Stone Cookies Artist Robin Antar from Brooklyn, New York, can create everyday objects from stone. Even though Robin is blind in one eye, she carves lifelike stone sculptures of iconic American items, such as a pair of Diesel jeans, a bag of Milano cookies, a Skechers' logger boot, a bag of M&M's®, and a giant Heinz Ketchup bottle. She usually works on her sculptures at night and spends up to six months on each piece. Her sculptures are so realistic that they have to be roped off to stop exhibit visitors trying to help themselves to a stone cookie or an M&M®!

Dirt Soda For its contract to supply soda to Qwest Field, home of the Seattle Seahawks football team, Jones Soda Co. came up with new flavors, such as Perspiration, Dirt, Sports Cream, and Natural Field Turf.

Cheese Lover Owing to a food phobia, Dave Nunley from Cambridgeshire, England, has eaten nothing but cheese for more than 25 years. He has never had a hot meal in his life—not even melted cheese—and survives by eating 238 lb (108 kg) of grated mild cheddar every year.

Giant Omelet Sixty thousand eggs were poured into a specially built 44-ft (13.4-m) pan to make a giant omelet weighing 6,510 lb (2,950 kg) at Brockville, Ontario, Canada in 2002.

Coffee Gum People in Japan can buy coffee-flavored chewing gum that leaves their breath coffee-fresh.

Varied Diet The ruffed grouse of North America enjoys a varied diet, from salamanders and snakes to flies and watercress. It eats on average at least 518 different kinds of animals and insects and 414 different plants.

Coconut Orchestra The cast and creators of the Monty Python musical *Spamalot* led 5,567 people in a mass coconut orchestra as they clip-clopped in time to "Always Look on the Bright Side of Life" in Trafalgar Square in London, England, in April 2007.

Huge Harvest A tomato tree at Walt Disney World's Epcot Center in Orlando, Florida, boasts a one-year harvest of more than 32,000 tomatoes with a total weight of 1,152 lb (522 kg).

Hungry Wolf In December 2007, customers at a crowded bar in Villetta Barrea, Italy, were shocked when a wolf strolled in, ate a steak sandwich, and walked out again. The hungry beast, which came from the nearby Abruzzo National Park, had been driven to drastic measures by a spell of cold weather.

Wizard Lizard The spiny-tailed iguana is eaten in the Sierra Madre Mountains of Mexico as a cure for depression.

Hard Fries British sculptor Keith Tyson made models of every item on a KFC menu, even down to the fries—in lead. His other weird and wonderful works have included pouring a thimble full of paint from a skyscraper and attaching 366 chopping boards to a wall.

Sheep's Eye In Outer Mongolia, a cure for a hangover consists of eating a pickled sheep's eye in a glass of tomato juice.

Pie Face

Winner Craig Bernston from Gloucester, Rhode Island, powers ahead during his assault on the pie-eating contest at the state's Washington County Fair held in the town of Richmond.

Desert Diet Eighty-year-old Ram Rati of Lucknow, India, eats 1 lb (450 g) of sand every day. She has been eating sand before each meal for the past 40 years and says it helps her to fight old age and stomach problems.

Peanut Gems Scientists at the University of Edinburgh, Scotland, say they can turn peanut butter into diamonds. They claim that the carbon in peanut butter can be transformed into precious gems by subjecting it to pressures of five million atmospheres—that's higher than the pressure found at the center of the Earth.

Costly Truffle A white truffle weighing 1 lb 10 oz (750 g) from Alba, Italy, was sold to a Hong Kong resident for $210,000 in 2007. Italian truffles were more expensive than usual in 2007 following a dry summer.

Color Change The first orange carrot was bred by Dutch farmers to honor their royal family, the House of Orange. Prior to that, most carrots were purple, yellow, or white.

Tea Bag In 2006, a German company made a tea bag that was 11 x 8½ ft (3.4 x 2.6 m). It contained more than 22 lb (10 kg) of tea.

Sound of the Sea At his restaurant in Berkshire, England, chef Heston Blumenthal serves a dish that comes with an iPod Nano in a clamshell—so that customers can listen to the sea as they eat their seafood.

Glass-eater An Indian fisherman eats crushed glass as part of his regular diet. Dashrath, known to residents of Kanpur as the "Glass Man," enjoys glass bulbs and bottles with his dinner and also eats lead bullets. He says that he's never had any health trouble and doesn't believe that the glass or bullets are causing him any ill effects.

Ripley's Believe It or Not!®

Big Breakfast

The proud winner of Britain's first All You Can Eat Breakfast Eating Championships is seen here with one of the 5½ breakfasts he ate in just 12 minutes at the contest held in London in July 2007. Each breakfast consisted of a delicious pile of eggs, bacon, sausages, mushrooms, and croissants.

Wobbly World

San Francisco may be expecting an earthquake some day soon, but this shaky city is ridiculous!

Liz Hickok has re-created San Francisco in Jell-O, constructing a whole scale model first and then using it to make molds for the Jell-O. She adds painted backdrops, model trees, and lights the Jell-O from underneath or behind. Then she snaps a photo before it decays and all her work becomes a sloppy mess.

Hung with fairy lights, Liz's Bay Bridge is a gravity-defying work of Jell-O.

Smashing Pumpkins

If you ever doubted that the pumpkin really is a squash fruit, the proof is at the Pumpkin Drop, a weird ritual that takes place each year before the Giant Pumpkin Weigh-off near Canby, Oregon. At 10 a.m. sharp, and watched by a crowd of around 4,000 admirers, a huge pumpkin (the 2007 specimen weighed 1,269 lb/575 kg) is loaded on to a crane and hoisted 100 ft (30 m) into the air above an old vehicle donated especially for the occasion. Once in position, the pumpkin is dropped from its great height onto the roof of the unoccupied van, crushing it to pieces.

Strange Combination Danny Partner of Los Angeles, California, used to eat 12 iceberg lettuces covered in chocolate sauce every day!

Dining Tomb At the Lucky Hotel Restaurant in Ahmedabad, India, guests dine among the 22 tombs that remain from an ancient burial ground.

Giant Kebab Using 3.8 tons of chicken meat, 250 students in Cyberjaya, Malaysia, created a kebab that was more than 1¼ mi (2 km) long.

Floating Pub A ship sailed 15,000 mi (24,000 km) from New Zealand to England in 2007 carrying an entire pub. When Tim Ellingham moved to London he asked friends back in New Zealand to send him his favorite Speights beer. Hearing of his predicament, the brewery decided to build a pub, fill it with beer, and ship it to the U.K. on board a cargo vessel. The pub was built in two 40-ft (12-m) containers joined together and came complete with bar, lounge, air conditioning, and plasma TV.

Beating Heart A delicacy in Japanese restaurants is the still-beating heart of a freshly killed frog! The dish is said to be particularly tasty if accompanied by lizard sake.

Frog Feast Dr. Matt Allen, a chemistry professor at Wayne State University, Detroit, Michigan, ate 1 lb 10 oz (750 g) of frogs' legs in only five minutes to win the first-ever World Frog Leg Eating Championship held at Madison, Wisconsin.

Grass Diet Lost in the hot Canadian bush for nine days in July 2007, 78-year-old Norm Berg, of Alberta, survived by eating grass and leaves.

Vintage Vodka In Moscow, Russia, there is a vodka museum containing 50,000 bottles of vodka, some as much as 200 years old.

Big Cheeses Troy Landwehr carved a sculpture of Mount Rushmore from a 700-lb (320-kg) block of Wisconsin Cheddar cheese. It took him four days to carve the replicas of U.S. presidents George Washington, Thomas Jefferson, Teddy Roosevelt, and Abraham Lincoln.

Popcorn Machines The Wyandot Popcorn Museum at Marion, Ohio, boasts the largest collection of popcorn and peanut roasters in the world, with some items dating back to the 1890s. It has more than 50 antique popping machines, including one used by movie star Paul Newman to promote his own popcorn in Central Park, New York.

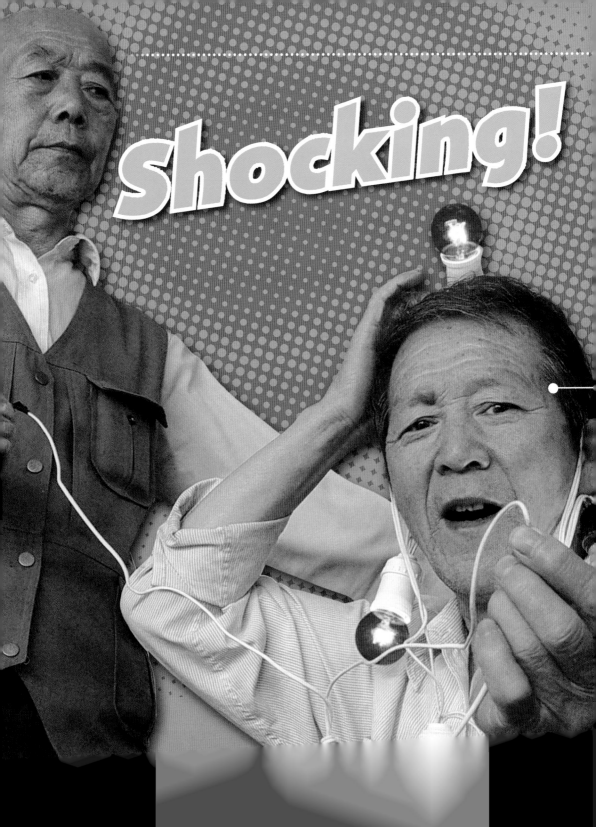

Zhang Deke can use his power as a human conductor of electricity to charge six 13-watt lightbulbs simply by placing them on his head and ears.

As the bulbs light up, he is even able to control their brightness. He has also cooked a fish, which he held in his hand as the current flowed through his body, in just two minutes!

Zhang, 71, a retired highway maintenance worker from Altay City, China, often exercises by hooking himself up to the electricity supply.

With both hands holding live wires, he allows 220 volts of electricity to run through his body without any ill effects, even though it is the same charge that an electric eel delivers to kill a human.

He first discovered his extraordinary ability when he was 47. While changing a lightbulb, he accidentally touched a live wire, but instead of receiving a shock or being electrocuted, he felt almost nothing. He tentatively tried it again and eventually realized that his body could conduct electricity. In 1994, he was examined at the Chinese Academy of Sciences, where experts said he has an unspecified physical dysfunction.

Zhang administers his electrical therapy to help friends and relatives who are suffering from ailments such as rheumatism, arthritis, and lumbago. One friend had been bedridden for some time with lumbar hyperplasia, but nine months after receiving Zhang's shock treatment he was out riding a bicycle.

Zhang demonstrates his electrical abilities by lighting up a string of lightbulbs being worn by a friend.

Zhang's incredible capacity to cook a fish with his body's electric current has amazed the world.

Jailhouse Rock

Hundreds of inmates at the Cebu Detention and Rehabilitation Center in the Philippines re-created the famous video dance routine to Michael Jackson's "Thriller." Their version proved so popular that by the end of 2007 it had been viewed more than 10 million times on YouTube—twice as many as had watched Jackson's original! The routine was an exercise program devised by security consultant Byron Garcia. Dancing is compulsory for all 1,600 inmates (except the elderly and the infirm) at Cebu and two former prisoners there have even gone on to become professional dancers.

Hands Apart Body parts from 16th-century Spanish missionary St. Francis Xavier were in such demand as relics that they are now scattered all over the globe. His left hand is in Cochin, India, while his right is in Malacca, Malaysia.

Wallpaper Museum

In France there is a museum devoted to wallpaper. Le Musée du Papier Peint at Rixheim has a history of wallpaper along with demonstrations of its manufacture.

Same Date

Lila Debry-Martin of Kingston Peninsula, New Brunswick, Canada, gave birth to triplets on August 10, 2000—the same day that she had given birth to twins three years before.

Seventh Heaven

Herbethe Elie of Birmingham, England, gave birth to her seventh baby in the seventh hour of the seventh day of the seventh month of 2007 —in hospital delivery room number seven.

Hot Wheels

Michael Zarnock of Deerfield, New York, has 8,128 different Hot Wheels cars—part of his collection of more than 25,000 model cars. Many of them are on display at the Children's Museum in Utica, New York, where they occupy seven glass cabinets, each 12 ft (3.6 m) in length. He says: "To this day, every birthday or holiday, everyone knows what to get me."

Birthday Bonanza

Michele Rosciano, his son Giovanni, and his grandson Miguel were all born as the second child, on the same day, of the same month, in the same hour—just in different years.

Murder Museum As well as scuptures of Charles Manson and notorious cannibals, the Serial Killer Museum in Florence, Italy, recounts the crimes of American murderers John Wayne Gacy and Ted Bundy. It also houses mock-ups of a gas chamber and an electric chair.

Artificial Legs The artificial legs of British World-War-II fighter pilot Douglas Bader are on display at the R.A.F. Museum in Stafford, England. Bader heroically flew in the Battle of Britain despite losing both of his legs in a plane crash 11 years earlier.

Bowling Alley Italian archeologists working in Egypt have found an indoor bowling alley that is nearly 2,000 years old. A large room, with a shallow lane running into a pit and two heavy stone balls lying nearby, was found at an ancient site that lies 55 mi (88 km) south of the Egyptian capital, Cairo.

Unique Attraction In the basement of his home at Onset, Massachusetts, Dick Porter has more than 5,000 thermometers—the result of some 25 years of collecting. He calls his collection the world's largest and only thermometer museum.

Cyanide Terror Nine villagers from Yangping, Henan, China, were killed in September 2007 when a floor collapsed and dumped them into an underground pool of deadly cyanide that no one had known was there.

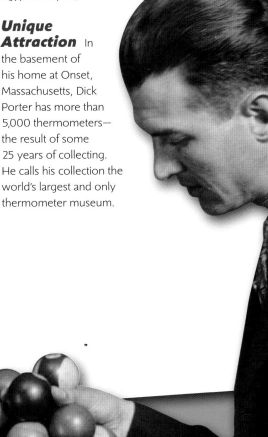

Pick-up King

In the 1930s, Julius Schuster of Jeannette, Pennsylvania, could pick up ten billiard balls in one hand, from a flat surface and without the aid of his other hand.

Playing Piggyback

Jack Trimbledon (bottom) led a novelty orchestra in the 1930s and 1940s. Here, two bandmates play while riding piggyback on Jack's back.

Hockey Ring

A Stanley Cup hockey championship ring that had been missing for more than 30 years has been found in the Gulf of Mexico. It belonged to former Toronto Maple Leafs' player Jim Pappin who later gave it to his father-in-law when he was traded to the Chicago Blackhawks. The ring was lost near Vero Beach, Florida, in the 1970s, but in 2007, a treasure hunter with an underwater metal detector found it with Pappin's name inscribed on the inside.

Blood Brothers

A bull that broke loose gored two American brothers—Lawrence and Michael Lenahan—simultaneously, catching one on each of its horns during the 2007 Running of the Bulls Festival at Pamplona, Spain.

Magical Marbles

As well as chronicling the history of marbles, the Marble Museum at Yreka, California, houses beautiful, hand-painted china marbles, as well as a collection of paintings all about marbles.

Body Found

While researching a story in August 2007, Seattle-based author Peter Stekel discovered the frozen body of a World-War-II aviator on a Californian glacier.

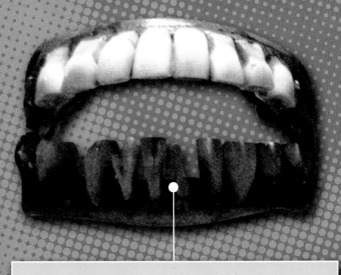

Tooth Truth

Laser scans performed on George Washington's teeth at the National Museum of Dentistry in Baltimore in 2005 showed that they were not made of wood as was commonly believed. Instead, his dentures turned out to be made from gold, ivory, lead, and human and animal teeth (probably horse and donkey). The dentures had springs to help them open and were held together by bolts.

Tie Pins

Since 1977, Kevin Godden of Kent, England, has been collecting tie pins—and he now has more than 1,300 of them.

Taping Dave

Judy Carter of Seymour, Indiana, created a sculpture of TV host David Letterman using duct tape!

Hitler's Head

What are believed to be Adolf Hitler's skull and jaw are stored at the Federal Archives Service in Moscow, Russia. The skull piece is stored on two sheets of tissue in a floppy disk container. Ironically, Hitler had ordered a German officer to burn his remains because he didn't want to end up on display in the Soviet Union.

She's Got Sole!

Darlene Flynn has certainly taken a shine to shoes. Since starting her collection in 2000, Darlene of Romoland, California, has accumulated around 9,000 shoe-related items.

"In 2006, I had a special dinner event with Raine and other shoe collectors at my home in California. Everything was shoes, shoes, shoes—we had Cinderella shoe bottle-openers, shoe silverware holders, and so on, and the big finale was the shoe dessert. It took me between six and eight months to figure something out that would be completely edible."

"These are mainly my shoe thimbles—they are all approximately an inch high."

"This curio cabinet contains some of my signed 'Just the Right Shoe' resin miniature shoe collection. 'Just the Right Shoes' were the first shoes I bought for my collection."

She has at least 500 different kinds of shoe memorabilia—among them shoe-shaped furniture, shoe curtains, shoe wallpaper, shoe lamps, shoe watches, shoe-themed art, shoe teapots, shoe soap, shoe purses, shoe thimbles, shoe spoons, shoe candles, shoe salt and pepper shakers, shoe-styled stationery, an electric shoe toothbrush, and a red stiletto shoe phone. Darlene's house is lined with display cases of beautiful miniature shoes. She has some 7,000 in total, including one named Ms. Vicky that is just 4 in (10 cm) wide and cost her $1,800.

Outside, a cowboy-boot birdhouse hangs from the wall and the patio is decorated with shoe-shaped flowerpots. Her collection also includes a replica of the Disney Cinderella glass slipper, Barbie shoes galore, and a shoe made from ash collected from the eruption of Mount St. Helens. She has ambitions to own a shoe-shaped car, and for her collection to appear on the "Oprah" TV show.

Giant Penguin Scientists have discovered fossilized remains of a sun-loving giant penguin that lived some 36 million years ago and, at 5 ft (1.5 m), was as tall as an adult human. The skeleton was discovered on the southern coast of Peru, indicating that this bird preferred the tropics to colder climes.

Multiple Jumps In 2006, Jay Stokes of Yuma, Arizona, celebrated his 50th birthday by jumping out of an airplane—640 times. Despite injuring a muscle around the 200th leap, he completed the jumps in 24 hours—averaging out at one jump every 2 minutes 15 seconds.

Filmed Flight In 2005, Francisco Gutierrez flew with a swarm of Monarch butterflies to film the flight of their 4,375-mi (7,040-km) migration from Canada to Mexico. Gutierrez flew among the thousands of insects in a small ultralight plane.

Twisted Logic In Dannebrog, Nebraska, there is a museum dedicated to liars. Nothing is as it seems at the Liar's Hall of Fame, where exhibits include a box of golf balls the size of hailstones!

Double Strike Lightning can strike twice! On July 27, 2007, Don Frick of Hamlin, Pennsylvania, was at a festival when lightning struck the ground nearby, leaving a burned zipper and a hole in the back of his jeans—27 years to the day of his first strike. On July 27, 1980, he had been driving a tractor-trailer when the antenna was struck by lightning, injuring his left side.

Jason's Journey British adventurer Jason Lewis completed a 46,000-mi (74,000-km), 13-year journey around the world. Between 1994 and 2007 he walked, cycled, roller-bladed, kayaked, swam, and pedaled across five continents, two oceans, and one sea. En route he was chased by a saltwater crocodile in Australia, questioned as a spy in North Africa, and suffered two fractured legs after being hit by a car in Colorado as he roller-bladed across the U.S.A. To help pay for his adventure, he worked as a cattle drover in North America and in a funeral parlor in Australia.

Car Kissing

A Chinese woman won a car in 2007 by kissing it virtually nonstop for more than 24 hours. Zhang Cunying was one of 120 people taking part in the endurance contest at a Beijing shopping mall, where the competitors had to kiss Chevrolet cars through plastic nipples attached to the bodywork but without touching the car itself. The person lasting the longest was declared the winner. They were allowed a ten-minute break every seven hours and, in order to speed up elimination, were eventually made to stand on one foot with their hands behind their back. Zhang owed her success to her dance training, although she was so exhausted at the finish that she could not stand up unaided.

Well-traveled Brain

When Princeton pathologist Dr. Thomas Harvey performed the autopsy on Albert Einstein in 1955, he chose to remove the physicist's brain. He later had it cut into 240 pieces, which he kept in two jars stored inside a cider box at his various homes across America. From time to time he sent pieces to researchers. In 1997, Harvey traveled to meet Einstein's granddaughter in California and took the brain with him in the trunk of his car. He accidentally left the brain at her house but she did not want it, so the following year she sent it back to its home in Princeton.

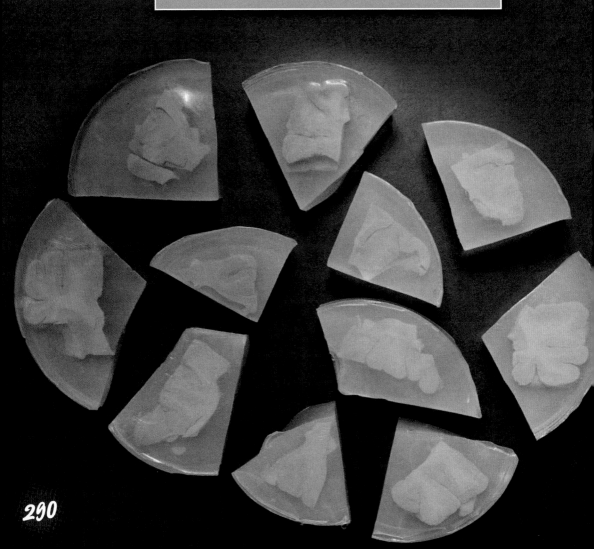

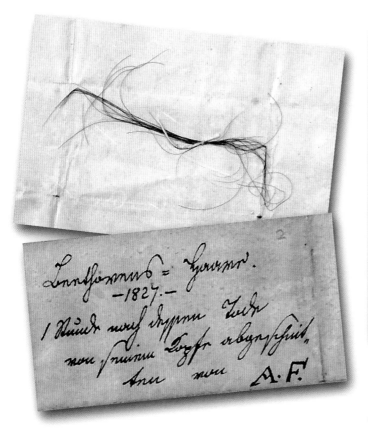

When Ludwig van Beethoven died in 1827, this lock of his hair was taken from his head as a keepsake of the great German composer. It became the property of the Royal Philharmonic Society in London, England, almost a hundred years later, and now belongs to the British Library.

Trash People
A thousand trash people—molded from tin cans, computer parts, and crushed plastic—have appeared in some of the world's most famous locations. The work of German artist H. A. Schult, the garbage army has been arranged on the Great Wall of China, near the Egyptian Pyramids, in Moscow's Red Square, at the base of the Matterhorn mountain in Switzerland, and in front of Cologne Cathedral in Germany.

Solo Crossing
Michael Perham of Hertfordshire, England, sailed solo across the Atlantic Ocean when he was just 14 years old. The schoolboy set off from Gibraltar in his 28-ft (8.5-m) yacht *Cheeky Monkey* on November 18, 2006, and arrived six and a half weeks later in Antigua in the West Indies on January 3, 2007. During the 3,500-mi (5,635-km) voyage, he had to contend with sharks, technical problems, and ferocious storms.

Ancient Tooth
Researchers in Spain have unearthed a human tooth that is more than one million years old. The fossil was discovered near Burgos and sets a new date for humankind's presence in western Europe—the previous oldest finds for the region being a mere 800,000 years old!

Bad Day
In 1945, Betty Lou Oliver of New York City survived a plane crash and a 1,000-ft (300-m) elevator fall on the same day.

Duck Overboard

In January 1992, a stupendous storm washed three containers off a ship that was bound from Hong Kong to Tacoma, Washington. One container spilled its contents into the sea—no less than 29,000 bathtub toys!

In 2007, retired teacher Penny Harris found the first plastic duck from the cargo to arrive in England when it washed up on a beach in Devon at the end of a 15-year round-the-world trip.

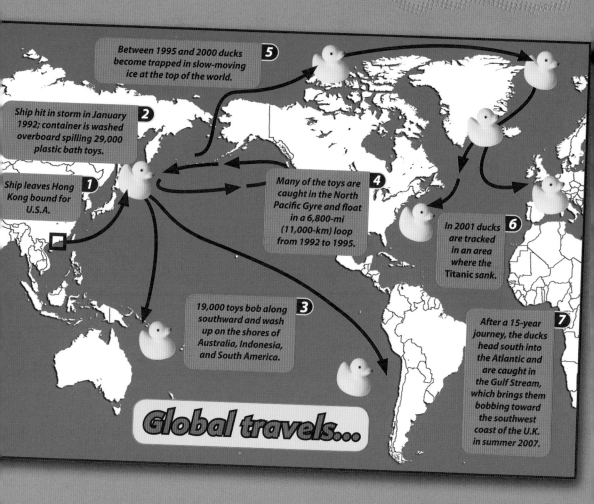

5 Between 1995 and 2000 ducks become trapped in slow-moving ice at the top of the world.

2 Ship hit in storm in January 1992; container is washed overboard spilling 29,000 plastic bath toys.

1 Ship leaves Hong Kong bound for U.S.A.

4 Many of the toys are caught in the North Pacific Gyre and float in a 6,800-mi (11,000-km) loop from 1992 to 1995.

6 In 2001 ducks are tracked in an area where the Titanic sank.

3 19,000 toys bob along southward and wash up on the shores of Australia, Indonesia, and South America.

7 After a 15-year journey, the ducks head south into the Atlantic and are caught in the Gulf Stream, which brings them bobbing toward the southwest coast of the U.K. in summer 2007.

Global travels...

Two-thirds of them bobbed off south through the tropics, landing months later on the shores of Indonesia, Australia, and South America. The remaining 10,000 plastic ducks, turtles, frogs, and beavers headed north and were soon off the coast of Alaska whereupon they turned back westward. Some of the ducks made their way south and were seen floating past Japan in 1995. Many, however, became trapped in the North Pacific Gyre. This giant clockwise spiral of water collects and gradually grinds the oceans' plastic debris. However, even this couldn't halt the plucky ducks, which eventually broke free and pressed on. They bravely steered a course for the Arctic where some became trapped in ice for several years.

They finally reached the North Atlantic in 2000 and, in the summer of 2007, more than 15 years and nearly 17,000 mi (27,500 km) after their journey's start, flotillas of ducks, bleached white by the sun and sea, hit the coasts of Great Britain and North America.

· · ·

Eraser Fan

Phoebe Syms from London, England, has collected nearly 4,000 erasers. Her obsession began at just two years of age, when she was attracted by the smell and feel of them. Fourteen years later, her collection is still going strong.

Naked Ambition

In 2007, a couple from Bedfordshire, England, climbed 15 Scottish mountains, each more than 3,000 ft (915 m) in height—naked. The naturists, known only as Stuart and Karla, commemorated each climb with a nude photo of themselves on the summit. There are 284 peaks in Scotland over 3,000 ft— known as the Munros—and Stuart and Karla intend to climb every one.

Firearm Art

Peace art project artists in Cambodia created original sculptures and furniture from decommissioned pistols and assault rifles.

Bull Attack

In 1912, 49-year-old "Granny" Anderson of Staples, Texas, had her intestines ripped out by a bull. A doctor washed the wound, replaced her innards, and sewed her up, and she went on to live to the age of 105.

Cone Zone

David Morgan's life is dedicated to traffic cones. Not only does he work for the world's largest producer of cones, but he has a collection of 500 of them at his home in Oxfordshire, England. He has been collecting them for more than 20 years, usually from roadworks, where he swaps a sought-after cone for a brand new one. Among his prized possessions are a Malaysian cone, found washed up on a beach in the Isles of Scilly off the southwest coast of the U.K., and a rare 1980 cone, which he picked up at an airport in Corsica while on his honeymoon.

Stone Riddle In September 2007, residents in northern England and in Scotland were puzzled to find strange stone heads left outside their homes in the dead of night. More than 50 gargoyle-like figures were deposited throughout a wide area, each bearing a carving that spelled out the word "paradox." A riddle was also attached. The culprit turned out to be eccentric artist Billy Johnson, who had hoped the recipients would use the cryptic clues to contact his website.

Wheelchair Ride

A wheelchair user was taken on a terrifying 50-mph (80-km/h) ride for 4 mi (6.4 km) along a U.S. highway in 2007 after the handles of his chair became wedged in the front grill of a truck.

"It was pretty scary," said Ben Carpenter of his ordeal. "I tried to yell for help, but no one could hear me."

The driver refused to believe there was a man stuck to the front of his truck... until he saw it for himself.

b A truck slowly pulls out of a gas station and hits Ben's wheelchair, which becomes attached to the front grill.

a Ben Carpenter crosses the road.

c Truck speeds up to 50 mph (80 km/h). Ben is carried along the highway.

d Passing vehicles call 911. Ben's chair is attached to the truck for 4 mi (6.4 km) before the police intervene.

Incredibly, Ben Carpenter emerged unharmed from his

Ben Carpenter, a 21-year-old muscular-dystrophy sufferer, was crossing the street in Paw Paw, Michigan, when the back of his motorized wheelchair was bumped by a truck leaving a gas station, the impact trapping the chair in the radiator grill. The truck driver then drove off down the highway, unaware that he had an involuntary passenger on the front of his vehicle.

Luckily, horrified passers-by saw Carpenter's predicament and alerted the police, who eventually managed to stop the truck. Carpenter was unhurt, having been held in place in his wheelchair by a seatbelt. Afterward he said: "It was quite a ride."

Bug Art

Los Angeles artist Steven Kutcher uses insects as living paintbrushes. He takes flies, cockroaches, and beetles in his hand and adds paint onto each leg, one leg at a time. He then releases them onto a prepared canvas, allowing them to create a trail of color. To ensure his insects come to no harm, he always uses water-based, nontoxic paints that wash off easily.

Discarded Objects Artist Rebecca Wolfram of Chicago, Illinois, has set up a Museum of Objects Left on the Sidewalk—a collection of items abandoned in the street, including used fireworks, broken dolls, sweat shirts, gloves, pots and pans, and a wire coat-hanger molded into the shape of a shark.

Stage Fan Andrea Schecter of Oceanside, New York, has a collection of approximately 2,300 playbills from the stage shows that she has seen, from New York to London.

Metal Addict The Swedish Employment Service granted disability payments to Roger Tullgren of Hassleholm, Sweden, because he is addicted to heavy-metal music. A heavy-metal fan since hearing Black Sabbath at the age of six, Tullgren attended 300 concerts in 2006, often skipping work to do so.

Lincoln Relics Part of President Abraham Lincoln's skull is housed at the National Museum of Health and Medicine in Washington, D.C. Also displayed there are bits of his hair and the bullet that killed him.

Golfing Double

Two members of a foursome scored back-to-back holes-in-one at a New Jersey golf club in 2007 — defying odds of more than 17 million to one! Immediately after nine-handicapper Thomas Brady landed an ace at the 179-yd (164-m) seventh hole at Forsgate Country Club in Monroe Township, Dennis Gerhart, a self-confessed "weekend hacker" who plays golf only 15 times a year, stepped upto the tee and emulated the feat.

Titanic Time

Watchmaker Romain Jerome of Geneva, Switzerland, has created a line of watches that use steel and coal that has been taken from the wreck of the R.M.S. *Titanic*. Incorporating steel from the stricken ship's hull and coal from the wreck site, the watches sell for anything between $8,000 and $175,000.

Snake's Tee

When a python was taken to a wildlife sanctuary near Brisbane, Australia, with four bumps in its belly, veterinarians were amazed to see four golf balls show up on an X ray. The snake had swallowed the balls after apparently mistaking them for chicken eggs. Unable to pass the golf balls naturally, the snake underwent a successful operation to remove them and was released back into the wild.

Chip and Pin
In February 2007, grandmother Olga Mauriello of San Giorgio Cremano, Italy, found a live World-War-II-era grenade—without its safety pin—in a sack of potatoes.

Land Swimmer

An over-sized sculpture of a man swimming through grass was unveiled on the banks of the Thames River in London, England, in 2007. The piece was commissioned to promote a reality TV show by Louis Molloy.

Curiosity Cabinet
Keswick Museum in Cumbria, England, is home to a "Cabinet of Curiosities," including a 14-ft-long (4-m), 1.5-ton xylophone made of slate, a 665-year-old cat, the Emperor Napoleon's teacup, poet Robert Southey's clogs, a spoon made from the leg bone of a sheep, and a man trap.

Elvis's Wart
Joni Mabe, "the Elvis Babe," of Cornelia, Georgia, keeps Elvis Presley's wart in a tube of formaldehyde. She bought the wart—part of her collection of Elvis memorabilia—in 1990 from a Memphis doctor who had removed it from Elvis's right wrist when Presley joined the army in 1958.

Green Light
A 14-year-old boy from Merseyside, England, has been given the green light to collect traffic signals. Simon Patterson already has six sets of lights, more than 30 beacons, and hundreds of photographs of traffic lights from around the world sent to him by friends on holiday. He has built up his collection, which also includes numerous road signs, by writing to councils or buying old sets on eBay at about $50 each.

Skeleton in Loft
A man's skeleton was discovered in the loft of his family home in Bergholz-Rehbrücke, Germany, in 2007—22 years after his disappearance.

Sick Remedy In April 2004, a Chinese man was arrested on suspicion of stealing 30 corpses from graveyards, cooking soup from their flesh, and crushing the bones in an attempt to heal his sick wife.

Edible Mozart Japan's Junko Terashima prepared an amazing likeness of the composer Wolfgang Amadeus Mozart—from food! Terashima is an expert in Bento Art— the Japanese craft of lunch sculpture—whereby incredible edible images are created from fruit, vegetables, and other foodstuffs.

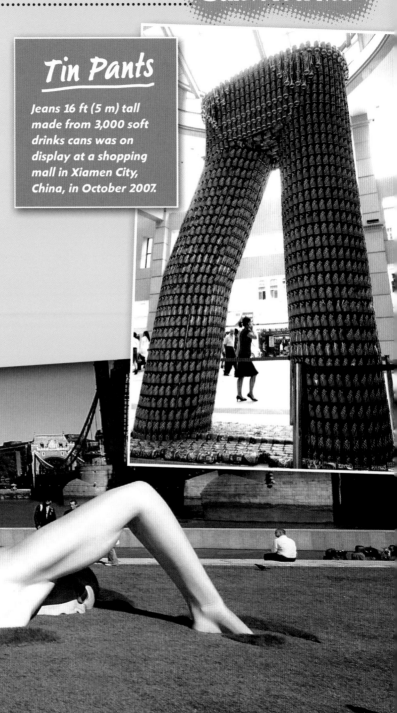

Tin Pants

Jeans 16 ft (5 m) tall made from 3,000 soft drinks cans was on display at a shopping mall in Xiamen City, China, in October 2007.

Be Our Guest

When comedian and filmmaker Mark Malkoff's New York City apartment had to be fumigated in January 2008, he obtained permission to move into an IKEA store for a week.

Mark in his IKEA bedroom.

Breakfast in Mark's IKEA pad was a relaxed affair.

Reasoning that hotels were too expensive, he lived, slept, and ate at the store in Paramus, New Jersey. Malkoff took full advantage of the free accommodation and fully furnished rooms at the IKEA store. He said the only problems were that the display sinks and toilets were not plumbed in (forcing him to shower in the staff locker room) and at night the lights in the store automatically came on at 2 a.m. Although his wife chose not to join him on his IKEA holiday, Malkoff had numerous visitors to his temporary in-store living quarters and even staged a housewarming party.

Mark in his showroom bathroom.

Mark sorts through his underwear drawer in one of the bedrooms.

Mark eating in his kitchen.

Mummified Dog

In 1980, a mummified dog was found lodged 20 ft (6 m) above ground in a tree near the Georgia–Alabama state line. The hollow tree created perfect conditions for the animal to be preserved some 20 years after its death. The dog became so popular that it was later given its own name—Stuckie.

Petrified Forest A forest of around 200 petrified trees has been discovered in Washington State, still standing on the spot where they were swamped by lava more than 15 million years ago. Clyde Friend used an excavator, a hammer, and a chisel to unearth the preserved hickory, maple, elm, and sweetgum trees on his land near Yakima.

Amputated Leg Even though his right leg was nearly blown off by a cannonball during the Battle of Gettysburg, Dan Sickles calmly smoked a cigar on his way to the medical tent. After the leg was amputated, Sickles donated it to the Army Medical Museum, where he would later take friends to impress them with his bravery.

Lighters Galore
Ted Ballard of Guthrie, Oklahoma, started collecting cigarette lighters when he was six years old and at the last count had a collection of more than 20,000.

Ring Returned
Clare Cavoli Lopez of South Euclid, Ohio, lost her class ring while scuba diving off the coast of South Africa more than 20 years ago. Her ring was found in 2007 by a professional diver in an underwater cave on Mauritius and returned to her.

Hot Work
Queensland shearers Dave Grant and Laurie Bateman shaved 709 Merino sheep in just eight hours at Hughenden, Australia, in October 2007. The pair trained for 12 months to build up the stamina necessary for the challenge, during which their bodies perspired up to 135 fl oz (4 l) of sweat every two hours.

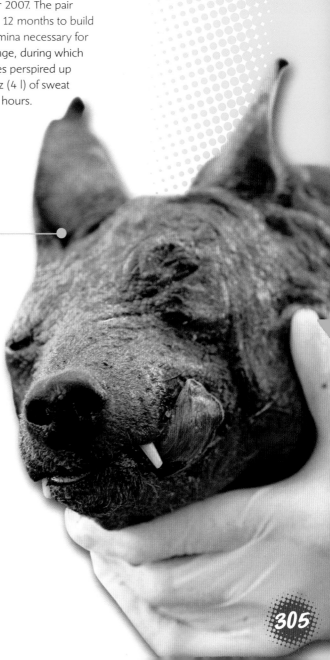

Mythical Beast?

When Phylis Canion found a strange animal dead outside her Cuero, Texas, ranch in August 2007, she thought it was a chupacabra, the mysterious beast blamed for killing 30 of her chickens. The state mammalogist suggested it was more likely to be a gray fox suffering from an extreme case of mange.

Beer Cans Australia's John Loveday has a collection of more than 6,000 beer cans from 78 countries—and he doesn't even drink! He has been collecting beer-related memorabilia for more than 15 years and also has 1,500 beer glasses, 900 beer bottles, plus assorted beer-themed coasters, matchboxes, key rings, bottle tops, and mirrors.

Extra Time Two soccer teams at Exeter, Ontario, Canada, played against one another continuously for 30 hours 30 minutes in May 2007. The final score was Stratford Enterprise 138, Exeter Fury 105. Players' injuries included a dislocated shoulder and a broken foot.

Hotel Fall Joshua Hanson, of Wisconsin, plummeted 16 floors after falling through the window of a Minneapolis hotel in 2007, but survived because he landed on the roof overhang one floor up from the street.

Unusual Case In 2007, a ten-year-old boy was hit by a car while walking to school in Lancaster, Pennsylvania, but escaped with only cuts and bruises because the violin case he was carrying took most of the impact.

Point Made

John Little never forgot being told off at school for not having a pencil sharpener, so now he has more than 1,500. John, from County Durham, England, has been collecting sharpeners for 20 years and has examples from all over the world in such diverse shapes as a kiwi, a banana, a red letter box, an apple, a wooden clog, and a shark.

Drain Tiles Housed in the 1822 home of John Johnston, a pioneer in tile drainage technology, the Mike Weaver Drain Tile Museum at Geneva, New York, boasts a collection of more than 500 drain tiles dating from 500 BC to the modern plastic version. Marion "Mike" Weaver worked in drainage for 20 years and started his collection in 1950.

Missing Arm British Admiral Horatio Nelson's right arm is said to be kept in the cathedral in Las Palmas, Gran Canaria. It was amputated after being shattered by grapeshot during an assault on Tenerife in 1797.

Call Center

The exterior of a small electronics store in Tokyo, Japan, is decorated with 6,000 used cell phones. The shop's owner, Masanao Watanabe, has been collecting them since 1994 and decided on the unusual display when he ran out of storage space inside. Now visitors come from all over the city to study the walls and see if they can find models they have owned.

Surprise Legacy Men carrying out plumbing work on Mike Sutton's new house in Bridport, Dorset, England, took up the cellar floor and found hundreds of artificial legs!

Mistaken Identity Bones long thought to belong to Joan of Arc were recently discovered to be those of an ancient Egyptian mummy and its pet cat.

Great Survivor A 50-ton bowhead whale caught off the coast of Alaska in 2007 had a weapon fragment embedded in its neck that showed it had survived a previous attack over a century before. The 3.5-in (9-cm), arrow-shaped projectile, thought to date from around 1890, was found deep under the whale's blubber.

Sewer Museum In Hamburg, Germany, there is a museum dedicated to objects found in the city's sewer system.

Tuxedo Travelers

Two men completed a five-month, 6,214-mi (10,000-km) trek from Hong Kong to London—dressed the entire way in tuxedos.

Briton Heath Buck and American Doug Campbell dreamed up their bizarre charity adventure in a Hong Kong bar in 2005 despite having known each other for only a few days. Before setting off on April Fool's Day 2007, the pair—who promoted themselves as "two fools, one adventure, no idea"—trashed their ordinary clothes and donned the tuxedos, which had been specially made for them in Bangkok, Thailand, from extra-resilient fabric and fitted with hidden pockets for valuables.

Apart from sleeping and showering, they wore their dinner dress every step of the way on a journey that took them through remote regions of China, Vietnam, Tibet, Nepal, India, Pakistan, and Kyrgyzstan—among other places.

In Vietnam, they plowed rice paddies, weeded corn crops, and built a wall—still wearing their black suits and bow ties. "It was quite a surreal experience," admitted Campbell. "At the end we brought a few of the local tribal women to tears when we donated fertilizer for the year's crop. In return they made us honorary tribe members."

The pair also went wrestling in India and had to deal with temperatures of over 120°F (50°C), but the tuxedos survived to the finish. Not surprisingly, the two men got some odd looks along the way. "Everyone asked if they could take a picture of us," said Buck. "They often asked us if we were getting married!"

Wearing Kyrgyzstani robes gave their tuxedos a local feel in Kyrgyzstan.

Posing with people dressed in traditional costume in Yangshuo, China.

Heath hosted an English tea party at the Everest Base camp.

Man-made Tornado

A museum in Stuttgart, Germany, has created its own 113-ft-high (34.4-m) tornado. In order to remove smoke from the building in the event of a fire, the Mercedes-Benz Museum has devised a system that uses 144 air jets to form a powerful tornado from 28 tons of air.

Watch Returned

A World-War-I veteran's engraved watch was returned to the owner's family in 2007 — nearly 90 years after William B. Gill lost it in France, where he served in the U.S. Army. It was later won in a poker game and then, with the help of a genealogist, returned to Gill's grandchildren in Sioux City, Iowa.

Dairy Delights

America's Ice Cream and Dairy Museum at Medina, Ohio, has artifacts on the history of ice cream dating back to ancient Egypt. Among the most cherished exhibits is a 1905 "gaslight" soda fountain.

Perfect Match

Joe DeGennaro of New York City, has a collection of more than 100,000 matchcovers and matchboxes. He is a leading light of the Rathkamp Matchcover Society—named after its founder and avid matchbox collector Henry Rathkamp—which boasts more than 1,000 members across North America.

Upside Down

The pilot of a light airplane escaped injury in July 2007 when it landed on its roof at Darwin Airport, Australia. The plane was spun upside down by a fierce crosswind as it came in to land.

Macabre Warning

Oliver Cromwell died in 1658, but three years later the reinstated English monarchy under King Charles II exhumed his body and had him posthumously executed. His head was then impaled on a spike in Westminster Hall, where it remained for 20 years as a warning to others. The head now rests in a chapel in Cambridge, England.

Croc Bait

Wearing only a swimming costume, Kerry Shaw was secured inside a reinforced steel cage and plunged into a pool full of 14-ft-long (4-m) crocodiles. She was lowered by crane into position at a wildlife park in Oudtshoom, South Africa, in 2007, and warned that under no circumstances should she reach through the bars!

Close Relatives

Unbeknown to each other, Dorothy Caudle lived just 300 ft (100 m) from her sister Gladys Clark for an entire year. The sisters, who had not seen each other for 38 years, were living in the same senior care facility at Tempe, Arizona, but did not realize it until celebrations were held to mark Clark's 100th birthday in 2007.

Fish Cure

British scientists believe that a tiny tropical fish could help find a cure for blindness in humans. The zebrafish has a unique ability to repair its own damaged and diseased eyes, and now researchers have identified that the special cells, which restore sight in zebrafish, can also be found in the human eye.

Bite Size

Sid the grass snake looked to have bitten off more than he could chew when tackling a goldfish more than ten times the size of his head at a garden in Kent, England. However, by dislocating his jaw he was eventually able to devour the tasty meal and continue his campaign to snatch fish up to 8 in (20 cm) long from the pond.

Plugged Hole Shot in the heart with a 3-in (7.6-cm) nail, 17-year-old Matt Robinson of Dexter, Missouri, survived the ordeal only because he didn't bleed. Miraculously, the nail in fact plugged the hole it had made until a doctor could operate.

Egg Returned A rare bird's egg was returned to a museum in the town of Salcombe in Devon, England, in 2006—43 years after it had been stolen. The bustard's egg arrived back in mint condition, accompanied by a letter signed only "John," apologizing for the theft in 1963.

Presidential Tumor President Grover Cleveland's tumor is kept in a jar at the Mütter Museum, Philadelphia, Pennsylvania. It was removed from the roof of his mouth in a secret operation.

Double Blow A man in Australia was attacked by a crocodile and then accidentally shot by his rescuer. Jason Grant had been collecting crocodile eggs at a reptile farm near Darwin when the saltwater croc seized him in his jaws. His colleague fired two shots at the crocodile and one struck Grant in the arm.

The Eyes Have It

Performing at Ripley's Chicago Odditorium in 1933, Harry McGregor of Philadelphia, Pennsylvania, could pull his wife Lillian around in a wagon—a load of 150 lb (68 kg) — with his eyelids!

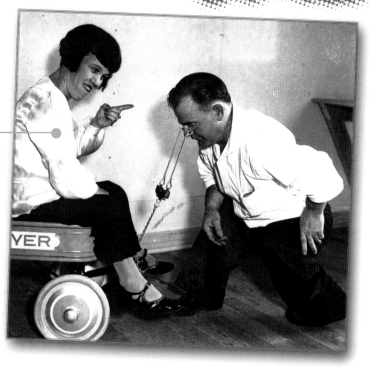

Cycling Phenomenon

Born with a deformed right leg, Emmanuel Ofosu Yeboah peddled his bike 379 mi (610 km) across Ghana in 2001 using only his left foot in order to challenge stereotypes about the disabled people of his country.

Neighborly Act

After two days adrift in the Caribbean, John Fildes was rescued by a cruise ship, which, amazingly, was captained by a neighbor from his hometown—Warsash, England.

Sweet Spot

The Marzipan Museum in Keszthely, Hungary, has displays of sculpture—including dragons, shields, and miniature palaces—all made out of marzipan.

Huge Nickel

Among more than one million vintage pieces at the Wooden Nickel Historical Museum at San Antonio, Texas, is a wooden nickel measuring 13 ft 4 in (4 m) in diameter and weighing 2,500 lb (1,135 kg).

Hammer Home

Germany's George Peters has been fascinated by hammers for 30 years and now has more than 3,500 in his collection. His hammers come from all over the world and range in weight from a tiny 0.0006 oz (0.017 g) to a hefty 155 lb (70 kg).

Parasite Paradise

The Meguro Parasitological Museum in Tokyo, Japan, has a collection of more than 300 parasites, including a tapeworm 30 ft (9 m) long that was pulled out of a person's body.

All the Eights

In 2007, a baby was born in Liverpool, England, at eight minutes past eight in the morning of the eighth day of the eighth month weighing eight pounds, and after her mother had been in labor for eight hours! The mother, Mel Byrne, was looked after by a midwife who delivered eight babies that day.

The Boy Behind the Mask

Little Joshua Taylor's family never know what he is going to look like from one minute to the next—because he has a collection of more than 400 masks.

Six-year-old Joshua from West Jefferson, North Carolina, has been fascinated by masks since he was 18 months old, when he watched the movie *The Haunted Mask* at every available opportunity. He started wearing a werewolf mask wherever he went before progressing to making his own masks... from food.

He would bite out eyes, nose, and mouth from bologna (sliced sausage) and even designed a mask from a tortilla. His mom Angie says: "He chewed out a face from the tortilla and put it in the refrigerator for days, and it had an old wooden look to it. It amazes me to watch his creativity."

Joshua has also made masks from papier mâché and for Christmas 2006 was given his first rubber-mask-making kit. Now the talented youngster is able to devise an amazing range of latex masks—from the grotesque to the humorous.

Young Joshua Taylor has more than 400 masks, many of which he has made himself. A variety of monsters, aliens, superheroes, and skeletons feature in his extensive collection.

Cookie-jar Monster

Starting in 1975, Lucille Bromberek of Lemont, Illinois, collected cookie jars and eventually amassed more than 2,000.

Spinal Column

Twelve days after murdering President Abraham Lincoln, John Wilkes Booth was fatally shot in the neck. His body was later buried in an unmarked grave in Baltimore but his third, fourth, and fifth vertebrae had already been removed during the autopsy to gain access to the bullet. These parts of his spinal column are on display at the National Museum of Health and Medicine in Washington, D.C.

Drum Dream

Alan Buckley of Walsall, England, started collecting drum kits at the age of eight—and now he has 110 of them. The 72-year-old musician, known as "Sir Alan" after his friends bought him a "knighthood," has snares dating back to 1809 and numerous other drums from the 1920s and 1930s. His collection includes a drum from London's Windmill Theatre, famous for never closing during World War II.

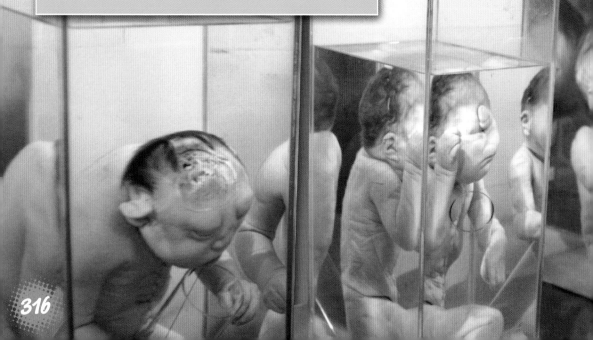

Brain Museum

A museum in Lima, Peru, houses almost 3,000 diseased human brains. Unlike most brain collections around the world, it is open to the public. Exhibits include the brain of someone who died from the human variant of "mad cow" disease, the brains of people who died of trichinosis—the most common brain disease in Peru—which is caused by eating undercooked meat, and several human fetuses with neurological disorders.

Wallet Recovered

A man who lost his wallet on a trip to the theater in 1964 got it back 43 years later. Construction workers renovating the Crest Theater at El Centro, California, discovered Epigmenio Sanchez's wallet jammed between the metal casings of a radiator.

TV Glut
The average U.S. home has more TV sets than it has people, and believe it or not, one in four Americans have actually appeared on TV!

Voodoo Experience

The New Orleans Historic Voodoo Museum brings together ancient and modern voodoo practices. It houses artifacts such as dolls and items relating to the 19th-century voodoo queen Marie Laveau.

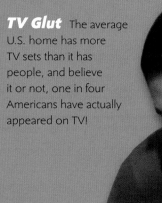

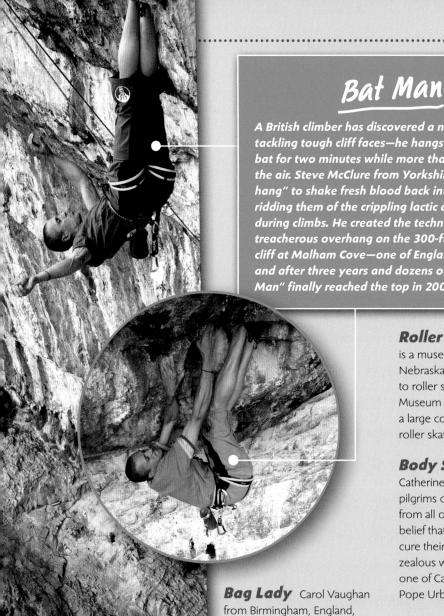

Bat Man

A British climber has discovered a new method of tackling tough cliff faces—he hangs upside down like a bat for two minutes while more than 100 ft (30 m) up in the air. Steve McClure from Yorkshire practices the "bat hang" to shake fresh blood back into his arms, thereby ridding them of the crippling lactic acid that builds up during climbs. He created the technique to conquer the treacherous overhang on the 300-ft (90-m) limestone cliff at Malham Cove—one of England's hardest climbs—and after three years and dozens of attempts, "Bat Man" finally reached the top in 2007.

Roller Skating There is a museum in Lincoln, Nebraska, that is dedicated to roller skating. The National Museum of Roller Skating has a large collection of historical roller skates and costumes.

Body Snatchers After Catherine of Siena died in 1380, pilgrims came to visit her body from all over Europe in the belief that touching it would cure their illnesses. One over-zealous worshiper removed one of Catherine's fingers and Pope Urban VI took her head.

Bag Lady Carol Vaughan from Birmingham, England, has collected more than 8,000 carrier bags in all shapes and sizes. The 64-year-old, who hates throwing things away, also has a house full of 52 other collections, including 2,500 bars of soap, 500 tins, and 400 mugs.

Hardened Criminal Following an attempted carjack, police easily captured the fleeing suspect in Reno, Nevada, in November 2007, after he got stuck in wet concrete as he tried to make his escape through a construction site.

Underwater Survivor

Hungarian escape artist David Merlini spent 10 minutes 17 seconds chained and handcuffed underwater in 2007, without air. His hands were tied by five sets of police handcuffs and he was bound by 60 lb (27 kg) of chains before being padlocked in a metal cage and lowered into a transparent tank of water in Hollywood, California.

319

The Last Word

Quick on the Draw

Some artists work in oils, others choose watercolors, but Jeff Gagliardi of Boulder, Colorado, prefers a different artistic medium—the Etch A Sketch® drawing toy. Using this much-loved children's toy of the 1960s, Gagliardi has been able to create wonderful works of art. He has had exhibitions at some of the U.S.A.'s leading galleries and his Etch A Sketch® version of Leonardo da Vinci's Mona Lisa has been valued at $10,000!

Leonardo da Vinci's The Mona Lisa, *by Jeff Gagliardi.*

Amazingly, Gagliardi never had an Etch A Sketch® as a child but developed an interest while playing with his nephew's. He first tried it out seriously while at art college in New York in the early 1970s. He says: "I did a drawing of the Taj Mahal, complete with reflecting pools. Quite frankly, I didn't think it was a big deal, but my family wouldn't let me erase it. From that point on it became apparent that I had some sort of gift for drawing on this little toy. People would walk past the serious work I was doing as a painter and want to see the Etch A Sketch® drawings."

Since then he has re-created details from Michelangelo's Sistine Chapel and copied paintings by Van Gogh.

His work requires enormous patience. Pictures are drawn by twiddling two knobs, which operate a stylus across the underside of the glass, scraping a line in the aluminum coating. The toy's system operates horizontally, which means that to create a vertical portrait—as in *The Mona Lisa* —Gagliardi has to draw sidewise!

MAGIC Etch A Sketch® SCREEN

Jeff's sketch of Grant Wood's American Gothic.

Cash Snatch During an art exhibition in Norway, artist Jan Christensen had his work, *Relative Value*, made out of 100,000 kroner ($16,300) worth of bank notes, stolen out of its frame by bandits in a gallery robbery.

Arctic Study Kristin Laidre, a researcher at the University of Washington, studies the depths of inaccessible parts of the Arctic Ocean by strapping scientific instruments to narwhals.

Marathon Effort Richard Takata of Toronto, Ontario, Canada, ran a marathon on seven different continents in just under 30 days in 2007. He took part in marathons in New Zealand, U.S.A., Egypt, Spain, Antarctica, Argentina, and Cyprus. Before his first race he had more than a foot of hair cut off that had taken him four years to grow.

Sleep Wash Mrs. Xu, of Wuhan City, China, regularly washes the family's clothes in the middle of the night—while she is still asleep. She has been sleepwalking for more than ten years and her husband has had to put locks on the door to stop her leaving the house and washing neighbors' clothes.

Shakespeare Recital In February 2004, more than 150 members of the Wellesley College, Massachusetts, Shakespeare Society read aloud the complete works of Shakespeare (a total of 39 plays, 154 sonnets and poetry) in 22 hours 5 minutes.

Mule Mission In 2007, Rod Maday of Boy River, Minnesota, rode his four-year-old mule, named Henry, 1,500 mi (2,415 km) to Gilette, Wyoming, in search of work. Maday, who had lost his driver's license ten years previously, rode up to 70 mi (112 km) a day and made the six-week trek in full cowboy gear.

Failed Crossing In March 2007, a man tried to cross the fast-flowing Niagara River from Canada into the U.S.A. on an inflatable air mattress. Hearing the man's screams, guards at the Ontario Power Generation plant at Chippawa plucked him from the water as he was being swept toward Niagara Falls on a small ice floe while still clinging to the mattress.

Thin Set The Japanese company Sony unveiled a new flat-screen TV set in 2007 that is about the same width as a coin.

One Size Fits All

Indian designer Shazneen Chiniwala made a dress that was an incredible 70 ft (21 m) long for a fashion week in Mumbai in March 2007—that's big enough to fit more than a dozen ordinary-sized women. It took the 26-year-old two months to finish the dress, which was made of plastic and colored jute.

In order to make the dress, Shazneen had to transport her sewing machine up to the terrace of the building. There she had to construct a tent to protect herself from the fierce heat.

Shazneen's dress was unveiled on a giant hanger—made of metal pipes—from the front of the Sunder Mashal building on Mumbai's Marine Drive.

Unicycle Marathon

Sam Wakeling, a 22-year-old student at Aberystwyth University in Wales, traveled 282 mi (455 km) on a unicycle in a single day in September 2007. The computer science undergraduate was so at home riding his customized unicycle, with 36-in (90-cm) wheels, around the university's running track that he covered the first 105 mi (170 km) without dismounting. He eventually completed 1,141 laps at an average speed of nearly 13 mph (21 km/h). In 2005, he had ridden a one-wheeler from the most southwesterly point of England (Land's End) to the northeastern tip of Scotland (John O'Groats)—a distance of 874 mi (1,406 km).

Mommy Dearest

Sisters Josephine and Valmai Lamas of London, England, have kept their mother Annie in a mortician's freezer for ten years—regularly replacing her cosmetics. Instead of burying her, they have spent more than $25,000 to keep her in cold storage so that they can visit her every weekend.

Compulsory Golf

Xiamen University in Fujian, China, requires all its business, law, economics, and computer students to take golf lessons.

Vacuum Shoes A new pair of shoes has been invented that vacuums as you walk. The "Shoover" has a tiny rechargeable vacuum cleaner inside the base that collects dust while the wearer walks around the house.

Favorite Jersey David Witthoft, a young Green Bay Packers' football fan from Ridgefield, Connecticut, was so excited by his 2003 Christmas gift—a Packers' jersey with Brett Favre's No.4—that he wore it every day for four years. By the end of 2007, 11-year-old David had worn the jersey for more than 1,450 consecutive days.

Finger Fun Eighteen hundred people, ranging from two-year-old children to senior citizens, created a 20,000-sq-ft (1,858-sq-m) finger painting in just one day at New Paltz, New York, in September 2007.

Runs in Family Thirteen sons and daughters of Janet Weisse of Oshkosh, Wisconsin—aged between 33 and 54—took part in the 2007 Fox Cities Marathon at Appleton. All 13 completed the course.

Gnom-adic The police station at Springfield, Oregon, was overrun by lawn gnomes in 2007. The 75 plastic and porcelain ornaments were recovered by officers from the front lawn of a house where they had been placed as a prank after being stolen from gardens around the town.

Hairy Eye Summitt, a dog living in Owensboro, Kentucky, has had hairs growing from the tissue of her right eye since she was a puppy.

Line Art

The famous portrait of George Washington that graces the front of every $1 bill and Emanual Leutze's well-known painting, "Washington Crossing the Delaware," are both re-created here in a 1932 drawing by Forest Ages McGinn—drawn in a single continuous line without lifting the pencil from the page!

Green Sheep A flock of 250 sheep in a Romanian village suddenly turned green overnight. Veterinarians discovered that the color change had been caused by a limestone solution that shepherd Cristinel Florea had given to the animals in order to cure a skin disease.

Field Art In a clover field at the Thomas Bull Memorial Park in New York, artist Roger Baker mowed an image of a Purple Heart medal, which is given to U.S. servicemen who are killed or wounded in action, that measured an astonishing 850,000 sq ft (79,000 sq m).

Multi-task Toilet The prize in a 2007 contest held by a U.S. plumbing company was an HDTV, DVD player, game system, laptop computer, digital music player, exercise machine, cooling fan, and refrigerator—all connected to a toilet.

Crash Premonition After suffering nightmares on ten successive nights about an impending passenger-plane crash involving an American Airlines DC-10, David Booth, a 23-year-old office manager from Cincinnati, Ohio, reported his fears to the relevant authorities on May 22, 1979. Three days later, an American Airlines DC-10 crashed at Chicago's O'Hare International Airport, killing 273 people.

Heavy Hedgehog

A hedgehog found in Surrey, England, weighed four times the size of a normal hedgehog. George tipped the scales at a whopping 4 lb 14 oz (2.2 kg) and was so fat that he had to be placed on a crash diet by an animal center.

328

Roadkill Toys

A British soft toy company has launched a range of animal characters that have all been run over. Twitch the roadkill raccoon has his tongue hanging out, one eyeball smashed in, and comes with a zipper that spills his innards and an opaque plastic body bag to keep out maggots. A label attached to his toe gives details of his grisly death. Other roadkill victims include Splodge the hedgehog and Pop the weasel.

Homemade Reactor

Thiago Olson, a 17-year-old high school student from Oakland Township, Michigan, built a functioning fusion reactor in his garage. It took him two years and more than 1,000 hours of research.

Guitar Gathering

In June 2007, Kansas City radio station KYYS (99.7FM) assembled a ballpark full of 1,721 guitarists—ages ranging from five to 60—to play Deep Purple's song "Smoke on the Water" simultaneously.

Chamber Music
Police in Bolzano, Italy, seized a toilet from an art gallery because it played Italy's national anthem while flushing.

Space Growth
Astronauts grow taller by several inches while in space, but gravity shrinks them to their normal size when they come back to earth.

Tuk to the Road

Two British women drove a little pink tuk-tuk (a three-wheeled motorized taxi, popular in Thailand) 12,000 mi (19,000 km) through 12 countries from Thailand to England in 2006. Antonia Bolingbroke-Kent and Jo Huxster, both 27, took three months to complete the journey in their tuk-tuk.

"We stopped at a salt lake in Xinjiang, northwest China, for a few hours of relaxation—the salty water making us look like this!"

Raising money for charity, they traveled through Thailand, Laos, China, Kazakhstan, Russia, Ukraine, Poland, the Czech Republic, Germany, Belgium, and France before finally reaching England. En route they passed such sights as the Great Wall of China and the Gobi Desert.

Although they had to repair two snapped accelerator cables and a failed suspension, the three-wheeler, with a top speed of 70 mph (115 km/h), stood up well to the test and averaged 150 mi (240 km) a day.

Huxster had thought up the idea for the adventure four years earlier during a visit to Thailand. "I was just driving around Bangkok with two friends, and the tuk-tuk driver let me sit in the front to pretend I was driving. I thought, 'One day I will drive one of these back to England.' And that's how it happened."

Wandering sheep were just one of the problems the women had to deal with on their drive across Asia.

331

Fridgehenge Falls

In Santa Fe, New Mexico, artist Adam Horowitz created a replica of Stonehenge from more than 100 old refrigerators. The refrigerators, stacked and arranged in a ring like the famous English landmark, became a popular tourist attraction. They stood for nearly a decade until, in 2007, the 80-ft (24-m) structure was demolished by a mixture of high winds and the city council.

Jailhouse Croc

A saltwater crocodile that measured 7 ft 9 in (2.4 m) was captured by Australian police and kept in a cell overnight after it had threatened local fishermen. Officers in Nhulunbuy, Northern Territory, put the croc in an unused cell at the town's police station and hosed it down with water throughout the night before taking it to a farm in the morning.

Sock Riddle

The Bureau of Missing Socks is the first website devoted exclusively to solving the riddle of what happens to single missing socks—with explanations from the occult to aliens.

Twisted Trees

The tree circus of Gilroy Gardens features one-of-a-kind tree sculptures—with various grafts, twists, and bends—all grown over 30 years by a farmer in California.

Waterfall Plunge

Tyler Bradt, 21, of Missoula, Montana, successfully paddled his kayak over a thunderous 107-ft (33-m) waterfall in September 2007. He made the daring drop at the Alexandra Falls on the Hay River in Canada's Northwest Territories—and landed at the bottom without flipping, even though part of the cockpit of his kayak exploded on impact.

The Law is an Ass

The chief witness in a 2007 court case in Dallas, Texas, was a donkey. Buddy was led into the courtroom to help resolve a dispute between two neighbors.

Think Small

Korean nanotechnology researchers used lasers and microscopic materials to create a copy of Rodin's sculpture *The Thinker* that is only twice the size of a red blood cell.

One-note Gig

The White Stripes finished their 2007 Candian tour by playing a show just one note long. Jack and Meg White took to the stage in St. John's, Newfoundland, played a C-sharp accompanied by a bang of the cymbals, announced that they had now officially played in every province and territory in Canada, and left the stage. Fans had been warned that the show would be just one-note long, but still hundreds turned up. Later, the band played a full-length set elsewhere in the city. Previous venues on their quirky tour had included a bowling alley in Saskatoon and a Winnipeg Transit bus.

Coughed Bullet

In October 2007, a month after he was shot in the mouth, Austin Askins of Liberty Lake, Washington, miraculously coughed up the bullet that surgeons previously had been unable to remove.

Card Tower

Using no tape or glue, Bryan Berg built a freestanding tower of playing cards measuring 25 ft 9½ in (7.86 m) high at the 2007 Texas State Fair in Dallas. The tower, which took Berg five weeks to complete, consisted of 1,800 decks of cards and was restricted only by the height of the building in which he was working.

Unwanted Gift Owing to a postal mix-up, Frank and Ludivine Larmande of Cascade, Michigan, accidentally received a preserved human liver and part of a head in the mail, both intended for a lab.

Lost in Translation

After having what she thought was the word "mum" tattooed on her back in Chinese letters, 19-year-old Charlene Williams was shocked to find that her tattoo actually said "Friend from hell." The mother-of-one from Dorset, England, did not realize that Chinese letters change their meaning when joined together. She has since had the tattoo covered over with a new design.

Sibling Birth A Canadian girl could give birth to her own brother or sister. The girl's mother, Melanie Boivin of Montréal, Quebec, has frozen her eggs so that Flavie, who cannot have children naturally, can later conceive.

Brick Dragon

A model dragon at the LEGOLAND® Windsor theme park in England has been built from nearly one million Lego® bricks. The "Ice Dragon" measures 30 ft (9 m) in length, weighs nearly 3 tons, and took 2,200 hours to build. It is so big that it had to be built in nine sections before being hoisted into place.

Costly Error Instead of sending out just one winning ticket, a marketing company in Roswell, New Mexico, mistakenly dispatched 50,000 scratch-off tickets that declared the ticket holder the winner of the $1,000 grand prize. The company blamed a typographical error.

Plastic Fantastic Luis Torres, a Metropolitan Transit Authority worker who lives in New York City, crafts sculptures from the transit credit cards that he collects during his day-job.

Discarded Gear A North American website shows pictures of clothing that have been discarded on sidewalks across the world. These include T-shirts, sneakers, baseball caps, and even a prosthetic leg in Singapore.

Dead Fish Millions of anchovies mysteriously washed ashore near Colunga, Spain, in September 2006, leaving the beach covered with three tons of dead fish.

Super Sleuth In just 25 years of searching for supernovae, Robert Evans of Australia has found more with his backyard telescope than all the astronomers in the 400 years before him.

The Best Medicine Scientists from Vanderbilt University in Nashville, Tennessee, believe that laughing for 15 minutes a day can help people lose weight. They say daily laughter can burn off up to 5 lb (2.3 kg) of fat a year.

Insured Eyes Cross-eyed silent movie star Ben Turpin was insured for $500,000 against the possibility of his eyes ever becoming normal again.

Restricted View In the 1760s, French astronomer Guillaume Le Gentil prepared for eight years to record the transit of Venus across the face of the Sun —only to have clouds block his view on his last chance to see it for a century.

Zombie Dogs In trials to develop suspended animation for humans, scientists in the U.S.A. have managed to bring dead dogs back to life. The Safar Center for Resuscitation Research in Pittsburgh, Pennsylvania, rendered the dogs clinically dead by draining their veins of blood and replacing it with an ice-cold salt solution. The animals stopped breathing, but three hours later they were revived with no ill effects after their blood was put back.

Solar Heating A Chinese farmer obtains hot water from a device made of beer bottles connected by lengths of hosepipe. Ma Yanjun from Shaanxi Province, has attached 66 beer bottles to a board on the roof of his house. Sunlight heats the water as it passes slowly through the bottles and it eventually flows into his bathroom as hot water.

Drunk Rider A German man rode his horse into the foyer of a bank to sleep off his hangover. Wolfgang Heinrich of Wiesenberg had been riding his horse, Sammy, when he stopped to have a few drinks. Too drunk to ride home, he used his bank card to open up a nearby bank foyer and spent the night there with Sammy.

Root Carver Micro-artist Shelvaraj from Nagapattinam, India, carves tiny ornate figures from the roots of trees. Shelvaraj, who has been pursuing his art since his teens, specializes in religious figures and has carved a row of elephants, ranging in size from a minute speck to ³⁄₈ in (1 cm) tall.

Alarm Mimic A pet parrot that loves to imitate sounds helped save a Muncie, Indiana, family from a house fire in 2007 —by mimicking a smoke alarm. As flames ripped through their home, Shannon Conwell and his son slept through the real smoke alarm but were woken by Peanut the parrot's squawking imitation of it.

Still Life Gisela Leibold of Munich, Germany, is blind to all movement and sees things only as a series of still frames.

Dream Team An Australian sports fan has quit his job, sold his house in Sydney, and moved his wife and two young children to the U.S.A. —just so that he can follow the Green Bay Packers. Wayne Scullino's love affair started when he was 15 and a friend gave him a videotape of a football game between the Packers and the Minnesota Vikings.

Judgment Day Immediately after being sentenced to five years in prison for theft, David Kite of Belleville, Illinois, was married in a civil wedding ceremony— by the same judge that presided over his criminal trial.

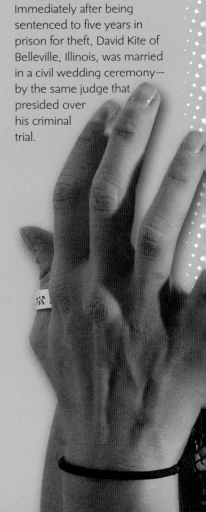

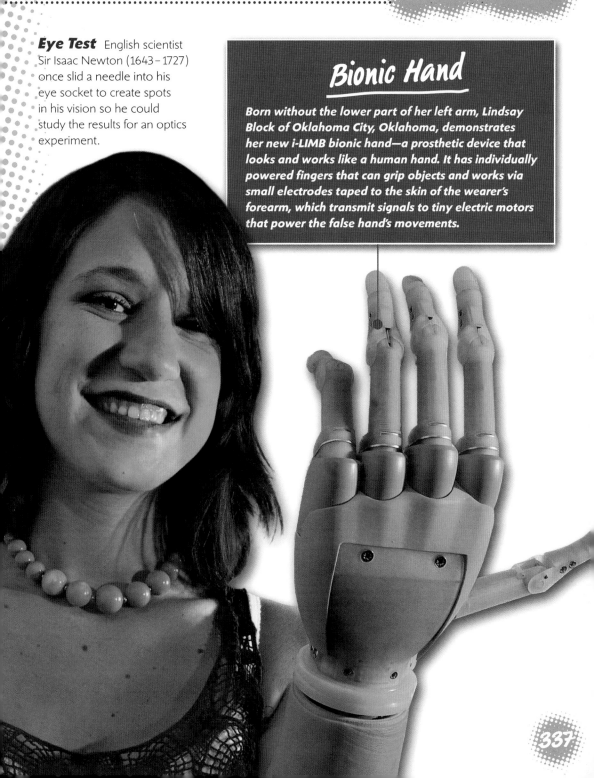

Eye Test English scientist Sir Isaac Newton (1643–1727) once slid a needle into his eye socket to create spots in his vision so he could study the results for an optics experiment.

Bionic Hand

Born without the lower part of her left arm, Lindsay Block of Oklahoma City, Oklahoma, demonstrates her new i-LIMB bionic hand—a prosthetic device that looks and works like a human hand. It has individually powered fingers that can grip objects and works via small electrodes taped to the skin of the wearer's forearm, which transmit signals to tiny electric motors that power the false hand's movements.

Boar Island

A 25
wild
Babe
of lux
own p
in the
Babe I
island
only tv
inhabit
Abbott
Wiethu
feed hin
apples, c
and wate
along the
go for a s
further re
enjoys a l
he has onl
day becau
more he ca
a bit boiste

Head-spinner

Eighteen-year-old Aichi Ono of Japan can do more than 100 spins in a minute—and he can do them standing on his head. Using his body as momentum, he demonstrated his remarkable head-spinning skills at a shopping mall in Hong Kong in December 2007.

Robert Ripley

Seen here in the 1940s drawing one of his famous cartoons, Robert Ripley used to receive thousands of letters from devoted fans every week, all hoping to have their unbelievable facts included in his cartoon strip.

ALL THE BEST! from Ripley

Believe I — or N

Huge Hairball
A barber for more than 50 years, Henry Coffer of Charleston, Missouri, has been collecting customers' clippings and has turned them into a huge hairball weighing more than 160 lb (73 kg).

Climbing Fanatic
Cheered on by 200 supporters, an Indian man scaled a 2,100-ft (640-m) hill 101 times in the space of 20 hours in August 2007. Bank employee Girish Kulkarni from Pune has been practicing running up hills for five years.

Belt Convention
The Niagara Aerospace Museum in Niagara Falls, New York, holds an annual convention dedicated to rocket belts—jet packs that can propel a person into the air.

Bullet Halted
Debbie Bingham of St. Petersburg, Florida, was struck by a stray bullet during a New Year's celebration—but was saved from serious injury when it lodged in her bra strap.

Kitty Cops
Thai police chiefs have come up with a new way to discipline officers who break rules—making them wear a Hello Kitty armband. The bright pink armband has a Hello Kitty motif and two embroidered hearts and is designed to shame the wearer.

Yodel-ay!
More than 1,000 American yodelers converge on Salt Lake City, Utah, each June for the Swiss Singing and Yodeling Festival.

Belated Graduation
A Utah woman received her high school diploma in 2007—at age 94. Leah Moore Harris Fullmer missed her graduation ceremony from Provo High School in 1931 because of illness and did not pick up her diploma, but her son persuaded the school to trace her records and present it to her before her 95th birthday.

Naked Shoot
More than 600 naked people were photographed as a living sculpture on a Swiss glacier in 2007. The photo shoot was arranged by New York artist Spencer Tunick to raise awareness of the effect of climate change on shrinking Swiss glaciers.

Balloon Bart

Here are the Simpsons as you have never seen them before—made entirely out of balloons. They are the work of Washington State balloon artist Adam Lee, whose other creations include balloon likenesses of Jay Leno, Austin Powers, Bill Gates, Martha Stewart, and the Statue of Liberty.

Accurate Tipster

Four days before the 1959 Kentucky Derby, psychic Spencer Thornton of Nashville, Tennessee, wrote his prediction for the first three horses to finish on a piece of paper. The paper was sealed, unread, in an envelope and placed in a vault of the Third National Bank. The vault could be unlocked only by a combination of three keys, kept by two vice-presidents and its custodian—and it was not until two days after the race that the three men opened the vault and the envelope to reveal that Thornton's prediction was 100 percent correct.

Speedy Sofa

A gardener from London, England, hit speeds of 92 mph (148 km/h) in May 2007—driving a sofa! Marek Turowski demonstrated the go-faster furniture at an airfield in Leicestershire. The rear-engined, street legal, high-speed sofa was built by Edd China, who has also designed an 87 mph (140 km/h) office desk.

Late Return

Robert Nuranen of Hancock, Michigan, paid $171 in late fees when he returned a library book 47 years after he had borrowed it.

Painted Pigs

Art students in China have been painting live pigs to create colorful images as the animals roam in a field. The students from Sichuan Fine Arts Institute chose pigs because they represent harmony and happiness.

Cloud Sprays

British professors John Latham and Stephen Salter have designed a fleet of yachts that would pump fine particles of seawater into clouds, thereby thickening them to reflect more of the sun's rays back into space and so reducing the impact of global warming.

Shoe Sniffer

A man in Nagoya, Japan, was arrested in 2006 for stealing 5,000 pairs of shoes, which he took only to smell them.

Inspired by Nature

Scientists from Northwestern University, Evanston, Illinois, have created a new super-sticky material based on the natural adhesive powers of geckos and mussels. The material, called "geckel," is effective because it is made from coating fibrous silicone—a substance similar in structure to a gecko's foot—with a polymer that replicates the powerful "glue" used by mussels.

Lizard Smuggler

In 2007, a man named Jereme James, from Los Angeles, California, was accused of smuggling three rare iguana lizards into the U.S.A.— by hiding them inside his prosthetic leg. He allegedly hollowed out a secret compartment inside his false leg and used it to smuggle Banded iguanas from Fiji. According to the prosecution, James had previously admitted to selling the rare lizards for up to $10,000 each.

Speed Surfer

A Swedish pensioner is able to surf the Internet many thousand times faster than anybody else in the world, thanks to a connection installed by her son. Seventy-five-year-old Sigbritt Lothberg of Karlstad has a 40-gigabits-per-second connection, so she can download a full-length movie in less than two seconds.

Scrap Elephants

Jim Powers of Gage, Oklahoma, has created giant insects, life-size elephants, and dinosaurs out of scrap metal from cars.

Light Movers

All electrons and protons moving through the wires, cables, and transistors of the Internet have a combined weight of less than 2 oz (57 g).

Cymbal of Courage

Despite being born without lower arms and a badly deformed leg, which was later amputated, 15-year-old Cornel Hrisca-Munn of Whittington, England, beat 420 able-bodied youngsters to take second place in a national drumming competition. He uses straps to attach the drumsticks to his upper arms and a false leg so that he can operate the bass pedal.

Ant Intelligence

Scientists from the University of Bristol, England, have observed that army ants form living bridges to help get jobs done. When ants are foraging on rough ground, some of them use their own bodies to plug tiny holes and allow their fellow ants to walk over them. It was even discovered that individual ants choose which of them is the best size to lie across a particular hole.

Lite Supper

Artist Mark Beekman from Charlestown, Pennsylvania, used more than 125,000 Lite-Brite pegs to create a 1:9-scale version of Leonardo da Vinci's painting The Last Supper that measured 5 ft (1.5 m) tall by 10 ft (3 m) wide.

Top Brass A band of German musicians staged a concert on a Bolivian mountain top in 2007. They played instruments at the summit of the Acotango Volcano for 30 minutes at an altitude of 19,855 ft (6,052 m).

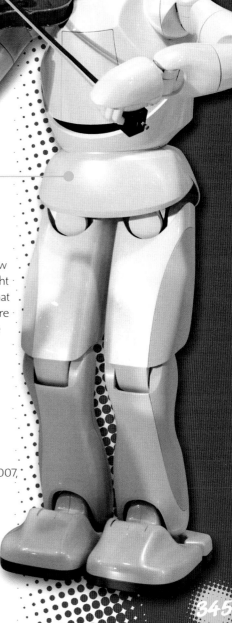

Robotic Violinist

A Japanese company has built a robot that can actually play the violin. Created by the Toyota Motor Corporation, the robot stands 5-ft-tall (1.5-m) and has 17 joints in its hands and arms to give it human-like dexterity. At the product launch, it used its mechanical fingers to push the strings correctly while bowing with its other arm to give a near-perfect rendition of Edward Elgar's "Pomp and Circumstance."

Name Change Scott Wiese of Forsyth, Illinois, bet that if his favorite team, the Chicago Bears, lost the Super Bowl in 2007, he would change his name to that of the opposing team's quarterback. The Bears did lose to the Indianapolis Colts and so Wiese filed to have his name legally changed to the Colts' quarterback—Peyton Manning.

Dazzling Sun In just one second, the Sun produces 35 million times the amount of electricity used annually by the whole of the U.S.A.

Truth Glasses A New York company has brought out a pair of sunglasses that can tell whether people are speaking the truth. The lie detector eyeglasses can monitor conversations in real time and provide an LED display of the truthfulness of people around the wearer with 95 percent accuracy.

Ghost Ship In April 2007, a yacht was found off the coast of Australia with its emergency equipment intact and dinner on the table—but its three-member crew gone without a trace.

Crystal Curiosities

Dutch artist Hans van Bentem makes beautiful crystal chandeliers in the most amazing, avant-garde designs—ranging from a Champagne bottle to a skull and crossbones. Abandoning the traditional chandelier shape, he has also created chandeliers in the design of a globe, a spider, an easel and brushes, a heraldic lion, a fighter plane, a seahorse, a violin, a pipe, and even a gun. He says he finds his inspiration in art history, comic strips, and the world of modern communication. Each piece takes up to two months to create and sells from $16,000.

Albino Birth

At Jamestown, North Dakota, in 2007, White Cloud, North America's only female albino bison, gave birth to an albino calf, named Dakota Miracle. The chances of this happening naturally in the wild would be one in ten million!

Wide Choice There were so many candidates in Bulgaria's 2007 local elections that the ballot papers were 6 ½ ft (2 m) long.

Slim Fit Artez Kenyetta Knox escaped jail in Gary, Indiana, by taking his clothes off and amazingly squeezing through the cell door's food-tray slot.

Nonstop Ride George Hood, of Aurora, Illinois, rode a stationary bike nonstop for nearly five days in 2007. He finally stopped pedaling at 111 hours 11 minutes 11 seconds because the time was easy to remember. He said that he started having hallucinations about eating donuts toward the end of his multi-marathon ride.

Robot Fly Scientists at Harvard University have created a life-size robotic fly. Weighing only 0.002 oz (60 mg) with a wingspan of 1 ³/₁₆ in (3 cm), the minute robot's movements are modeled on those of a real fly. It is hoped that the mechanical insects might one day be used as spies or for detecting dangerous chemicals.

Ice Queen

In 2007, sculptors Ivo Piazza and Rainer Kasslatter created a huge sculpture of Marilyn Monroe—from ice. It earned them first prize in an annual ice-sculpture contest in Austria.

Sheep Accommodation

A man in Apex, North Carolina, shared his house with 80 sheep. David Watts lived upstairs while the flock, which he considered to be pets, lived downstairs. He sometimes took selected sheep for walks on a leash around the neighborhood.

Cow Crusher

A couple driving through Washington State on vacation to celebrate their first wedding anniversary miraculously survived after a cow weighing 600 lb (270 kg) fell off a cliff 200 ft (60 m) high and landed on their moving minivan. Charles and Linda Everson from Westland, Michigan, escaped unhurt by the incident, but their van was badly damaged and the windshield smashed. A shocked Mr. Everson said: "It was just bam—you just saw something come down and hit the hood!"

See-through Frog!

Scientists in Japan have bred transparent frogs whose organs, blood vessels, and eggs can be seen clearly through their skins. Experts say the frogs will be invaluable for research into diseases such as cancer, because scientists can study organ growth and development without having to dissect the frog... which is good news for the frog, too.

Multi-purpose

The Wenger company of Basel, Switzerland, has produced a Swiss Army Knife with no fewer than 85 different tools capable of performing more than 100 functions. The knife weighs 2 lb 11 oz (1.2 kg), is just under 9 in (23 cm) wide, and its features include seven blades and three types of pliers, plus screwdrivers, saws, wrenches, tweezers, a can opener, and a key ring.

TOP 10 UNIQUE FEATURES OF THE KNIFE

1. Bicycle chain rivet setter
2. Cupped cigar cutter with double-honed edges
3. Fish scaler, hook disgorger, line guide
4. Laser pointer with 300-ft (90-m) range
5. Golf divot repair tool
6. Nail file, nail cleaner
7. Tire tread gauge
8. Toothpick
9. Golf club face cleaner
10. Watch caseback opening tool

Subway Sprint

Armed only with beef jerky and water, college friends Don Badaczewski and Matt Green rode the entire New York subway system nonstop in just over 24 hours in August 2006. They set off from Queens and finished in the Bronx after passing through all 468 stations on the city's 26 lines... with no bathroom breaks. Don had the idea for the underground adventure after reading about riding the subway on the Internet.

Mail Tower

Artist Anne Cohen from Newcastle, England, turned a year's worth of unwanted junk mail into a garden sculpture. She put all the junk mail she received on a large metal spike outside her front door and by the end of 2007 the tower was more than 6 ft (1.8 m) tall.

Prolific Author

At her most prolific, British romantic author Barbara Cartland completed a novel every two weeks. Altogether, she published 723 novels in her 70-year career!

Religious Sign?

Visitors flocked to the home of Eric Nathaniel in Port Blair, Andaman Islands, India, in 2007, after two of his paintings of Jesus began to drip red fluid. Experts suggested it was more likely to be red paint from the pictures melting in the humidity, than blood.

Invincible Opponent

Computer scientists at the University of Alberta, Canada, have created a program for playing checkers that cannot be beaten. The program's name is Chinook.

Ice Course

Charlie Gandy of Colorado built an 18-hole golf course on the ice of the Twin Lakes Reservoir and used microchips in the white balls so that radar could keep track of them.

Synthetic Trees

A U.S. scientist has invented an artificial tree to clean up the atmosphere and combat global warming. Dr. Klaus Lackner of Columbia University says his trees would be a thousand times more effective than living trees at cleaning the air, and that just one could remove 40,000 tons of carbon dioxide in a year.

Electric Charge

Human sweat is able to create an electrical charge in coins that have two different alloys—like the Canadian Toonie or the 1 and 2 euro coins.

Nice Profit

In 2005, Ed Lee of Merrimack, New Hampshire, sold a 1913 nickel coin for $4.15 million—that's a staggering 83 million times its original value!

Rampant Rat

A prehistoric skull found in a museum in Montevideo, Uruguay, has led scientists to conclude that a rodent the size of a cow roamed the forests of South America four million years ago. The monster rat stood 5 ft (1.5 m) tall, was 10 ft (3 m) long and weighed almost a ton, making it 14 times bigger than any rodent alive today.

Space Images

Natalie Meilinger of Chicago, Illinois, found that instead of turning on the TV for the latest news on NASA's 2007 Atlantis space shuttle, all she had to do was switch on her baby's monitor. The monitor mysteriously picked up black-and-white video images from inside the shuttle.

Cardboard Cars

Chris Gilmour makes full-sized replicas of cars, bicycles, and motor scooters out of cardboard. Using nothing more than cardboard and glue—and with no supporting wood or metal framework—the English-born artist creates amazingly lifelike models. His "Pussy Galore" car, exhibited in New York in 2006, is an exact replica of James Bond's famous Aston Martin, right down to tire-slashers, machine guns, and rocket launchers. Although made of cardboard, it is valued at $30,000.

Gilmour's cardboard typewriter is so realistic that visitors to his exhibitions are often tempted to press the keys.

Gilmour uses cardboard partly because it is so easy to find—he collects discarded pieces from dumpsters near his base in Udine, Italy. Sometimes he even leaves the original printing, tape, and labels on to emphasize the fact that he is creating coveted items from what is merely waste material.

His first big piece was a cardboard cow—"to replace the cattle destroyed by B.S.E., so that the fields don't look empty"—and he has since created such diverse everyday objects as a grand piano, guitars, a coffee set, a wheelchair, and a typewriter.

He also built a series of small churches from cardboard packaging. "I needed lots of different packets," he says, "so we bought a lot of things just because of the packaging. Buying one of every item in the supermarket was fun but it did leave us with a cupboard full of food we didn't much like and couldn't tell what it was because I'd taken the wrappings off!"

Chris Gilmour's cardboard replica of a Fiat 500 car extends way beyond the simple exterior.

Daring Juggler

Nathan Zorchak, an American entertainer based in Brighton, England, can not only juggle scythes and bowling balls, but also three live chainsaws.

Shot by Dog A hunter in Iowa was shot in the leg by his own dog. James Harris of Tama was hunting pheasants in October 2007 when his dog stepped on his shotgun and tripped the trigger, dispatching more than 100 pellets into his master's calf.

Long Note In September 2007, saxophonist Aaron Bing of Jacksonville, Florida, held a single, continuous low G note on his saxophone for 39 minutes 40 seconds while standing on a windy New York City street.

Pigeon Control Scientists in Shandong, China, have learned to control the flight of pigeons by implanting electrodes in the birds' brains. The researchers have designed a computer system that allows them to instruct the pigeons to fly left, right, up, or down.

Converted Cart Bill Lauver of Middleburg, Pennsylvania, converted an electric golf cart into a remote-controlled snowplow so that he could clear his driveway of snow from the comfort of his living room.

Tiny Scissors In 2003, Chen Yu Pei of China, designed a pair of stainless steel scissors that measured just 0.068 in (1.75 mm) long and 0.054 in (1.38 mm) wide—and they actually worked!

Card Confusion Manhattan accountant Frank Van Buren ordered two replacement credit cards but received 2,000 of them instead—all with his name and account number. It took him hours to shred the surplus cards.

Gator Wrestling

For $100 you can buy a day's tuition in... alligator wrestling. Colorado Gators, near Alamosa, is an alligator farm where people can learn to wrestle reptiles up to 11 ft (3.4 m) long and weighing 600 lb (270 kg). The key to success is a stealthy approach, although even experienced wrestler Jay Young gets bitten at least once a year. "These are not mild-mannered animals," he says, "and if they're breathing, they're in a bad mood."

Half Share To protest against his pending divorce, a 43-year-old man from Sonneberg, Germany, cut his house in half with a chainsaw and then used a forklift truck to take his half away.

Moon Pull Even though the Moon is 239,000 mi (385,000 km) away, it has hundreds of times more gravitational pull than the action of a person hugging you.

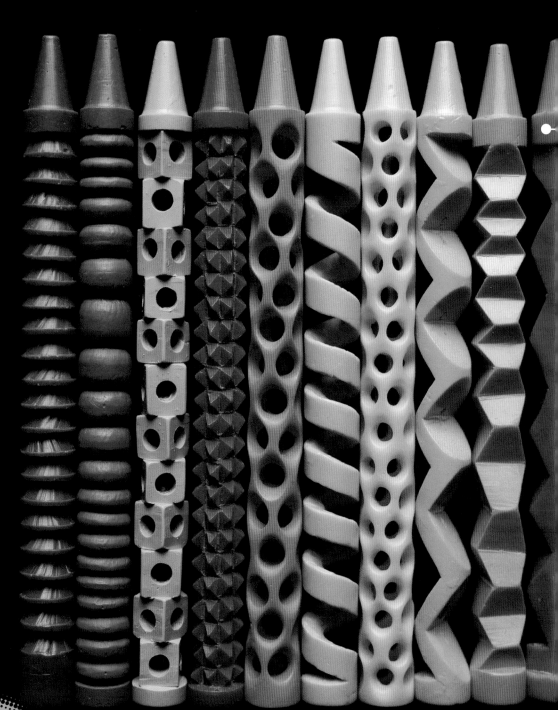

Crayon Sculpture

No school bag ever housed a set of crayons like these, but U.S. sculptor Pete Goldlust has turned art on its head by carving intricate designs into ordinary wax crayons.

Baboon's Butt Matthew Roby from Lancashire, England, creates characters from old bits of machinery and scrap metal. Nothing goes to waste—he even used the bright orange ballcocks from a toilet system for a baboon's butt!

Carousel Contest Four couples spent seven days on a rotating carousel in Xiamen, China, in an endurance contest to win a house. They had to stay on the fairground horses to eat, drink, and sleep—and were allowed to climb off only for toilet breaks. The contestants wore safety belts so that they did not fall off their horses while sleeping.

Dual Purpose Gala Contemplating the Mediterranean Sea Which at Twenty Meters Becomes a Portrait of Abraham Lincoln, painted by Spanish artist Salvador Dali in 1976, is both a painting of his wife and a pixilated portrait of U.S. President Abraham Lincoln!

Slow Start Invented by King Camp Gillette, the safety razor first went on sale in the U.S.A. in 1903, but only 51 were sold in the first 12 months. In 1904, Gillette sold 90,000!

Yard Theft In May 2006, a thief stole an entire front yard from a house in Adelanto, California, taking the grass, plants, and even the sprinkler system.

Croc Frock A woman tried to cross the border between Egypt and Gaza with three crocodiles strapped to her waist. The 20-in-long (50-cm) crocodiles had their jaws tied shut with string and were concealed under a loose robe, but the woman's "strangely fat" appearance alerted guards at the crossing.

Birthday Reminder Vanda Jones of Penygroes, Wales, had the birthdays of all her five children tattooed on her arm so that she could be sure never to forget them.

Mountain Dash Austria's Marcus Stoeckl, reached a speed of 130.7 mph (210 km/h) while traveling down a snow-covered mountain in Chile—on a mountain bike—in September 2007. His icy dash made him the fastest man on two wheels without an engine.

Leg Hair Medical student Wes Pemberton from Tyler, Texas, has a leg hair that is 5 in (13 cm) long. He spotted the stray strand growing from his left thigh in the summer of 2007 and began nurturing it by washing it daily with shampoo and conditioner.

Special Goats A U.S. biotech company breeds goats that produce a nerve gas antidote in their milk.

Slow Seasons Because the planet Uranus is tilted to 98 degrees on its axis (meaning that it is practically lying on its side), it has the longest seasons in the solar system—winters and summers each last for the equivalent of 21 Earth years.

The Hills are Alive The city of Salzburg, Austria, has a cable channel that plays the movie *The Sound of Music* 24 hours a day, every day of the year!

Counting Chicken

A hen in Shenyang, China, can apparently do simple arithmetic. The bird's owner says the chicken can peck the answer to simple calculations when he points to numbers on a board and asks her questions. She also knows and can point to the 26 letters of the alphabet when asked to do so.

算 算 数

$8 + 2 = 10$

$4 = 5$

$\times 3 = 9$

$5 = 2$

Flying Hovercraft

An inventor from New Zealand has devised a hovercraft with wings that flies 6 ft (1.8 m) above the water. Rudy Heeman has spent 11 years designing the Hoverwing, a two-passenger vehicle with an ability to lift off that leaves other water-based craft in its wake. It sets off like an ordinary hovercraft but on reaching its top speed of 60 mph (97 km/h), its wings can be extended, enabling it to take to the air.

Giant Coin A 220-lb (100-kg) gold coin the size of a pizza was produced by the Royal Canadian Mint in 2007. Worth $2 million, the coin featured maple leaves on one side and Queen Elizabeth II on the other.

Memory Loss British musician Clive Wearing cannot remember anything from 1985 to the present day owing to a brain infection, but he can remember everything prior to 1985.

Wooden Horse Saimir Strati of Albania, has created a mosaic of a leaping horse that is 13 ft (4 m) long—from more than half a million toothpicks. It took him 40 days to construct, working 13 hours a day.

Computer Flotsam Hundreds of computer monitors from an unknown source washed ashore in September and October 2006 on Tai Long Wan Beach in Sai Kung, Hong Kong,

Amazonian Man

Dodging pirates, piranhas, whirlpools, sharks, and crocodiles, Martin Strel swam the mighty Amazon River in just 66 days.

On April 7, 2007, Martin, a 53-year-old from Slovenia, completed his colossal 3,274-mi (5,268-km) swim. From the Amazon's near-source in dense jungle around Atalaya in Peru across the vast width of Brazil to Bélem on the Atlantic coast, he swam a jaw-dropping average 50 mi (80 km), 10 hours a day, emerging from the water on the final afternoon exhausted and delirious, with blood pressure at near heart attack levels. He staggered to the ambulance still wearing the wet suit that had protected him from the snakes, spiders, and carnivorous fish that had chewed at his body during his remarkable adventure.

Martin wore a pillowcase mask to help protect against sunburn.

Throughout the mammoth journey, support crews in a boat beside him had tipped vast bucketloads of pig and chicken blood into the water in an attempt to lure the predators away. To work, the blood had to be old and the stench was revolting. The theory wasn't always successful—Martin was once pulled from the water yelling in agony, as a piranha gnawed into his leg. Other obstacles were women wielding machetes, murderous drug smugglers, and almost constant diarrhea (which had to be released into the said wetsuit and attracted more pests, including parasitic fish). But Strel was happy to add the Amazon to his list of conquests, and even happier to be on dry land!

Martin receives extra oxygen at the end of a particularly hard day's swim.

Not all of the creatures that Martin encountered were bad for his health!

Bark Analysis

Hungarian scientists have developed computer software that will enable humans to understand dog barks. Following the analysis of 6,000 barks, the amazing software can differentiate between a dog's various barks to be able to tell when it has seen a ball, when it meets a stranger, or when it wants to be taken for a walk.

Complaints' Choir

A Finnish couple have put together a series of choirs that complain in four-part harmony about subjects ranging from bad dates to people who chew gum too loudly. Oliver Kochta-Kalleinen and Tellervo Kalleinen have started more than 20 complaints' choirs all over the world, from Melbourne, Australia, to Chicago, Illinois. In Birmingham, England, the choir sang about the country's expensive beer; in Helsinki, Finland, singers bemoaned boring dreams; and in Budapest, Hungary, choristers ranted about a neighbor practicing folk dancing in an upstairs apartment. Participants do not need to come from a musical background, but they must offer at least one complaint for possible inclusion in the performance.

Falling Cat

A woman from Chongqing, China, was taken to hospital in 2007 after being knocked out by a cat falling from a high-rise apartment building. The tumbling cat hit Tang Meirong on the head as she walked along a footpath. Tang survived her ordeal but, sadly, the cat had used up its ninth life and was pronounced dead at the scene.

Epic Adventure

Using only human power, Colin Angus of Vancouver Island, British Columbia, Canada, circumnavigated the world in 720 days between 2004 and 2006. Starting and finishing in Vancouver, he cycled, skied, canoed, walked, and rowed through 17 countries, going through around 4,000 chocolate bars, 550 lb (250 kg) of freeze-dried foods, and 72 bicycle inner tubes. He hiked 3,125 mi (5,000 km) across Siberia, was blown 375 miles (600 km) off course while traversing the treacherous Bering Strait and, together with his fiancée Julie Wafaei, rowed for five months across the Atlantic Ocean.

Gun Play

Colombian musician and anti-violence advocate Cesar Lopez creates and plays guitars built from guns.

Computer Error

Denis Dixon of Dorset, England, was sent a quarterly gas bill for his two-bedroom rented apartment, which mistakenly asked for a payment of £11 million ($22 million)!

Swell Idea

Scientists in Naples, Italy, have invented a new weight-loss pill that swells up to the size of a tennis ball in the stomach. The pill, which is made out of diaper material, makes people feel full for about two hours.

R.A.P. Artist

Portuguese artist Leonel Moura has built a Robotic Action Painter—a robot that creates its own art. He has also constructed "the first zoo for artificial life," filled with 45 robots (each representing a different creature) housed in cages and enclosures.

Tiny Sun

Using a new nanoprinting technique, Swiss computer experts have created an image of the Sun that is just 80 microns wide— less than one-tenth the size of a pinhead!

Lightning Heat

The spark from lightning can reach more than 5 mi (8 km) in length and raise the temperature of the air by 50,000°F (27,000°C).

Motorcycling Frog

When it comes to talented pets, Oui the frog must be unique—because she can ride a miniature motorcycle and predict winning lottery numbers! The frog's owner, Tongsai Bamnungthai of Pattaya, Thailand, says local people used to come and read Oui's stomach to determine lucky numbers, and that Oui loves to play with children's toys and to pose for photographs.

Page numbers in *italic* refer to the illustrations

Abbott, Luke 339, *339*
Ableman, Scott 42, *42-43*
abseiling, blind man 59, *59*
acrobat, legless 213
adhesives, super-sticky 343
advertisements, as tattoos 230
Agrawal, Subhash Chandra and Madhu 41
Ahmed, Arif 243
Ahmed, Iqbal 176
airplanes
    blind pilot *58-59*, 59
    cat hides in suitcase 120
    cockpit in bedroom *86-87*, 87
    double survivor 291
    flying hovercraft 359, *359*
    flying round world 92, *92*
    lands on highway 155
    lands on its roof 311
    nightmares predict crash 328
    passenger wears too many clothes 90
    pulling with ear 51
    "virtual journeys" on 165
airports
    antiques verified in 166
    eagle keeps runway clear 131
    sightseers 163
Akash 34
al Mualla, Firas 98
Alaska, record temperature 167
albinism 227, 348, *348*
Aldrin, Buzz 171
algae, oxygen production 31
Allen, Camille 216, *216-217*
Allen, Dr. Matt 275
alligator wrestling 355, *355*
Alves, Edson 230
Amazon River, swimming down 360-361, *360-361*
Anderson, Danny 112
Anderson, "Granny" 294
Andrews, Megan 227
Anglesey, Mark 37
Angus, Colin 362
Antar, Robin 269

Antarctica
    solo trek across 28
    thickness of ice 176
antelopes, lion adopts 109
antiques, verification 166
ants
    ant cookies 236
    eating 251
    fire ant festival 91
    grow own food 130
    living bridges 344
anvils, shot into air 77
apartments
    full of beer cans 156, *156*
    in shopping mall 186
apples, speed-picking 253
Arabian Sea, first cyclone 165
Arfons, Tim 150, *150*
arm-wrestling match, woman loses driver's license 156
armchairs, motorized 148, *148*
armor, cardboard 170
armpits, bacteria in 230
arms
    crocodile bites off 102-103, *102-103*
    four-armed people 197, 198, *198-199*
    hands grow from shoulders 207
    Nelson's 306
    prosthetic 226
    reattached 225
    woman without forearms 192
Arnheim, Tim 263
Askins, Austin 332
asparagus, speed-eating 244
asthma, cures for 221, 225, *225*
astronauts, growth in space 329
Atlantic Ocean
    boy sails across 291
    rowing across 79
Atulkar, Shyam 259
Austin, Matt 200
autograph, multiple signings 35
autopsy, corpse wakes up in 221

babies
    all born on same day 63
    born in saunas 73
    born with teeth 227
    devils jump over 73, *73*

babies (*cont.*)
    family share birthday 282
    from frozen eggs 333
    significant numbers 281, 313
    tiny sculptures 216, *216-217*
    triplets born on twins' birthday 281
    twins give birth on same day 82
    very premature 195, *195*
    very strong 37, *37*
    very tiny 230
baby monitor, picks up space shuttle images 351
bacteria, in armpits 230
Badaczewski, Don 351
Baddick, Jane 185
Bader, Douglas 283
bagel, very expensive 239, *239*
bags, large collection of 318
Baker, Roger 328
Ballard, Ted 305
balloons
    flying with *14-15*, 15, 71
    Simpsons made of 342, *342*
    very long journey for 16
    wedding dress made of 67, *67*
balls
    holding in hand 283, *283*
    horse ridden inside giant 45
    juggling with mouth 25
    mass basketball dribble 18
    in python's stomach 299, *299*
bananas
    causing accidents 259
    huge bunch of 256
banks
    horse ridden into 336
    robot-shaped 159
Bao Xishun *210*, 211
Barlow, Edith 230
Barnum, P.T. 217
Barr, Brady 140
Barr, Jay 256
barrels
    hotel bedrooms in 176
    man lives in 51

bars
  bottle cap decoration *70-71*, 71
  hungry wolf walks into 269
  made of ice 178
  stress-relief for customers 167
  very young bartender 63
barstool, jet-powered 150, *150*
baseball
  breaking bats 41
  visiting all major-league stadiums
    63
basketball
  mass dribble 18
  very tall player 203
Bass, Jennie 91
Bateman, Laurie 305
bathtub
  dog survives fire in 107
  regatta 77
bats, fishing 118
battles, with cardboard armor 170
Baumann, Daniel 176, *176*
Baumberger, Quinn 82, *82*
Beane, Stephanie 148
beards
  bearded woman 213
  bee beard contest 206
  very long 49, *49*
bears
  fainting cure 216
  has own postal zip code 158
  killed with log 91
  raids van 263
Beaton, Rob 243
beauty contest, for large ladies
    84, 85
bedbugs, dog hunts 132
Beekman, Mark 344, *344*
beer
  carrying glasses of 16, 256, *256*
  for dogs 113
bees
  bee beard contest 206
  elephants frightened of 121
Beethoven, Ludwig van, hair 291,
    291
Behrs, Matt 71
Bejano, Emmitt 213
bells, attached to eyebrows 19, *19*
belt, made of soda can tabs 45
Benitz, Max 83

Bentem, Hans van 346, *346-347*
Berberich, Olga 18
Berendsen, Gerrie 113
Berent, Stanislaus 207
Berg, Bryan 333, *333*
Berg, Norm 275
Bernston, Craig 270, *270*
Bertoletti, Patrick 243
Bevan, Kerry 90
Bhati, Nangaji 29, *29*
Bias, Ezra 216
bicycles
  blind man rides 40
  disabled man's long ride 313
  fast ride down mountain 357
  fish-shaped 158
  marathon ride on stationary bike
    348
  for seven riders 159
  tall 154
  Tour de Fat 35
  very long journey 82, *82*
Bielunski, Kelvin 16
bikinis, huge photoshoot 51
Bilenka, Iryna 31
billboard, chocolate 238
Bing, Aaron 354
Bingham, Debbie 341
birds
  attack fishing boat 150
  brain implants control 354
  dizziness cure 216
  giant fossil penguin 288
  hand-rearing cranes 107, *107*
  medicine from saliva 221
  mimicry 140
  mynah bird's bad language 127
  owner stuck in tree 135
  pelican eats pigeon 109, *109*
  penguins eat garlic 143
  pigeons as spies 133
  seagull shoplifter 141
  stolen egg returned 312
  tries to hatch Easter eggs 125
  underwater film of penguins 118
  varied diet 269
  very large appetites 104, *105*
bison, albino 348, *348*
Biwer, Renee 98
Blackthorne, Thomas 74, *74-75*
bladder stone, enormous 195

Blair, Paul 36, *36*
Blankenship, Chris 120
blind people
  abseiling 59, *59*
  climbing 58, *58*
  fish's cure for 311
  pilot *58-59*, 59
  scuba diving 58, *58*
  sculptor 70, *70*
  unable to see movement 336
  uses echolocation 40
blindfolded people
  driving car 60
  juggling 31
  riding unicycle 44, *44*
  text messaging 28
Block, Lindsay 337, *337*
blood
  consumption by mosquitoes 226
  green 203
  very rare blood group 217
blouses, Ripley's Believe It or Not!
    cartoons on 93, *93*
Blue Hole, Belize *154*, 155
Blumenthal, Heston 270
boats and ships
  birds attack fishing boat 150
  boy sails across Atlantic 291
  earthquake reveals 181
  like dolphin 164, *164*
  made of beer cans 90
  made of plastic bottles 186
  pilot wears gorilla suit 45
  reducing global warming with
    343
  rescue ship captained by
    neighbor 313
  shop on 158
  Viking ship found under car park
    87
  yacht found abandoned 345
Boehm, Marco 40, *40*
Boerdihardjo, March Tian 93
Boivin, Melanie 333
Boland, Jason 163
Bolingbroke-Kent, Antonia
    330-331, *330-331*
bomb, used as doorstop 66
bones
  dinosaur bone medicine 211
  not Joan of Arc's 307

bones (*cont.*)
  skeleton found in loft 300
Bonnett, Thelma 66
books
  bound in human skin 71
  extremely small 51
  on first manned space flight 171
  long overdue library book 63,
    343
  oddest title 83
  prolific author 351
boomerang, very small 92
Booth, David 328
Booth, John Wilkes 316
boots, hanging upside-down in 156
Borbilas, Hugo 192
bottle caps, bar decorated with
    70-71, 71
bottles
  boat made of plastic bottles 186
  house built of 156
  solar heating using 336
  wedding vows found in 71
Bowen, Eli 213
bowling alley, ancient 283
boxing, chessboxing 54
bra, stops bullet 341
Bradbury, Richard 236
Bradt, Tyler 332
Brady, Thomas 299
brain
  eating 236, *236*
  Einstein's 290, *290*
  implants control pigeons 354
  living with half a brain 200
  museum of *316-317*, 317
Bravo, Gonzalo 49
Bravo, Joe 234-235, *234-235*
bread sculpture 257
break dance, very long 22
breakfast
  robot serves 263
  speed-eating 271, *271*
  tattoo on head 222, *222-223*
breath-holding, by diver 60
Breton, Claude 253
bricks
  car apparently made of 149
  splitting with hand 30, *30*
bridesmaid, chicken as 98
bridge, mass bounce on 49

Bridges, R.C. 110, *110-111*
Bromberek, Lucille 316
brooms
  and impotence 227
  purifying houses with 82
Browcott, Kris 236
Brown, David H. 156
Brown, Leven 79
brush, hedgehogs adopt 130, *130*
Bryans, Steve 206
Buck, Heath 308-309, *308-309*
Buckelew, Bill 37
Buckley, Alan 316, *316*
buffalo
  as cure for plague 227
  pet 110, *110-111*
buildings
  crazily shaped 171, *171*
  elephants demolish 115
  gingerbread 254-255, *254-255*
  painted to lower crime rate 165
  robot-shaped bank 159
  rotating section 162, *162*
  very long dress on 324-325,
    325
bullets
  coughed up 332
  lodges in bra strap 341
bulls
  gores brothers together 285
  piglet thinks it is 126, *126*
  rips out intestines 294
bumper stickers, stolen from truck
    163
buns
  made of cardboard 258
  tower of plastic 71
  very old 244
Burge, William *180*, 181
burgers
  long journey to buy 256
  speed-eating 262, *262*
Burkitt, Ken and Annie 160,
    160-161
Burns, Robert 152, *152-153*
Burrell, Stuart 45
burrs, man covered in 99
bus, cat travels on daily 115
butter sculpture 243
butterflies, flying with 288
buzkashi 66

Byars, Russ 51
Byrne, Mel 313

"Cabinet of Curiosities" 300
cables, pickup truck driven on 43
Cai Dongsheng 208
Cain family 126
cakes
  full-sized car 239
  giant birthday cakes 251
  St Paul's Cathedral replica 245
  very large cream cake 244
  very old fruitcake 263
Caldwell, Don 67, *67*
Caldwell, Rebecca 179
Callan, Pat 18
Calvin, Max 227, *227*
Camejo, Carlos 221
camels, sweating 130
cameras
  on cat's collar 128, *128-129*
  elephant-dung camouflage 142
  on golden eagle 138
  pigeons as spies 133
Campbell, Doug 308-309, *308-
    309*
Canales, Eduardo 49
cancer, tobacco as cure for 227
Canion, Phylis 305, *305*
cans
  apartment full of 156, *156*
  boat made of beer cans 90
  cheeseburger in 258
  fish found wearing 98
  fridge throws beer cans 243
  jeans made of 301, *301*
  large collections of 17, 306
cardboard
  armor 170
  buns made of 258
  full-sized replicas made out of
    352-353, *352-353*
  sleds 85
carousel, week spent on 357
Carpenter, Ben 296-297, *296-297*
Carrington, Alfie 185
carrots, color 270
cars
  apparently made of bricks 149
  at high altitude 49
  blindfolded driver 60

cars (cont.)
  cardboard replica 352-353, 353
  covered in artificial grass 181
  covered in chocolate 181
  covered in crystals 160, 160-161
  covered in kitchen utensils 181
  covered in plastic fruit 157
  covered in sticky notes 42,
    42-43
  custom-made 149, 149
  driver without license 170
  driving backward 173
  drunk driver arrested by husband
    173
  eco-friendly 155
  full-size cake 239
  gargoyle-themed 180, 181
  Hot Wheels collection 282, 282
  leopard car 181
  life-size LEGO® replica of 29
  lifting 37
  like cathedral 179
  limbo-skating under 20-21, 21
  long parade of 163
  man steals to visit girlfriend 165
  pig-like car 167
  pushing 37
  scrap metal sculptures 343
  sheep follow shepherd's 139
  speedy limousine 151
  stolen twice in one day 167
  tearing license plates in half 41
  tornado throws into air 70
  upside-down car on top of 172
  very careful driver 176
  very expensive 178
  very long journey in 83
  winning by kissing 288-289,
    289
  young stock-car driver 148
Carter, Eyvonne 85
Carter, Judy 285
Cartland, Barbara 351
cartoons, truck decorated with
    182-183, 182-183
cash machines, dogs use 143
casino, lost money found 63
Castrission, James 88, 88-89
catapults, firing pumpkins 90
caterpillars
  caterpillar race 98

caterpillars (cont.)
  rapid growth 141
  tea made from droppings 224
cathedral, car looks like 179
Catherine of Siena, St. 318
cats
  bus travel 115
  camera on collar 128, 128-129
  different-colored eyes 115, 115
  dog gives birth to kitten 130
  dog rescues 119
  enormous 132, 132
  flying 71
  fur spun 122-123, 122-123
  head stuck in jar 118, 126
  hides in suitcase 120
  knocks out woman 362
  locked in shed 126
  new breed of 106, 107
  save woman from snake 115
  saves diabetic boy 104
  saves family from fire 139
  as stationmaster 135
  superstitions 73
  survives fire 132
  survives long sea voyage
    138
  talking 132
  winged cat 124, 125
Caudle, Dorothy 311
Cavallaro, Cosimo 244
caves
  Blue Hole, Belize 154, 155
  giant crystals 184, 185
  living in 185
  village in 181
Cawley, Dan 151
cell phones
  store decorated with 307,
    307
  surgery by light of 213
cells, number in body 218
cemetery, bodies decapitated 63
centenarian, rides in motorcycle
    sidecar 18
centipedes, eating 258, 258
chainsaws
  juggling with 354, 354
  sculpture with 96, 96
chandeliers, crystal 346, 346-347
Chandler, Bob 187, 187

Chang Po-yu 102-103, 102-103
Charles II, King of England 311
Chaudhary, Phulram 92
checkers, computer program 351
cheese
  bribes 244
  canned cheeseburger 258
  concrete 155
  enormous 155
  living on diet of 269
  Mount Rushmore sculpture 275
  watching it mature 259
Chege, Patrick 49
Chen Huanxiang 215
Chen Yu Pei 354
Cheng Yanhua 92
Chenoweth, Mark 194, 194
chess
  chessboxing 54
  chocolate chess set 28
Chestnut, Joey 244, 262, 262
chewing gum
  coffee-flavored 269
  paintings on 28, 28-29
  very old 97
  whistling while chewing 43
chick, dog adopts 134
chickens
  addicted to playing soccer 126
  alive in freezer 142
  as bridesmaid 98
  chicken wing hunt 85
  cow eats 118
  killed by heat surge 176
  math ability 358, 358
  speed-eating 244
  tornado plucks 167
Chidiac, Sid 251
chili
  addiction to 252
  in prehistory 239
  resistance to effects of 25
  speed-eating 245
chimpanzee, memory ability 141
China, Edd 343
Chindak, Aniket 20-21, 21
Chiniwala, Shazneen 324-325, 325
chocolate
  billboard 238
  car covered in 181
  chess set 28

chocolate (cont.)
chocolate-covered lettuces 274
cockatoo tries to hatch Easter
eggs 125
finger found in 265
igloo 253
model of Sir Elton John 263
painting with 251
sculpture 244
squirrel raids store for 133
as temptation of the devil 259
very expensive 252, 252
choirs, for complaints 362
chopsticks, eating single grains of
rice 243
Christensen, Jan 324
Chudleigh, Tom 177, 177
chupacabra 305, 305
churches
leaning steeple 181
tiny 178, 178
cigarette lighters, large collection
of 305
circus, elephants escape from 130
clapping
very fast 51
very loud 17
Clark, Gladys 311
Clay, Dennis 172
Cleveland, Grover, tumor 312
cliffs
dog survives on ledge 132
hanging upside down on 318, 318
clothes
air passenger wears too many
90
balloon wedding dress 67, 67
discarded on sidewalks 335
dress made of hair 49
dressed mummies 228-229,
228-229
football fan wears jersey every
day 327
made from meat 239
made of newspapers 51
miniature knitting 32-33, 32-33
sleepwalker washes 324
very long dresses 66, 324-325,
325
clouds, thickening to reduce global
warming 343

cockroaches
eating 238
medicinal properties 230
cocktail, very expensive 248
coconut orchestra 269
coffee
believed to be poisonous 236
drinking in every Starbucks in
world 266-267, 266-267
flavored chewing gum 269
giant cup of 263
latte art 248, 248
Coffer, Henry 341
Cohen, Anne 351
coins
electrical charge 351
giant 313, 359
holding in ear 227, 227
long lines of 31, 51
very valuable 351
color blind artist 19
Columbus, Christopher 79
comas
language skills after 192
woman briefly wakes from 197
combs, superstitions 72
comic book characters, truck
covered in 182-183, 182-183
computer disks, sculpture 90,
90-91
computers
monitors washed ashore 359
sculpture made from 60, 60
unbeatable at checkers 351
understanding dog barks 362
concrete, thief stuck in 318
contact lenses, eating 269
continental drift 173
Conway, John Joseph 217
Conwell, Shannon 336
Cook, Dr. M.T. 141, 141
cookie jars, large collection of 316
cookies, ant 236
cooking, large number of recipes
37
Cope, Tim 26-27, 26-27
coral reefs, lifted by earthquake 181
corks
production by tree 171
truck decorated with 166
corkscrews, large collection of 243

Cornett, Gravil 141, 141
Cornwell, John 243
corpses
kept in freezer 326
kept in jars 201
stolen from graveyard 301
wakes up in autopsy 221
Cotton, Jenna 63
Couch, Ken 14-15, 15
coughs, unusual cures 227, 230,
231, 236
court case, donkey as witness
332
Courtney, Jess 197
cowboys, poetry gathering 63
cows
conjoined calves 141, 141
eats chickens 118
eight-legged calf 131
falls onto minivan 349
music improves milk production
115
six-legged calf 132
tea made from manure 230
two-faced calf 113, 113
two-nosed calf 132
Cox, Lynne 76
Cramer, Nicole 82
crayons, sculpture 356, 357
credit cards
multiple replacements 354
sculpture from 335
crème brûlée, enormous 264
crime, buildings painted pink to
lower rate of 165
crocodiles
arrested by police 332
attacks man 102-103, 102-103
man hides in tree to escape 106
protect endangered animals 181
smuggled across border 357
studying disguised as 140
survives fall 104
victim shot by rescuer 312
woman in pool full of 311
Crolla, Domenico 244
Cromwell, Oliver, posthumous
execution 311
crossword puzzles
giant 25
marriage proposal in 91

crystals
car covered with 160, *160-161*
chandeliers 346, *346-347*
giant *184-185*, 185
Cummins, Scott 246-247, *246-247*
cyanide, underground pool of 283
cyclone, in Arabian Sea 165
cyst, enormous 220
Czislowski, Ben 200

Dae Yu Quin 220
Dakin, Laura 67, *67*
Dali, Salvador 357
Dallas, Aaron 209, *209*
dance
as cure for illness 225
prison video 280, *280-281*
very long break dance 22
very long line dance 43
with hooks in skin 97, *97*
Dashrath 270
dating agency, for parrots 121
D'Aubney, George 245
Davies, Wayne 90
Davis, John *86-87*, 87
Davis, Lowell 76
dead man turns up alive 209
Debry-Martin, Lila 281
Declaration of Independence, found in thrift store 60
DeGennaro, Joe 311
del Rio, Jackie 196, *196*
Delefortrie, Julian 179
Dellagrotti, Philip 37, *37*
Dennison, Thomas 209
dentures
George Washington's 285, *285*
swallowed in kiss 207
depression, iguana cure for 269
deserts
golf course in 172
running across 71
desk, made of LEGO® 22
dessert, very expensive 248
Diamond, Rich 226
diamonds
peanut butter turned into 270
visitors search mine for 165
Diana, Princess of Wales 61, *61*

diapers, on donkeys 126
Dickinson, Blane 222, *222-223*
Diefenbaker, John G. 151
dieting, extreme 45
dinosaur bones, medicinal uses for 211
diploma, presented very late 341
Disney bridal dresses 22
diving
blind diver 58, *58*
disabled man walks after 194, *194*
holding breath 60
into tiny pool 64, *64-65*
lightning kills diver 154
making a big splash 93
Dixon, Denis 362
dizziness, bird cure for 216
DNA, having two sets of 224
Dobson, John 18
doctor, elderly 217
dog food, eating 252
dogs
adopts chick 134
adopts pig 127, *127*
beer for 113
brought back to life 336
computer understands barks 362
eating paws 253, *253*
eats cash 105
escapes from tiger 112
fortune left to 138
French-speaking 139
friendship with monkey 142
fur spun 122-123, *122-123*
gives birth to kitten 130
grass in stomach 108
hairs growing from eye 327
high jumping 120
house painted to look like Dalmatian 132
hunts bedbugs 132
hymn-singing 134
kiss-of-life saves puppy 119
as lifeguard 119, *119*
marrying 92, 112
monocled markings 140, *140*
mummy found in tree 304, *304*
paintings by 113
puppies without front legs 114, *114*
rescue drowning people 118, *118*

dogs (*cont.*)
rescues cats 119
rescues dolphins 120
save boys 120, 121
saves family from fire 113
saves woman from choking 133
serves shop customers 120
shoots owner 354
spoils pie eating contest 140
surfing 121, *121*
survive falls 115, 132
survives fire in bathtub 107
swallows underpants 237
two-nosed 120, *120*
ugliest 104, *104*
use cash machines 143
white-star marking 141, *141*
dollhouse, covers grave 185
dolphins
dog rescues 120
prosthetic tail 105, *105*
save surfer from shark 125
watercraft like 164, *164*
Dombalis, Paul 245
domino-toppling 49
donkeys
chief witness in court case 332
diapers on 126
friendship with wolf 140
donut, enormous 240, *240-241*
Dotzauer, Robert 220, *220*
dragon, made of LEGO® 334-335, 335
drain tiles, museum of 306
drawings
autistic's ability 94-95, *94-95*
made from words of New Testament 98, *98*
dreams, predict air crash 328
drill, swallowing 74, *74-75*
driver's licenses
lost after arm-wrestling 156
man without 170
Drossel, Arnd 136-137, *136-137*
drums
disabled drummer 344
large collection of 316, *316*
Dubendorf, Fred and Lynnette 71
ducks
alive in freezer 132
four-legged 118

ducks (*cont.*)
  plastic ducks travel round world
    292-293, *292-293*
  trapped duck rescued 115
duct tape sculpture 285
Dunbar, Alice 221, *221*

eagles
  carries camera 138
  keeps runway clear 131
Earles, Nadine 185
ears
  holding coins in 227, *227*
  pulling weights with 45, 51
  spiders nest in 197
  stretching lobes 215
earthquake, lifts coral reefs 181
Easter eggs, cockatoo tries to hatch
    125
Easter Island statues, topiary 29
echolocation, blind man uses 40
eggs
  boiled by machine 263
  giant omelet 269
  holding large number of 35, *35*
  reducing fever with 230
  standing on end 35
  stolen egg returned 312
Egmont, Aric 91
Einstein, Albert, brain 290, *290*
elections, long ballot papers 348
electricity
  produced by human body *278-
    279*, 279
  production by Sun 345
  sweat creates 351
elephants
  demolish buildings 115
  escape from circus 130
  frightened of bees 121
  holds up traffic 125
  rock shaped like 151
  secret camera films 142
Elftmann, Jan 166
Elie, Herbethe 281
Ellis, Rick 22
Endris, Todd 125
Engle, Charlie 71
erasers, large collection of 294,
    294
Eriksen, Marcus 186

escape artists, underwater 34, 319,
    319
Etch a Sketch®, famous paintings
    322-323, *322-323*
Etzweiler, George 31
Eusebio, Ephraim 181
Evans, Robert 335
Everhart, Chris 91
Everson, Charles and Linda 349
exam, wearing wedding dress 87
eyebrows, bells attached to 19, *19*
eyelids
  pulling weights with 313, *313*
  weight lifting with 31, *31*
eyes
  burning leaves cure 213, *213*
  cat with different-colored 115,
    115
  chemical burn improves sight 215
  cross eyes insured 335
  dog with hairs growing from 327
  glass under 211
  horse with two-tone eye 112, *112*
  needle in 337
  popping out of sockets 200
  sheep's eyes as hangover cure
    269

face, enormous tumor 206
fainting, bear cure for 216
Fairchild, Lydia 224
falls
  crocodile survives 104
  cushioned by human excrement
    85
  dog survives 115
  man survives 306
  umbrella slows 66
fan, stopping with tongue 40, *40*
Fanti, Marco 253
Fast, Reverend Kevin 51
Fauser, Wayne 259
feet
  six-toed man 227
  three-toed woman 192
Feng, Granny *124*, 125
fever, reducing with egg whites 230
Fildes, John 313
finger painting, giant 327
fingernails, very long 224
fingerprints, on mummy 230

fingers
  found in chocolate bar 265
  fused together 230
  loud snapping 208
  pulling taxis with finger 54
  re-grows 207
  six on each hand 227
  very long 225
  very thick 195, 230
  weight lifting with 78, *78*
fire
  cat saves family 139
  cat survives 132
  dog saves family 113
  dog survives in bathtub 107
  horses jump across 68, *68-69*
  parrot saves family 336
  spitting fire while floating 34, *34*
  squirrels start 106
firecrackers
  explode on chest 48, *48*
  long chain of 60
fireworks, dangerous festival 76, *76*
fish
  asthma cure 225, *225*
  cure for blindness 311
  fish-shaped bicycle 158
  human electricity cooks 279, *279*
  jellyfish kills salmon 134
  large number caught 41
  "lucky" fish in restaurant 245
  mystery deaths 335
  parasitic tongue 138
  snake eats goldfish 312, *312*
  tattoos 139
  wearing can 98
fish hook, stuck in tongue 251
fishing, by bats 118
flags
  "human" 99, *99*
  planted below North Pole 51
  small child can identify 76
Fleming, Elmer 181
floating, for long time 40
Florea, Cristinel 328
fly, robotic 348
flying saucer, built in garage 185
Flynn, Darlene 286-287, *286-287*
fog
  forest watered by 164
  tiny particles 179

food
landscapes made of 260, *260-261*
sculptures 269, 301
squirrels fake burials 106
tattoos of 213, 222, *222-223*
football
fan changes name after team loses match 345
fan wears jersey every day 327
obsessive fan 336
soda for 269
Force, Amia 200, *200*
forest, watered by fog 164
fossils
ancient tooth 291
giant penguin 288
foxes
lives with family 135, *135*
mythical beast 305, *305*
Francis, Steve 243
Francis Xavier, St. 280
Frankel, Laurence J. 218, *218*
Fransson, Fredrik 146-147, *146-147*
Frazier, Gregory 83, *83*
freezers
chicken alive in 142
duck alive in 132
mother's body kept in 326
Frick, Don 289
Friend, Clyde 304
Froerer, Ryan 156
frogs
eating 230, *231*, 236, 269, 275
mock weddings with 73
motorcycling 363, *363*
toothache cure 215
transparent 349, *349*
front yard, thief steals 357
fruit
car covered in plastic fruit 157
exploding 167
Fu Yingjie 17
fudge, giant slab of 252
Fuller, Jeshuah 227
Fullmer, Leah Moore Harris 341
fungus, puffball 163
fur, spinning 122-123, *122-123*
Furman, Ashrita 51

furniture, race on skis 85
fusion reactor, built in garage 329

Gagliardi, Jeff 322-323, *322-323*
Galpin, Alastair 22
Gan Shugen 142
Gandy, Charlie 351
Gangaram 263
garbage, people made of 291
Garcia, Byron 280
Garcia, Oliver 45
gargoyle-themed car *180*, 181
garlic, penguins eat 143
Garside, Robert 22
gas, enormous bill 362
Gaulin, Mario and Angie 227
geckos, super-sticky adhesive 343
Geiger, Michael 29
Genghis Khan 26
Gentry, Howard 131
George, David 106
Gerhart, Dennis 299
ghost town, statues in 25
Giese, Jeanna 195
Gilbey, Dayne 222, *222-223*
Gill, William B. 311
Gillette, King Camp 357
Gilmore, Johnny 211
Gilmour, Chris 352-353, *352-353*
gingerbread buildings 254-255, *254-255*
glaciers
frozen body found in 285
naked people photographed on 341
Gladwin, Muriel 176
glass
eating 16, *16*, 270
living in glass room 43
under eye 211
Glenn, John 120
global warming, combating 343, 351
Glum, Steve 263
gnomes, stolen 327
goats, produce nerve gas antidote 358
Goddard, Robert 171
Godden, Kevin 285

Godson, Lloyd 31
gold
heart-shaped crowns on teeth 214, 215
size of 149
tongue decorations *214*, 215
Goldlust, Pete *356*, 357
golf
back-to-back holes-in-one 299
course on ice 351
desert course 172
lessons for students 326
underwater 48
golf balls, in python's stomach 299, *299*
golf cart, becomes snowplow 354
Gonzalez, Philip 119
gorillas
finger-painting 142
table manners 130
Grady, Columbus 85
Grant, Dave 305
Grant, Jason 312
grass
car covered in artificial 181
in dog's stomach 108
eating 263, 275
growing in lung 221
grasshopper, giant statue of 185
graves
corpses stolen from 301
cure stiff necks 213
dollhouse covers 185
gravy wrestling 259
Gray, Chadwick 190-191, *190-191*
Green, Matt 351
grenade, in sack of potatoes 300
Grewcock, Greg 125
Grieves, Patrick 62, *62*
Gu, Wenda 87
guinea pigs, hairless 133, *133*
guitars
made from guns 362
playing simultaneously 329
Guo Huochun 35, *35*
Gupta, Anil 204, *204-205*
Gurchin, Randy 119
Gustav III, King of Sweden 236
Gutierrez, Francisco 288

Haddrill, Barbara 97
Hadjiev, Taso and Asen 85
hair
  Beethoven's 291, *291*
  cutting underwater 37
  dress made of 49
  grows from dog's eye 327
  hairiest man contest 97
  hairy stone 167, *167*
  huge ball of 341
  huge hairball in stomach 224
  medicinal properties 227
  sculpture 87
  soaks up spilled fuel 192
  very long 220
  very long leg hair 358
  whole body covered in 201, *201*,
    213
Hairong Tiantian 43
ham, very old 245
hammers, large collection of 313
hamster, revived after cooking
    107
hands
  bionic 337, *337*
  enormous 203
  finger re-grows 207
  fingers fused together 230
  growing from shoulders 207
  holding lots of eggs 35, *35*
  holding lots of balls 283, *283*
  rotating 360 degrees 211
  six-fingered man 227
  splitting bricks with 30, *30*
  very long finger 225
  very thick fingers 195, 230
hangover cure, sheep's eyes 269
Hanson, Joshua 306
Haraguchi, Akira 97
Hardacre, Chris 63
Harding, Steven 87
Harris, Jackie 157
Harris, James 354
Harris, Penny 292-293, *292-293*
Harris, Sam 221, *221*
Harshbarger, Eric 22
Hart, William 135
Harvey, Dr. Thomas 290, *290*
Hatch, Robert 208
Hawkins, Judy 72
hay ride, very long 37

head
  breakfast tattoo on 222, *222-223*
  breaking toilet lids with 22
  eating sheep's 237, *237*, 238
  headbanging 18
  horned people 193, *193*, 200,
    226
  impaled on steel bar 216
  larvae growing in 209, *209*
  pencil removed from 203
  sent in post 333
  shark swallows 195
  sleeper shot in 78
  smashing plates on 17
  spinning on 340, *340*
  stone heads found 295
  surviving decapitation 209
  tooth in forehead 200
  two-faced calf 113, *113*
  two-faced piglet 113
  two-headed snake 125
  two-headed turtle 138, *138*
  walking down stairs on 192, *192*
heart
  blood pressure 219
  eating frogs' 275
  man without pulse 209
  nail shot into 312
  snakes digest own 109
  stops beating for long time 218
heaviest people 221, *221*
hedgehogs
  adopt brush 130, *130*
  enormous 328, *328*
Heeman, Rudy 359, *359*
Heiden, York 167
Heinrich, Wolfgang 336
helicopters
  dogs rescue drowning people
    118, *118*
  moose attacks 126
  pulling with ear 45
  rescues bird owner from tree
    135
Helmsley, Leona 138
Helsby, Colin 213
Herbert, Ada 244
Herbert, Victoria 167
Hewer, Susie 17
Hewison-Jones, Blaine 82
hiccups, long attack of 203

Hickman, Ian 253
Hickok, Liz 272, *272-273*
Hill, Al 79
Hill, Benjamin 192
Hill, Nanny Mae 192
hill, running up many times 341
Hilton, Taquela 220
Hilton-Barber, Miles 58-59, 59
Hitler, Adolf, skull 285
Hoekstra, Eric 51
Hoeller, Carsten 29
hog, monster shot 142, *142*
Holt, F.G. 19, *19*
Honrubia, Francisco Tebar 25
Hood, George 348
Hopkins, Jenna 207
Horden twins 141, *141*
horns
  on people's heads 193, *193*, 200,
    226
  on rooster's head 139, *139*
Horowitz, Adam 332
horses
  dangerous race 77, *77*
  jump across fires 68, *68-69*
  plays soccer 120
  psychic predicts winners 343
  ridden inside giant ball 45
  ridden into bank 336
  traveling across Eurasia on 26-27,
    26-27
  two-tone eye 112, *112*
horseshoes, tower of 155
hospitals
  snake in intensive care 106
  themed restaurant 249, *249*
  uses vodka 196
hot cross bun, very old 244
hotels
  bedrooms in wine barrels 176
  one-room 176, *176*
  in prison 171
  very remote 185
houses
  built of embalming-fluid bottles
    156
  in caves 185
  in cement pipes 151
  crazily shaped 170, *170*
  cut in half 355
  divided with barbed wire 85

houses (cont.)
gift-wrapped 163
knitted 34
looks like redwood tree 178, *178*
murals of famous paintings 152,
152-153
painted to look like Dalmatian
dog 132
pencil mosaics 168, *168-169*
purifying with broom 82
sheep live in 349
shoe-shaped 156
suspended in trees 177, *177*
thief steals front yard 357
tornados damage 163, *163*, 179,
179
towed across river 165, *165*
hovercraft, flying 359, *359*
Howard, Patricia 255, *255*
Hrisca-Munn, Cornel 344
Huang Chuncai 206
Huang Liqian 230
Huenefeld, Nicholas 50, *50*
hug, mass 51
hula hoops
running with 36, *36*
underwater 51
Hulleman, Debbie 105
Hundertwasser, Friedensreich 171,
171
Hunt, Nicholas 243
Hussain, Aazer 76
Huxster, Jo 330-331, *330-331*
hymn-singing dog 134

ice
bar made of 178
golf course on 351
sculpture 38, *38-39*, 349
swimming in icy water 76
thickness in Antarctica 176
ice cream
enormous sundaes 237, 253
museum of 311
savory flavors 264, *264*
speed-eating 256
ice hockey, playing under ice 45
igloo, chocolate 253
iguanas
depression cure 269
smuggled in prosthetic leg 343

impotence, brooms and 227
Innes, Rob 164, *164*
insects, as paintbrushes 298, *298*
Internet
speedy surfer 343
weight of 343
Inuit mummies 213
iron, in human body 230
Irvington, Barrington 92, *92*
islands
birth of 146-147, *146-147*
in lake on island 173
for wild boar *338-339*, 339

Jack, Andrew 106
Jackson, Michael 280
Jacobs, Benno 97
James, Jereme 343
Janus, Tim 265
Jarvis, Ed 256
jeans, made of cans 301, *301*
jell-O, model of San Francisco 272,
272-273
jellyfish
invasion of 134
octopuses use stings from 138
Jerome, Romaine 299
Jesus Christ
image of on garage floor 157
paintings drip blood 351
jewels, cobras guard 25
Ji Fengshan 54, 78, *78*
Jiang Musheng 230, *231*, 236
Joan of Arc 307
John, Sir Elton 263
Johnson, Billy 295
Johnson, Levi 244
Johnston, John 306
Jones, Justin 88, *88-89*
Jones, Wanda 357
juggling
blindfolded 31
with chainsaws 354, *354*
with mouth 25
Jumsai, Sumet 159
junk mail, sculpture from 351

Kahn, Leopold 217
Kalam, A.P.J. Abdul 40
Kalleinen, Tellervo 362
kangaroo, killed by shark 106

Karason, Paul 202, *202*
Kasslatter, Rainer 349
Kattan, Sadir 92
Kaya, Hasip 264
kayaks
cross Tasman Sea 88, *88-89*
long journey in 54
paddled over waterfall 332
kebab, very long 274
Keen, James 226, *226*
Kelly, Kirstie 22
Kersey, Hannah 211
ketchup
giant packet of 251
speed drinking 50, *50*
Khalil, Moneera 195
King, Joel *150-151*, 151
Kish, Daniel 40
kiss-of-life, saves puppy 119
kissing
false teeth swallowed in 207
by lion 143, *143*
winning car *288-289*, 289
woman kisses painting 34
kitchen utensils, car covered in
181
Kite, David 336
Kloska, Melody 71
Kmet, Bob 37
knees, faces on 200, *200*
knife, multi-functional 350, *350*
knitting
houses 34
miniature 32-33, *32-33*
while running marathon 17
Knox, Artez Kenyetta 348
Koch, Julius 203
Kochta-Kalleinen, Oliver 362
Koehler, Donald 201
Kolodziejzyk, Greg 85
Krombholz, Mark 132
Kulkarni, Girish 341
Kus, Matej 192
Kutcher, Steven 298, *298*
Kyzer, Nancy 255, *255*

Lacasse, Dominic 99, *99*
Lackner, Dr. Klaus 351
ladybugs, clear parasites 125
Lahan, Jayanta 252
Laidre, Kristin 324

lakes
  island in lake on island 173
  submerged town reappears 155
  vanishing 186
Lam, Nancy 263
Lamas, Josephine and Valmai 326
Lambert, Jenna 78
Lambert, Natalie 78
landscapes, made of food 260,
  260-261
Landwehr, Troy 275
Lang, Sabina 176, 176
Langevin, Gerard 209
language skills, after coma 192
Larmande, Frank and Ludivine 333
larvae, growing in head 209, 209
Latham, John 343
latte art 248, 248
laughing, weight loss with 335
Lauther, Percilla 213
Lauver, Bill 354
Laveau, Marie 317
lawn mowers, balancing on chin
  220, 220
Le Gentil, Guillaume 336
Lee, Adam 342, 342
Lee, Ed 351
Lee, Mr. 128
Leff, William J. 155
LEGO®
  desk made of 22
  giant figure found in sea 54
  human body made of 24, 25
  life-size replica of car 29
  model dragon 334-335, 335
  The Last Supper recreated in 19
legs
  amputated 304
  artificial legs found under floor
    307
  artificial legs in museum 283
  eight-legged calf 131
  four-legged duck 118
  four-legged girl 198, 198-199
  iguanas smuggled in prosthesis
    343
  legless acrobat 213
  lower part of body missing 211
  mermaid's tail for legless woman
    217
  motorcycle rider loses 208

legs (cont.)
  ownership dispute 217
  puppies without front legs 114,
    114
  robotic 226
  self-amputation 79
  seven-legged lamb 140
  six-legged calf 132
  six-legged piglet 142
  three-legged man 197
  wrong leg lengthened 225
Leibold, Gisela 336
Lenahan, Lawrence and Michael
  285
Leonardo da Vinci
  Etch a Sketch® version of The
    Mona Lisa 322, 323
  LEGO® version of The Last
    Supper 19
  Lite-Brite peg version of The Last
    Supper 344, 344
  tattoo of The Last Supper 204,
    204-5
leopard car 181
Letourneau, R.G. 165, 165
Letterman, David 285
letters, multiple published 41
lettuces, chocolate-covered
  274
Leutze, Emanuel 327, 327
Levenkovas, Jurijus 37
Lewis, Jason 289
Li Chuanyong 31, 31
Li Enhai 41, 41
Li Jianping 224
liars, museum of 289
library books, overdue 63, 343
lie-detecting sunglasses 345
lifeguards, dog as 119, 119
lightbulbs, human electricity 278-
  279, 279
lightning
  kills diver 154
  numbers of strikes 185
  strikes twice 289
  temperature of 362
Lilly, Christa 197
limbo-skating under cars 20-21,
  21
Lin, J.J. 35
Lin, Kevin 71

Lincoln, Abraham
  assassination 316
  in double portrait 357
  skull 298
Linton-Smith, Christopher 263
lions
  adopts antelopes 109
  kissing 143, 143
Lipes, Wheeler 211
liposuction, eating fat from 257
Lite-Brite pegs, version of The Last
  Supper 344, 344
Little, John 306, 306
Liu Hua 195, 225, 230
Liu Suozhu 43
liver
  growing in lung 207
  sent in post 333
Livingston, Ed 51
lizards
  eats rubber lizard 105
  smuggled in prosthetic leg 343
  soup 227
lobsters, set free from market 134
Loch Ness Monster, topiary 18
locomotive, as piggy bank 172
log rafts 72, 72
Lombardo, Rosalia 229
Loosley, Sheila 85
Lopez, Cesar 362
Lopez, Clare Cavoli 305
lost property, museum of 298
Lothberg, Sigbritt 343
lottery
  all tickets winners 335
  double win 91
  mistake wins 185
  tree predicts winning numbers
    151
Loveday, John 306
Lucenay, Peter 140
Lucius, Natalie 195
Luczun, Robert 182-183, 182-
  183
luge board, jet-powered 150-151,
  151
lungs
  grass growing in 221
  liver growing in 207
Luntiala, Hannu 66
lychee, very expensive 245, 245

Lyle, Mark 245
Lyles, Kelly 181

Ma Yanjun 336
Mabe, Joni 300
McAuley, Andrew 88
MacCallister, Trish 254, *254*
McClure, Steve 318, *318*
McGinn, Forest Ages 327, *327*
McGregor, Harry and Lillian 313, *313*
Mach, David 25
McKeand, Hannah 28
Mackenzie, Mike *58*
McMahon, Kasey 239
Maday, Rod 324
magic tricks, waiters perform 151
magnet, human 196
mail
    human body parts sent in 333
    sculpture from junk mail 351
Malkoff, Mark 302-303, *302-303*
Malloy, Shannon 209
Manilow, Barry 90
manure, medicinal properties 230
marathons
    knitting while running 17
    large family in 327
    running on all continents 324
marbles museum 285
Marquis, Pat 60
marriage proposal, in crossword 91
Martell, Mary 120
marzipan sculpture 313
masks, large collection of 314, *314-315*
Mason, Pete 61, *61*
Massingale, Emma 120
matchcovers, large collection of 311
math
    chicken's ability 358, *358*
    child prodigy 93
Mauriello, Olga 300
mayors, weighing 149
meat
    clothes made from 239
    rock like slice of 172, *172*
mechanical man 150
Mecier, Jason 168, *168-169*

medicines
    birds' saliva 221
    burning leaves 213, *213*
    caterpillar droppings 224
    cockroaches 230
    cow manure 230
    dinosaur bones 211
    hair 227
    live fish 225, *225*
    lizard soup 227
    magical statue 225
    mummies 211
    scorpions 224, *224*
    seahorses 221
    urine 208
Mediterranean Sea, swimming across 98
Mee, Jennifer 203
Meilinger, Natalie 351
melon, very ancient 243
memory
    autistic's drawings 94-95, *94-95*
    child's phenomenal 96
    chimpanzee's ability 141
    loss of 359
    reciting pi 97
Mendez, Nelson 236
Merback, Althea Crome 32-33, *32-33*
Mercer, Ross 45
Merlini, David 319, *319*
mermaid's tail, for legless woman 217
meteor, damage by 164
meteorite, sacred 73
Meyer, Dan 54, *54*
mice
    cat gets head stuck in jar 118
    regurgitating *44-45*, 45
Middleton, Charlotte 87
milk
    huge in-store dairy plant 265
    milk spitting contest 71
    music improves production 115
mimicry, by birds 140
mines
    very deep 171
    wedding in 90
Mireles, Shayna 70
mirror, brings sun to village 170

Modoran, Alina 87
Moffatt, Brent 206, *206*
Molloy, Louis 300, *300-301*
money
    bank note artwork stolen 324
    dog eats 105
    dogs use cash machines 143
    fake million-dollar bill 158
    pig's tusks as currency 73
monkeys
    friendship with dog 142
    loud screams 107
Monroe, Marilyn, ice sculpture of 349
Monroe, Mark 149
Montagno, Antonio 85
Montague, Julian 83
Moon
    book sent to 171
    gravitational pull 355
Mooney, Michael 154
Moore, Charlotte and Mike 173
Moorer, Eelko 156
moose, attacks helicopter 126
Morales, Jay Lonewolf 19
Morgan, David 295, *295*
Morgan, Kerry 245
Morris, Terry 98
mosaics
    made of toothpicks 359
    of pencils 168, *168-169*
mosquitoes
    blood consumption 226
    giant statue of 167
    mosquito-calling contest 83
motorcycles
    centenarian rides in sidecar 18
    frog rides 363, *363*
    giant 164
    poker players 83
    rider loses leg 208
    riding round world on 83, *83*
Mount Rushmore, cheese sculpture 275
mountains
    blind climber 58, *58*
    concert on top of 344
    fast cycle ride down 357
    mirror brings sun to village 170
    naked climbers 294
    painted green 167

mountains (*cont.*)
  toilets on top of 172
  underwater 150
Moura, Leonel 362
mouth
  juggling with 25
  muscular strength 221
  painting with 40
  snake in 22, *23*
movie, cable channel plays
    continuously 358
Moyer, David 28
Mozart, Wolfgang Amadeus 301
mud, health benefits 196, *197*
Mudliar, Krishnaveni 37
Mueller, Wolfgang 93
mules
  lifting with teeth 18, *18*
  very long journey on 324
mummies
  displayed to friends 216
  dog found in tree 304, *304*
  dressed 228-229, *228-229*
  fingerprints 230
  Inuit 213
  medicinal properties 211
  wrappings 215, 218
murder, Serial Killer Museum 283
Murray, Alison 34
muscles, strength of mouth 221
mushrooms
  enormous 166, *166*
  very old 257
music
  addiction to heavy metal 298
  Barry Manilow as punishment for
    noisiness 90
  bells attached to eyebrows 19, *19*
  complaints' choirs 362
  elderly band 96
  improves milk production 115
  mountain-top concert 344
  musical roads 151
  note held for long time 354
  one-note concert 332
musical instruments
  coconut orchestra 269
  guitars made from guns 362
  guitars played simultaneously 329
  playing piggyback 284, *284*
mussels, super-sticky adhesive 343

nails
  breaking with teeth 208
  sculpture made from 134, *134*
  shot into heart 312
names
  all people met in lifetime 76
  banned 73
  changed after team loses match
    345
  longest town name 157, *157*
  town name chosen out of hat 179
nanotechnology sculpture 332
Narayanam, Nischal 96
Nathaniel, Eric 351
national anthems
  restaurant customers sing 72
  toilet plays 329
neck
  boy lives with broken neck 218
  graves cure stiffness 213
  huge tumor 230
needles, multiple piercings 206,
  206
Nelson, Admiral Horatio, missing
  arm 306
Nerhus, Eric 195
nerve gas antidote, produced by
  goats 358
New Testament, drawing made
  from words of 98, *98*
New York, riding subway nonstop
  for day 351
Newman, Paul 275
newspapers
  dresses made of 51
  multiple letters published in 41
Newton, Sir Isaac 337
Nicholls, Elliot 28
nickel, huge 313
Nicot, Jean 227
Nieber, Tilo 164
nightmares, predict air crash 328
noise, Barry Manilow as
  punishment for 90
noodles, very fine 41, *41*
North Pole, Russian flag planted
  below 51
noses
  dog with two 120, *120*
  extremely long 192
  snake in 22, *23*

noses (*cont.*)
  two-nosed calf 132
numbers
  chicken recognizes 358, *358*
  typing 18
Nunley, Dave 269
Nuranen, Robert 343

oceans, narwhals help study 324
octopuses, use jellyfish stings
  138
Oenhauser, Rita 121
oil, hair soaks up spill 192
oil field, in State Capitol grounds
  176
Oliver, Betty Lou 291
Olson, Thiago 329
omelet, giant 269
Ono, Aichi 340, *340*
Oprea, Ioan-Veniamin 52, *52-53*
optical illusions 80, *80-81*
oranges
  as diabetes cure 249
  very old 265
orangutans, friendship with tigers
  131
orchestra, coconut 269
Osborne, Jessica 243
outhouse, jet-powered 186, *186*
owls
  attacks man 139
  stuffed toy as surrogate mother
    131, *131*
oxygen, for train passengers 185

paintings
  body paintings 190-191, *190-
    191*
  by dogs 113
  by pigs 108, *108*
  on chewing gum 28, *28-29*
  chocolate portraits 251
  color blind artist 19
  double portrait in 357
  Etch a Sketch® versions 322-323,
    322-323
  famous paintings as tattoos 204,
    204-205
  finger-painting by gorillas 142
  giant finger painting 327
  insect paintbrushes 298, *298*

paintings (*cont.*)
  murals of famous paintings 152, *152-153*
  optical illusions 80, *80-81*
  paintings of Jesus drip blood 351
  on pigs 343
  robotic painter 362
  on tortillas 234-235, *234-235*
  very long 43
  with mouth 40
  with thumbnail 29, *29*
  woman kisses 34
pancakes, squirrel 257
Pappin, Jim 285
parachute jumps, multiple 288
paragliding, in tornado 91
parasites, museum of 313
Pariente, Shai 238
park, owned by Cuba 163
Parker, Jesse 139, *139*
Parkhurst, Debbie 133
parrots
  dating agency for 121
  intellectual ability 105
  large vocabulary 125
  saves family from fire 336
  teaches autistic boy to speak 99
Partington, Gina 209
Partner, Danny 274
Parton, Allen 143
Pataraia, Lasha 45
Patnaik, Sudarsan 85
Patterson, Simon 300
Patty, Alexandre 192, *192*
peanut butter, turned into diamonds 270
Pearce, Jordan 51
Pece, Marco 19
pedal boats
  long journey on 85
  swan in love with 106
pelican, eats pigeon 109, *109*
Pellegnno, Margo 54
Pemberton, Wes 358
pen-knife sculpture 79, *79*
Pena, Maria Moral 163
pencil sharpeners, large collection of 306, *306*

pencils
  mosaic of 168, *168-169*
  removed from head 203
Peng Shulin 226
penguins
  eat garlic 143
  giant fossil 288
  underwater film of 118
penis restaurant 256
Pepperberg, Dr. Irene 105
Perham, Michael 291
Peters, George 313
Pettigrew, Victoria 122-123, *122-123*
Pez dispenser, large 268, *268*
photo album, huge 91
photography, very young paparazzi 82
Piazza, Dan 164, *164*
Piazza, Ivo 349
Pichl, Clemens 256, *256*
Pickin, Sarah 97
picnic, for Betty's 87
piercings, multiple 206, *206*
pies
  dog spoils pie-eating contest 140
  making huge number of 265, *265*
  pie-eating contest 270, *270*
pigeons
  brain implants control 354
  pelican eats 109, *109*
  as spies 133
piggy bank, enormous 172
pigs
  brings up tiger cubs 138
  car looks like 167
  dog adopts 127, *127*
  painted 343
  paintings by 108, *108*
  piglet thinks it is a bull 126, *126*
  six-legged piglet 142
  tusks as currency 73
  two-faced piglet 113
  wild pigs in Australia 107
Pilarz, Virginia 254, *254*
Pilenga, Ferrucio 118
Pinto, Claudio Paulo 200
pipes, home built in 151
pizza
  enormous 253
  speed-eating 243

pizza (*cont.*)
  tattoo of 213
  very expensive 244
plant, dies after flowering 158
playbills, large collection of 298
playing cards, tower of 333, *333*
plowing, mass 43
poachers, crocodiles protect endangered animals 181
poetry, cowboys read 63
poker, motorcycle players 83
police
  arrest crocodile 332
  Hello Kitty armbands as disciplinary measure 341
Ponder, Joe 18, *18*
pools, different colored 159, *159*
popcorn
  giant ball of 265
  huge batch made 239
  museum of 275
poppadums, tall stack of 236
porridge, huge bowl of 259
Porter, Dick 283
Portnoy, Rich and Andra 263
portraits
  chocolate 251
  double portrait 357
  drawn with single line 327, *327*
  made with postage stamps 61, *61*
postage stamps
  enormous 151
  portraits made with 61, *61*
postcards, giant picture of racehorse from 25
potato, man knocked out with 238
Powers, Jim 343
Pozgar, Morgan 35
prairie-dog colony, enormous 126
Pratt, Sarah 243
pregnancy
  twins in different wombs 211
  very long 211
Presley, Elvis, wart 300
Pretou, Fabien 195
priests, large number of 41
prisons
  dance routine 280, *280-281*
  escape via food-tray slot 348
  hotel in 171
  land ownership 163

prisons (cont.)
  prisoner married by judge who
    found him guilty 336
pubs
  in hollow tree 157
  moved to England 275
  private 245
puffball fungus 163
pulse, man without 209
pumpkins
  carving 246-247, 246-247
  dropping onto van 274, 274-
    275
  firing from catapults 90
Purple Heart medal, mowed 328

Qasem, Abdul-Karim 25
Quigley, Karen 104
Quiroz, Manuel 25

rabies, surviving 195
Radcliffe, Daniel 211
Rafi, Mohammed 214-215, 215
rafts, log 72, 72
Raikkonen, Kimi 45
Raileanu, Aurel 196
rain, praying for 92
Rajendran, S. 40
Rathkamp, Henry 311
Rati, Ram 270
rats
  eating 236, 242, 242
  enormous 126, 351
razor, invention of 357
Rees, Nona 134
refrigerators
  replica of Stonehenge 332
  throws beer cans 243
restaurants
  chicken wing hunt 85
  free sandwich for naked
    swimmers 249
  hospital-themed 249, 249
  long-distance takeout 243
  "lucky" fish 245
  national anthem sung in 72
  penis restaurant 256
  sounds of the sea in 270
  tombs in 274
  very expensive dessert 248
  very large tip for waitress 243

restaurants (cont.)
  very narrow 257, 257
  waiters perform magic tricks 151
resuscitation, dogs 119, 336
Reynolds, Matt 85
Rhee, Gwang Hyuk 98, 98
Rhodey, Vincent 120
Rhymes, Simon 263
rice, eating single grains 243
rice crackers, wasps in 259, 259
Richardson-Leitman, Zacheri 139
Ricore, Giuseppe 244, 244
Rider, Chris 41
rings, long-lost 285, 305
Ripley, Robert 70, 70, 157, 157,
  341, 341
Ripley's Believe It or Not!, cartoons
  on blouses 93, 93
rivers
  house towed across 165, 165
  man rescued from 324
  swimming down Amazon 360-
    361, 360-361
roadkill soft toys 329, 329
roads
  airplane lands on highway 155
  musical 151
Robbins, Leah 28
Roberts, Joseph 265
Robinson, Matt 312
robots
  bank shaped like 159
  fly 348
  painter 362
  serves breakfast 263
  shark 115
  violinist 345, 345
Roby, Matthew 357
rocket belts, annual convention
  for 341
rocket festival 76, 76
rocks
  colored 158, 158
  elephant-shaped 151
  hairy stone 167, 167
  like slice of meat 172, 172
Rodgers, Joseph & Sons 79, 79
Rodin, Auguste, nanotechnology
  version of The Thinker 332
Rodriguez, Richard 46-47, 47
Rogiani, Mike 237

roller coaster, multiple rides on
  46-47, 47
roller skating
  museum of 318
  under cars 20-21, 21
Romeo, Dave 41
roofs, tornado rips nails out of
  151
rooster, horns on head 139, 139
Rosciano, Michele 282
Rose, Alex 104
Rothman, Dagmar 44-45, 45
rowing, across Atlantic Ocean 79
Royal, Rick 264
running
  across Sahara Desert 71
  elderly runner 31
  round world 22
  while hula hooping 36, 36

Saayman, Eubie 237
Sahara Desert, running across 71
St. Onge, Achille J. 171
saints, relics 280, 318
Salazar, Alberto 218
Sale, Naomi 82
Salter, Stephen 343
Salzman, Barbara and Barry 91
San Francisco, Jell-O model of 272,
  272-273
Sanchez, Epigmenio 317
sand
  burial in 212, 212
  eating 270
  replica of Taj Mahal 85
Sandler, Adam 82
sandwich, giant 249
Santiago, Alejandro 25
Santos, Rudy 197
sari, very long 37
saucepan lids, biting 55, 55
saunas, babies born in 73
Saunders, Andy 149, 149
sausage, very long 250-251,
  251
Sawaya, Nathan 24, 25
scalpel, left in body 213
Schechter, Andrea 298
Schult, H.A. 291
Schuster, Julius 283, 283

scissors
  left in stomach 225
  tiny 354
scorpions
  eating 258, *258*, 264
  medicinal properties 224, *224*
Scullino, Wayne 336
sculpture
  blind sculptor 70, *70*
  bread 257
  butter 243
  cheese Mount Rushmore 275
  chocolate 244
  computer 60, *60*
  computer disks 90, *90-91*
  crayon *356*, 357
  credit cards 335
  drought exposes 37
  duct tape 285
  of food 269
  from weapons 294
  in ghost town 25
  giant mosquito 167
  huge driller 171
  human hair 87
  ice 38, *38-39*, 349
  junk mail 351
  KFC menu 269
  lunch sculpture 301
  marzipan 313
  medicinal properties 225
  minute replica of Lloyd's of
    London building 98
  nails 134, *134*
  naked people on glacier 341
  nanotechnology 332
  pen-knives 79, *79*
  sand replica of Taj Mahal 85
  scrap metal 343, 357
  tiny babies 216, *216-217*
  tiny tree root carvings 336
  trash people 291
  tree 332
  very large swimmer 300, *300-301*
  with chainsaws 96, *96*
seahorses, asthma cure 221
Searles, Kathleen 179
seasons, on Uranus 358
Seconda, Bill 134, *134*
Senft, Didi 158

Serial Killer Museum 283
sewer museum 307
Shakespeare, William, complete
    works read aloud 324
sharks
  dolphins save surfer from 125
  kills kangaroo 106
  new species discovered 125
  refuses to let go 208, *208*
  robot 115
  swallows man's head 195
Shaw, Kerry 311
Shearon, Brigham and Todd 63
sheep
  in city 79
  dyed red 106
  eating heads 237, *237*, 238
  eyes as hangover cure 269
  follow shepherd's car 139
  live in house 349
  seven-legged lamb 140
  speed-shearing 305
  turn green 328
Shelley, Kevin 22
Shelvaraj 336
shoes
  large collection of 286-287,
    286-287
  shoe-shaped house 156
  stealing to smell 343
  vacuuming with 327
Shoesmith, Mark 70, *70*
shopping mall, secret apartment
    in 186
short people 207, *207*
  firefighter 217
  marries tall man 195, *210*,
    211
shovels, races on 60
Sickles, Dan 304
Sietas, Tom 60
"Simon Says", mass game of 22
Simpson, Frazer 215
Simpsons, made of balloons 342,
    342
Singh, Manjit 51
Singh, Paramjit 51
sisters, unknowingly live in same
    care facility 311
skateboard, enormous 150
skiing, furniture race 85

skin
  blue 202, *202*
  book bound in 71
  dancing with hooks in 97, *97*
  hanging from hooks in 22
  scaly 213
skipping
  contest for large ladies *84*, 85
  mass display of 37
  speed 18
skulls
  Hitler's 285
  Lincoln's 298
skunk festival 66
skydiving, lucky escape 97
sleds, cardboard 85
sleep
  sleeper shot 78
  sleepwalker washes clothes 324
  Sleepyhead Day 73
slides, as art exhibit 29
slot machines, money found under
    63
Smith, Edwin 49, *49*
Smithson, Robert 37
snails
  medicinal properties 230
  protective discharge 138
snakes
  cats save woman from 115
  cobras guard jewels 25
  decapitated head bites man 112
  digest own hearts 109
  dog saves boy from 121
  eating live 259
  eats goldfish 312, *312*
  enormous python 125
  golf balls in stomach 299, *299*
  in intensive care ward 106
  in mouth and nose 22, *23*
  rattlesnake bite in mouth 209
  two-headed 125
snow
  colored 163
  shovel races on 60
  snow donuts 174, *174-175*
snowmobile, high jump on 45
snowplow, golf cart becomes 354
soccer
  all players score 43
  chickens addicted to playing 126

soccer (*cont.*)
  horse plays 120
  very long match 306
socks
  missing 332
  wearing multiple 22
soda, football flavors 269
soda can tabs, belt made of 45
Soder, Stephan 181
sofa, extremely fast 343
solar heating, using bottles 336
soldiers, reburied 61
soup
  enormous pot of 238
  lizard 227
space shuttle
  baby monitor picks up images
    from 351
  speed on land 165
space travel
  astronauts' growth 329
  book sent to Moon 171
Spacehopper toys, mass bounce
  49
spaghetti, speed-eating 244, *244*
Sparks, Michael 60
Spector, Laura 190-191, *190-191*
spiders
  eating 238, *238*
  enormous web 125
  nest in boy's ear 197
spies, pigeons as 133
Spievack, Lee 207
spinsters, superstitions 72
spoons
  accidentally swallowed 230
  as surgical instruments 211
squirrels
  dig up ancient tool 93
  fake food burials 106
  pancakes made from 257
  raids store for chocolate 133
  start fires 106
Stadelbacher, Mary 113
stairs, descending on head 192,
  192
Staite, Prudence Emma 28
Staller, Eric 159
Stanford, Mike 174, *174-175*
Starbucks, drinking coffee in every
  branch 266-267, *266-267*

Starr, Teri 37
stars, number in galaxy 218
stationmaster, cat as 135
steam engine, very small 176
steel bars, swallowing 17, *17*
Steele, Ray 43
Steiner, Dave 158
Steinlauf, Fred 44, *44*
Stekel, Peter 285
Stender, Paul 186, *186*
Stewart, Ian 48, *48*
Stewart, Les 18
sticky notes, car covered in 42,
  42-43
Stiles, Grady Jr. 230
stir-fry, enormous 263
stocking, enormous 51
Stoeckl, Marcus 357
Stokes, Jay 288
Stoldt, Frank 54
stomach, pulling weights with 17
Stone, Jamison 142, *142*
stone heads, found outside houses
  295
stone-skipping 51
Stonehenge, refrigerator replica
  of 332
stores
  on boat 158
  cell phone decoration 307, *307*
  dog serves customers 120
  man lives in 302-303, *302-303*
  seagull shoplifter 141
Strati, Saimir 359
Strel, Martin 360-361, *360-361*
Su Chuandong 34, *34*
subway
  hanging upside-down in 156
  riding nonstop for day 351
sugar, sense of taste 195
suitcase, cat hides in 120
Sullivan, Jesse 226
sumo squats, multiple 35
Sun
  electricity production 345
  minute image of 362
  mirror brings sun to village 170
  transit of Venus obscured by
    clouds 336
Sun Ming Ming 203
sunglasses, lie-detecting 345

supernovae, amateur searches for
  335
surfing
  by dogs 121, *121*
  dolphins save surfer from shark
    125
  mass surfers on one wave 41
surgery
  by light of cell phones 213
  hand towel left behind 217
  scalpel left in body 213
  scissors left in stomach 225
  to look like Bruce Willis 217
  to look lucky 226
  using spoons 211
sushi, tiny 251
Sutton, Mike 307
swans
  in love with pedal boat 106
  superstitions 97
sweat
  camels 130
  creates electrical charge 351
swimming
  across Mediterranean Sea 98
  disabled swimmer 78
  down Amazon River 360-361,
    360-361
  in icy water 76
  mermaid's tail for legless woman
    217
  tiger enjoys 116, *116-117*
  very young swimmers 28, 78
Swiss Army knife 350, *350*
swords, swallowing underwater
  54, *54*
Syms, Phoebe 294, *294*
Szancer, Jan Marcin 170, *170*
Szopinski-Wisla, Andrzej 40

Tabasco® sauce, speed-drinking
  244
tails
  prosthesis for dolphin 105, *105*
  mermaid's tail for legless woman
    217
Takata, Richard 324
tall people 207, *207*
  basketball player 203
  tall man marries small bride 195,
    210, 211

tall people (cont.)
  twin differences 201
Tang Meirong 362
taste, sense of 195
Tatma, Lakshmi 198, 198-199
Tatma, Poonam 198
tattoos
  advertisements as 230
  breakfast on head 222, 222-223
  children's birthdays 357
  famous paintings 204, 204-205
  on fish 139
  over entire body 226
  of pizza 213
  unfortunate wording 333
taxis
  pulling with finger 54
  very long journeys in 179, 330-331, 330-331
Taylor, Amillia Sonja 195, 195
Taylor, Rev. Bryan 167
Taylor, Darren 64, 64-65
Taylor, Joshua 314, 314-315
Taylor, Sean 45
Taylor, Stephen 225
tea bag, giant 270
teeth
  ancient fossil 291
  baby born with 227
  biting saucepan lids 55, 55
  breaking nails with 208
  cleaning with sticks 215
  embedded in forehead 200
  false teeth swallowed in kiss 207
  George Washington's dentures 285, 285
  heart-shaped crowns 214, 215
  weight-lifting with 18, 18, 196, 196
television, very thin 324
temperatures
  heat surge 176
  of lightning 362
  record in Alaska 167
Terashima, Junko 301
text messages
  blindfolded 28
  novel made from 66
  sending large numbers of 35
Thanksgiving meal, speed-eating 265

theater, playbill collection 298
thermometers, large collection of 283
Thienna, Dr. 35
Thornton, Spencer 343
thumbnail, painting with 29, 29
thunderstorms, numbers of 185
tie pins, large collection of 285
tigers
  different colored cubs 112
  dog escapes from 112
  enjoys swimming 116, 116-117
  friendship with orangutans 131
  man in rolling globe 136, 136
  only speaks French 108
  pig as surrogate mother 138
Times Square, New York 165
tire inner tube, travel down river on 92
Titanic, watches made from 299
tobacco, as cancer cure 227
Todorovic, Zoran 257
toilets
  breaking lids with head 22
  jet-powered 186, 186
  multi-tasking 328
  plays national anthem 329
  on top of mountain 172
Tomasic, Goran and Karmen 132
tomatoes, huge harvest 269
tombs, in restaurant 274
Tongsal Bamnungthai 363, 363
tongue
  enormous 225
  fish hook stuck in 251
  gold decorations 214, 215
  parasitic 138
  split 226, 226
  stopping electric fan with 40, 40
  very flexible 214-215, 215
  whistling with tongue stuck out 43
toothache, frogs to cure 215
toothpicks, mosaic made of 359
topiary
  Easter Island statues 29
  Loch Ness Monster 18
tornados
  created in museum 310, 311
  damage houses 163, 163, 179, 179

tornados (cont.)
  lifts paraglider up 91
  pluck chickens 167
  rips nails out of roofs 151
  throws car into air 70
Torres, Ana Julia 143, 143
Torres, Luis 335
tortillas, paintings on 234-235, 234-235
Towler, Mike 135, 135
towns
  longest name 157, 157
  name chosen out of hat 179
  submerged town reappears 155
toys, roadkill 329, 329
tractors
  long journey on 93
  mass plowing 43
traffic cones, large collection of 295, 295
traffic signals, collecting 300
trains
  commuters push 176
  oxygen for passengers 185
trees
  artificial trees to combat global warming 351
  cork production 171
  eats metal 157
  helicopter rescues bird owner 135
  house built to look like 178, 178
  houses suspended in 177, 177
  image of tree inside 173, 173
  man escapes crocodiles in 106
  man survives upside down in 85
  mummified dog found in 304, 304
  petrified forest 304
  predicts winning lottery numbers 151
  pub in hollow tree 157
  sculpture 332
  tiny tree root carvings 336
  water pours from 179
Tresoglavic, Luke 208, 208
tricycle, electric 181
Trimbledon, Jack 284, 284
triplets, born on twins' birthday 281
Trout, Sara Jane 249

trucks
bumper stickers stolen from 163
comic book characters on
182-183, *182-183*
driven on cables in air 43
enormous 187, *187*
pulling 51
run over chest 49
wheelchair stuck in grill 296-297,
296-297
wine corks on 166
truffle, very expensive 270
tsunami, enormous 181
tube, gymnast in 52, *52-53*
Tujague, Frank 239, *239*
tuk-tuk, very long journey in
330-331, *330-331*
Tullgren, Roger 298
tumors
enormous 206, 215, 219, *219*,
230
Grover Cleveland's 312
Tunick, Spencer 341
Turcott, Alan 106
turkey, cooking giant 263
Turner, A.M. 132, *132*
Turowski, Marek 343
Turpin, Ben 335
turtle, two-headed 138, *138*
tuxedos, long journey dressed in
308-309, *308-309*
twins
conjoined 198, *198-199*, 203,
203
in different wombs 211
give birth on same day 82
height differences 201
parasitic 197, 218
triplets born on birthday of 281
Twister, mass games of 54
Twombly, Cy 34
typewriter
full-sized cardboard replica
352-353, *352*
tossing 63
typing numbers 18
Tyson, Keith 269
Tyson-Brown, Alfie 218

umbrella, slows fall 66
underpants, dog swallows 237

underwater
algae and urine produce oxygen
31
degree ceremony 16
escape artists 34, 319, *319*
feast 31
golf 48
haircut 37
hula hooping 51
ice hockey 45
mountains 150
submerged town reappears 155
sword-swallowing 54, *54*
unicycles
riding blindfold 44, *44*
very long journeys on 60, 326,
326
universities
golf lessons for students 326
underwater degree ceremony 16
Updegraff, Mrs W.E. 265, *265*
Uranus, long seasons on 358
Urban VI, Pope 318
Uribe, Manuel 45
urine
medicinal uses 208
oxygen produced by 31

vacuum cleaner, in shoes 327
Valle, Bonnie 217
Van Buren, Frank 354
Van Zyl, Ron 156
Vaughan, Carol 318
ventriloquists' wedding 85
Venus, transit across Sun obscured
by clouds 336
vertebrae, John Wilkes Booth's 316
Vessey, Nadya 217
villages
in cave 181
mirror brings sun to 170
violin case, saves boy 306
violinist, robot 345, *345*
Visschedyk, Austin 82
Vlasto, George 83
vodka
museum of 275
used in hospital 196
volcano, concert on top of 344
voodoo museum 317
Vox, Valentine 85

Wafaei, Julie 362
waitress, very large tip for 243
Wakeling, Sam 326, *326*
walking
across Eurasia 26-27, *26-27*
disabled man walks after scuba
diving 194, *194*
solo trek across Antarctica
28
wallet, long-lost 317
wallpaper museum 281
Wang Gongfu 16, *16*
Wang Wei Min 253, *253*
Warburton, Evelyn 18
Warner, Carl 260, *260-261*
warts
cures for 218
Elvis Presley's 300
washing machine, child stuck in
62, *62*
Washington, George
dentures 285, *285*
portrait drawn with single line
327, *327*
runs whiskey distillery 256
wasps, in rice crackers 259, *259*
Watanabe, Masanao 307, *307*
watches
long-lost 311
made from *Titanic* 299
water, pours from tree 179
water pistol battle 90
waterfall, kayak paddled over
332
waterspout, shower of worms in
164
Watts, David 349
weapons
grenade found in sack of potatoes
300
guitars made from guns 362
sculpture made from 294
Wearing, Clive 359
Weaver, Marion "Mike" 306
Wedders, Thomas 192
wedding dresses
Disney characters 22
made of balloons 67, *67*
taking exam in 87
very long 66
worn by whole family 87

weddings
  chicken as bridesmaid 98
  marriage to dog 92, 112
  milk spitting contest 71
  mock weddings with frogs 73
  prisoner married by judge who
    found him guilty 336
  in slate mine 90
  tall man marries small bride 195,
    210, 211
  ventriloquists' 85
  vows in bottle 71
Wegner, Margaret 203
weight loss
  expanding pill 362
  very large 45
  with laughter 335
weights
  balancing on chin 220, *220*
  lifting car 37
  lifting with eyelids 31, *31*
  lifting with finger 78, *78*
  lifting with teeth 18, *18*, 196, *196*
  multiple lifts 45
  pulling trucks 51
  pulling with ear 45, 51
  pulling with eyelids 313, *313*
  pulling with finger 54
  pulling with stomach 17
  trucks run over chest 49
  very short weight lifter 28
Weisse, Janet 327
Wenner, Kurt 80, *80-81*
West, Booker 121
whales
  enormous blood vessel 142
  exploding 131
  scientific instruments strapped
    to 324
  weapon fragment found in 307
wheelchair, stuck in truck grill
  296-297, *296-297*
wheels, burning 97
whiskey
  distillery run by George
    Washington 256
  very old bottle auctioned 263
Whisnant, Shannon 217
whistling, with tongue stuck out 43
White, Jack and Meg 332
Whitstine, Bill 132

Wiese, Scott 345
Wiethuchter, Mona 339, *339*
Wigan, Willard 98
wild boar, island for *338-339*, 339
Wilkinson, Matt 209
Williams, Betty Lou 218
Williams, Charlene 333
Williams, Dave 140
Willis, Bruce 217
Wilson, Dan 17
Wilson, Richard 162, *162*
Wiltshire, Stephen 94-95, *94-95*
wine barrels
  hotel bedrooms in 176
  man lives in 51
winged cat *124*, 125
Winter 266-267, *266-267*
Wisnierska, Ewa 91
Witthoft, David 327
Wolfram, Rebecca 298
wolves
  friendship with donkey 140
  walks into bar 269
wombs, twins in different 211
Wood, Grant *323*
Wood, John 217
world, traveling round 289
  flying 92, *92*
  human power 362
  plastic ducks 292-293, *292-293*
  motorcycles 83, *83*
  running 22
worms
  eating 259
  shower of 164
  weight of 125
  worm race 98
wrestling, with alligators 355, *355*
Wurz, Reinhard 16

Xia Shujuan *210*, 211
Xiao Zhu 211
Xin Yucai 151
Xu, Mrs. 324

Yang Decai 139
Yang Yuyin 30, *30*
Yankow, Maurice 217
yarn, spinning from pet fur
  122-123, *122-123*
Ye Fu 43

Yeboah, Emmanuel Ofosu 313
yodeling festival 341
Young, Jay 355, *355*
Yu Zhenhuan 201, *201*

Zahab, Ray 71
Zaleski, Szotynscy 170, *170*
Zarnock, Michael 282, *282*
Zeng 166
Zhang, Mrs. 126
Zhang Cunying 288-289, 289
Zhang Deke 278-279, 279
Zhang Haijing 66
Zhang Quan 17
Zhao, Granny 200
zip code, bear has own 158
Zokos, George 139
Zorchak, Nathan 354, *354*

Acknowledgments

FRONT COVER AND TITLE PAGE (c) Rex Features (b) Solent news/Rex Features; **13** (c) ©Veniamin's Human Slinky Author; Ioan ®Veniamin Oprea President of ®Veniamin Shows, Inc.; **14–15** Kent Couch - www.couchballoons.com; **16** ChinaFotoPress/Photocome/PA Photos; **17** AFP/Getty Images; **20–21** Simon de Trey-White/Barcroft Media; **23** UPPA/Photoshot; **24–25** www.brickartist.com; **26–27** www.timcopejourneys.com; **28** Alex Macnaughton/Rex Features; **29** Reuters/Amit Dave; **30** CNImaging/Photoshot; **31** UPPA/Photoshot; **32–33** Althea Crome Merback; **34** Jin Siliu/ChinaFotoPress/Photocome/PA Photos; **35** ChinaFotoPress/Photocome/Press Association Images; **36** Phil Mesibar www.mesibar.com/Paul Blairww.DizzyHips.com; **38–39** Timothy O'Rouke/RexFeatures; **40** Reuters/PoolNew; **41** ChinaFotoPress/Photocome/PA Photos; **42–43** ScottAbleman; **46** (c) Martin Rickett/PA Wire/PA Photos; **46–47** (b) Courtesy of Pleasure Beach, Blackpool; **47** (r) Images courtesy of Pleasure Beach, Blackpool; **48** Babineau Photography; **50** Brad Meyer; **52–53** ©Veniamin's Human Slinky Author; Ioan ®Veniamin Oprea President of ®Veniamin Shows, Inc.; **55** Reuters/Claro Cortes; **57** Jasper Juinen/GettyImages; **58–59** Jon Cook and Miles Hilton-Barber; **60** Photocome/PA Photos; **61** Caters News Agency Ltd/Rex Features; **62–63** Peter Lawson/Rex Features; **64** (t/r) Stefan Nemec, (b/r) Eric Land; **65** Eric Land; **66** ChinaFotoPress/Photocome/PA Photos; **67** Don and Laura Caldwell www.AcmeBalloon.com; **68–69** Jasper Juinen/Getty Images; **72** Kazuhiro Nogi/AFP/Getty Images; **73** Denis Doyle/Getty Images; **74–75** Hermann J. Knippertz/AP/PA Photos; **76** Jerome Favre/AP/PA Photos; **77** Ron Wurzer/Getty Images; **78** Reuters/China Daily China Daily Information Corp – CDIC; **80–81** Chris Jackson/Getty Images; **82** Quinn Joseph Baumberger; **83** Dr. Gregory W. Frazier www.horizonsunlimited.com/gregfrazier; **84** Reuters/Sergei Karpukhin; **86–87** David Burner/Rex Features; **88–89** www.crossingtheditch.com.au; **90–91** (b) Hu Xuebai/ChinaFotoPress/Photocome/PA Photos; **92** (c) Jon Ross, (t/l) Juan Rivera Just Film Media, LLC; **94** (c, t/r) Gary Bishop/Rex Features, (l) Steve Geer/iStockphoto; **95** Gary Bishop/Rex Features; **96** AFP/Getty Images; **97** Reuters/Mariana Bazo; **99** Hermann J. Knippertz/AP/PA Photos; **101** Rick Murphy, Six Flags Discovery Kingdom; **102–103** (b) Reuters/Frank Lin; **103** (r) Reuters/Frank Lin, (t) Steve Chen/AP/PA Photos; **104** Ben Margot/AP/PA Photos; **105** Reuters/Yuriko Nakao; **106** Rex Features; **107** Barry Batchelor/PA Archive/PA Photos; **108** Richard Austin/Rex Features; **109** Cathal McNaughton/PA Archive/PA Photos; **110–111** Sherron Bridges; **112** Douglas Fretz; **113** Jean Farley/AP/PA Photos; **114** Gary Roberts/Rex Features; **115** Reuters/Ali Jarekji; **116** Rick Murphy, Six Flags Discovery Kingdom; **117** Robyn Beck/AFP/Getty Images; **118** Reuters/Alessandro Garofalo; **119** Colin Shepherd/Rex Features; **121** Denis Poroy/AP/PA Photos; **122–123** www.vipfibers.com; **123** (b) Ashne Lalin; **124–125** Camera Press/ChinaFotoPress; **126** S Chalker/Newspix/Rex Features; **127** ChinaFotoPress/Zhong Zhibing/Photocome/PA Photos; **128–129** Mr.Lee/J.Perthold; **130** Simon Czapp/Rex Features; **131** Chris Balcombe/Rex Features; **133** Phil Yeomans/Rex Features; **135** Caters News Agency Ltd/Rex Features; **136** Reinhold Kringel Münster/Germany; **137** Oliver Krato/DPA/PA Photos; **138** Matt Rourke/AP/PA Photos; **142** Mike Stone; **143** Inaldo Perez/AP/PA Photos; **146–147** Fredrik Fransson; **147** (c) NASA; **147** www.Armchaircruisers.com; **149** Phil Yeomans/Rex Features; **150** Tim Arfons; **150–151** Joel King/Wrigley's Airwaves®; **152–153** Robert Burns of Brighton; **154** (r) Image Copyright 2007 – Tony Rath Photography www.trphoto.com; **156** Ryan Froerer; **158** Reuters/Darrin Zammit Lupi; **159** Reuters/Finbarr O'Reilly; **162** Richard Wilson Turning the Place Over 2007 Courtesy Richard Wilson and Liverpool Biennial; **164** Dan Piazza; **166** AFP/Getty Images; **167** Yang Fan/ChinaFotoPress/Photocome/PA Photos; **168–169** Richard Barnes www.jasonmecier.com; **170** Borys Czonkow/Rex Features; **171** Peter Foerster/DPA/PA Photos; **172** ChinaFotoPress/Zhang Yanlin/Photocome/PA Photos; **173** Bournemouth News & Pic Service/Rex Features; **174–175** Mike Stanford WSDOT; **176** Sipa Press/Rex Features; **177** Rex Features; **180–181** Martin Meissner/AP/PA Photos; **182–183** Robert Luczun; **184** Javier Trueba/MSF/Science Photo Library; **186** Michael.J.Gallagher; **187** Bigfoot 4x4 Inc; **188–189** Manichi Rafi; **190–191** Chadwick and Spector www.chadwickandspector.com; **193** ChinaFotoPress/Wang Zi/Photocome/PA Photos; **194** Gary Roberts/Rex Features; **195** Reuters/Ho New; **197** Reuters/China Daily China Daily Information Corp – CDIC; **198** Aijaz Rahi/AP/PA Photos; **199** AP/PA Photos; **200** Amia Fore; **201** AFP/Getty Images; **202** NBCUPhotoBank/Rex Features; **204–205** www.anilgupta.com; **206** Reuters/Shaun Best; **208** Reuters/Stringer Australia; **209** Kelley Cox/AP/PA Photos; **210** Reuters/Jason Lee; **212** Reuters/Apichart Weerawong; **213** Reuters/Stringer Shanghai; **214** (t) Reuters/Kim Kyung Hoon, (c) Reuters/Marcos Brindicci; **214–215** (b) Manichi Rafi; **216–217** Camille Allen www.camilleallen.com; **219** Reuters/STR New; **222–223** Peter Byrne/PA Archive/PA Photos; **224** Reuters/Stringer Shanghai; **225** Reuters/Stringer India; **226** Joe Imel/AP/PA Photos; **228–229** Yann Arthus-Bertrand/Corbis; **231** Reuters/China Daily China Daily Information Corp – CDIC; **233** Scott Cummins; **234–235** Tortilla Paintings © 2007 Joe Bravo; **236** Daniel R. Patmore/AP/PA Photos; **237** Reuters/David Mercado; **238** Tang Chhin Sothy/AFP/Getty Images; **239** Reuters/Jacob Silberberg; **240–241** Newspix/Rex Features; **242** Reuters/China Photos; **245** Reuters/China Photos; **246–247** Scott Cummins; **248** N Connolly/Newspix/Rex Features; **249** Reuters/Richard Chung; **250** Srdjan Ilic/AP/PA Photos; **252** Reuters/Yuriko Nakao; **253** Toru Yamanaka/AFP/Getty Images; **254–255** Berkson Photography; **258** ChinaFotoPress/Photocome/PA Photos; **259** Reuters/Staff Photographer; **260–261** www.carlwarner.com; **262** The Krystal Company; **264** Paul Cooper/Rex Features; **266–267** Winter; **268** Gary R. Doss; **270** Joe Giblin/AP/PA Photos; **271** Lindsey Parnaby/EMPICS Entertainment/PA Photos; **272–273** Liz Hickok; **274–275** Your Country Escape, LLC; **277** Gabriel Bouys/AFP/Getty Images; **278–279** Zhang Xiuke/ChinaPhotoPress/Photocome/PA Photos; **280–281** Reuters/Victor Kintanar; **282** Michael Zarnockwww.MikeZarnock.com; **285** Keith Srakocic/AP/PA Photos; **286–287** www.darsshoeheaven.com/www.justtherightshoeshoeheavenworldwide.com; **288–289** ChinaFotoPress/Photocome/PA Photos; **290** Steve Pyke/Getty Images; **291** Peter Macdiarmid/Rex Features; **292** SWNS.com; **294** Phoebe Syms; **295** Ben Cawthra/Rex Features; **296–297** AP/PA Photos; **298** Steven R Kutcher; **299** AP/PA Photos; **300–301** Peter Macdiarmid/Getty Images; **301** ChinaFotoPress/Photocome/PA Photos; **302–303** Reuters/Lucas Jackson; **304** Michael Steve Bean; **305** Eric Gay/AP/PA Photos; **306** Simon Jones/Rex Features; **307** Masatoshi Okauchi/Rex Features; **308–309** Heath and Doug, The Tuxedo Travellers; **310** Daimler AG; **312** KNS News; **314–315** Angie & Jimmy Taylor; **316** Daniel Graves/Rex Features; **316–317** Reuters/Pilar Olivares; **318** Keith Sharples/Rex Features; **319** Gabriel Bouys/AFP/Getty Images; **321** www.coloradogators.com; **322–323** Etch-A-Sketch art by Jeff Gagliardi; **326** Steve Colligan; **328** Solent News/Rex Features; **329** Rex Features; **330–331** Antonia Bolingbroke-Kent and Jo Huxster www.tuktotheroad.com; **333** Courtesy of Bryan Berg; **334–335** SWNS.com; **337** Brandi Simons/Getty Images; **338–339** Gary Roberts/Rex Features; **340** Mike Clarke/AFP/Getty Images; **342** Adam Lee www.adamlee.net; **344** Mark Beekman; **345** Katsumi Kasahara/AP/PA Photos; **346–347** Gavin Bernard/Barcroft Media; **348** John Steiner; **349** Masayuki Sumida/AP/PA Photos; **350** Wenger N.A.; **352–353** Courtesy Perugi Artecontemporanea Italy; **354** Roger Bamber/Rex Features; **355** www.coloradogators.com; **356** Courtesy of Pete Goldlust/Amy Mac Williamson; **358** ChinaFotoPress/Photocome/PA Photos; **359** Barcroft Media; **360–361** www.amazonswim.com; **363** Reuters/Sukree Sukplang

Key: t = top, b = bottom, c = center, l = left, r = right, sp = single page, dp = double page

All other photos are from Ripley's Entertainment Inc.
Every attempt has been made to acknowledge correctly and contact copyright holders and we apologize in advance for any unintentional errors or omissions, which will be corrected in future editions.